GREAT LIVES OBSERVED

Gerald Emanuel Stearn, *General Editor*

EACH VOLUME IN THE SERIES VIEWS THE CHARACTER AND
ACHIEVEMENT OF A GREAT WORLD FIGURE IN THREE PER-
SPECTIVES—THROUGH HIS OWN WORDS, THROUGH THE OPIN-
IONS OF HIS CONTEMPORARIES, AND THROUGH RETROSPECTIVE
JUDGMENTS—THUS COMBINING THE INTIMACY OF AUTOBI-
OGRAPHY, THE IMMEDIACY OF EYEWITESS OBSERVATION, AND
THE OBJECTIVITY OF MODERN SCHOLARSHIP.

HUGH DAVIS GRAHAM, *editor of this volume in the Great Lives
Observed series, is Associate Professor of History at the Johns
Hopkins University and Acting Director of the Institute of
Southern History. He is author of* Crisis in Print, *is co-director
of the History Task Force of the National Commission on the
Causes and Prevention of Violence, and is co-editor of* Vio-
lence in America.

GREAT LIVES OBSERVED

Huey Long

Edited by HUGH DAVIS GRAHAM

Ill fares the land, to hastening ills a prey,
Where wealth accumulates and men decay.

—OLIVER GOLDSMITH

A SPECTRUM BOOK

PRENTICE-HALL, INC., ENGLEWOOD CLIFFS, N.J.

Current printing (last number): 10 9 8 7 6 5 4 3 2 1

C–13-444612-7

P–13-444604-6

Library of Congress Catalog Card Number: 77–96968

Printed in the United States of America

PRENTICE-HALL INTERNATIONAL, INC. (*London*)
PRENTICE-HALL OF AUSTRALIA, PTY. LTD. (*Sydney*)
PRENTICE-HALL OF CANADA, LTD. (*Toronto*)
PRENTICE-HALL OF INDIA PRIVATE LIMITED (*New Delhi*)
PRENTICE-HALL OF JAPAN, INC. (*Tokyo*)

Contents

v

PART TWO
HUEY LONG VIEWED BY HIS CONTEMPORARIES

PART THREE
HUEY LONG IN HISTORY

Introduction

Huey Pierce Long never reached the American presidency. His political career spanned less than twenty years and his lifetime only forty-two. Yet these years coincided with America's fundamental transformation from a predominantly rural society to an urban industrial one. Long's lifespan thus links nineteenth century Populism to Franklin Roosevelt's New Deal. Indeed, in a fundamental way it links the modern era to its antecedents in slavery and secession, Civil War and Reconstruction, for Huey Long was a Southerner and his political environment reflected the tragic legacy of the Lost Cause—of failure, poverty, and guilt.

And Huey was an American, fully in the Horatio Alger tradition. Clawing his way up from the pine barrens of Winn Parish (county), Louisiana, to the U.S. Senate, Huey Long became a national and even international figure with astonishing speed. In the 1930s, the Western world was slumped in economic paralysis, and with worldwide depression came a crisis in parliamentary government. In response, radical political leaders of the left and right surfaced in the Western democracies. The fragile Weimar Republic could not withstand Hitler's Nazi putsch; Italy had already succumbed to Mussolini's Caesarism; Franco's Insurgents crushed the republican Loyalists in Spain; Leon Blum's socialist coalition triumphed in France, only to be swamped by the fascist Vichy. England—one of the exceptions—survived Sir Oswald Mosley. In Russia, Stalinists boasted that the Soviet system was "depression-proof." And in America, Franklin Roosevelt and the Democrats were given their chance. But by 1934–35 they were floundering, and from the political wings came forward a congeries of dissatisfied radicals. They varied widely in their styles and appeals, but none matched the electric appeal—or, to those who feared him, the political threat—of the senator from Louisiana.

Long's truncated career can be summarized briefly enough. Born in 1893 in Winnfield, Louisiana, he attended high school without graduating and college without earning his diploma. In 1914 he borrowed money to enroll in the Tulane University law school, and in an astonishing one-year blitz he emerged a certified lawyer at the age of twenty-one. His political career formally began in 1918 when he won election as railroad commissioner for the northern district of Louisiana, a public regulatory post he shrewdly employed to flay the "corporate interests"

1

in a neo-populistic crusade in behalf of Louisiana's dispossessed common man. Defeated in the gubernatorial race of 1924, he successfully waged in 1928 a class-based crusade for the governor's chair. The following year he survived impeachment, and in 1930 he consolidated his mass support by winning a seat in the U.S. Senate while still sitting as governor.

A Democrat (inevitably, in Louisiana) and early supporter of Franklin Roosevelt, Long soon broke with the New Dealers—ostensibly over their unwillingness to support his radical program calling for a national soak-the-rich redistribution of wealth. As a freshman senator Long was decidedly a maverick. He boldly castigated his staid senior colleagues and used the Senate as a strategic forum for launching his nationwide Share Our Wealth movement and denouncing the New Deal for failing to end the depression. By 1935 he was clearly embarked on a drive for the presidency, having secured his power base in Louisiana through a puppet regime armed with essentially dictatorial powers. But in September of 1935 an assassin gunned him down in Baton Rouge. The Chronology following this introduction records the milestones of his career, which is fleshed out in Huey Long's own words in Part One. Part Two presents views of Long as seen by contemporary observers, and in Part Three Long is assessed in the light of history—brief as that hindsight has been since 1935.

What can we learn from this tumultuous career, both about the nature of the man and, more importantly, about American social and political behavior and our national character? Much of the discussion of Huey Long—too much—has focused on the question of his political genre. Was Huey Long a demagogue, a fascist, a communist, a dictator, a populist democrat . . . ? Long once dismissed such speculation with the cryptic observation that he was *sui generis*. His impatience with the popular game of political categorization probably reflected the politician's natural instinct to avoid being too restrictively labeled, but it stands as a useful admonition to students of history. Speculation over whether Huey Long was, for instance, a demagogue *or* a democrat remains largely a profitless exercise because his unique political amalgam was indeed *sui generis*, in that no single political label can adequately describe him.

The character of Huey Long, then, reflected all of these generic strains: democrat, demagogue, populist, capitalist, political boss—and all of them are firmly rooted in the American political tradition. Long was a white Southerner, literally born in a log cabin and destined to rise in a Southern political version of the classic Alger tradition. His background and populistic rhetoric suggest a kind of genuine visceral equalitarianism that is altogether plausible and in no way inconsistent with his admittedly demagogic appeals. His rustic antics disguised a mind that was electric in its agility and almost totally retentive. His wealth-sharing panacea, however economically naive or politically cynical it be judged, in no way fundamentally challenged American capitalism. (Long once even debated socialist Norman Thomas in defense of the system; his demand for wealth-sharing represented a call not for repudiation but for radically corrective readjustment.) The widespread and fearful speculation by liberals in the thirties that Long was a proto-fascist probably tells us more about their preoccupations with Hitler and Mussolini than it does about Huey Long, who was innocent of the kind of systematic ultra-right-wing ideology necessary to sustain fascism —or, on the left, communism. Far too much attention has been devoted to linking Huey Long to European "isms" or to determining whether he was a scoundrel.

To be instructive the debate over Long's political significance should avoid exclusive categories and European ideological frames of reference and focus on questions of motivation and patterns of behavior. The former concern, the shadowy question of intention, is clearly crucial, yet it remains problematical owing to the nature of the evidence. How sincere was Long in insisting that his prime concern in life was to alleviate the lot of the dispossessed, and that he would gladly lay down the burden of political life once his dream for America was achieved? Or did that appeal cynically mask and serve only as a convenient vehicle for an insatiable lust for power? The evidence is inconclusive, for his assassination abruptly terminated his performance and so far as we know he left no candid memoir or diary or body of manuscript that might enlighten us. So we must turn in the final analysis to his performance, truncated as it was by his murder at midpassage. And here again we find contradictory evidence. On the one hand we confront a Long program of class reforms and socially constructive enterprise in Louisiana, and in the U.S. Senate a liberal-equalitarian speaking and voting record that must be weighed as reflective of his intentions. On the other hand, we also find erected by Long in Louisiana a governmental structure that both contemporary liberal and conservative critics labeled as an unvarnished dictatorship in which Long adhered to the forms and retained the paraphernalia of constitutional democracy while perverting its substance. And we find charges of ruthlessness, and supportive evidence that is damaging. But the process of historical understanding constitutes far more than a logical exercise in legal judgment; the evidence must be weighed and the charges assessed within their historical context. For all his unique drive and genius, Huey Long was very much a creature of time and circumstance in his native South.

Students of Southern politics have long complained that a romantic thrust of irrationality has confounded its logic. Such a prejudgment seems to demand logic in politics from men who by nature are not altogether logical, but a strong case can be made that class divisions in the South have been so consistently blurred by emotional considera-

tions of race and caste that the have-nots have been easily exploited
by a dominant and conservative elite minority. Thus the "rich man's
war" of 1861 was largely fought by those three quarters of the whites
who owned no slaves. Similarly, the stark specter of Yankee and Negro
Republican rule during the Reconstruction led the mass of Southern
whites to support the successful efforts of conservative "Redeemers" to
repudiate and oust the Radical regimes, even though much of the social
legislation of Radical Reconstruction was designed to benefit lower-
class whites and Negroes alike. These conservative Redeemer govern-
ments fostered a system of farm tenancy and crop liens, largely yoked
to the one-crop tyranny of cotton, that mired the rural masses in a morass
of peonage. When these acutely distressed white and black dirt farmers
threatened to make common class cause against the conservative "Bourbon" Democrats in the Populist revolt of the 1890s, the conservatives
were able successfully to invoke the sacred icon of white supremacy to
shatter the Populist alliance (aided, to be sure, by a generous measure
of vote fraud and, ironically, by the votes of black belt Negroes who
perhaps wisely preferred the paternalism of the conservative Bourbons
to the inconstant liberalism of the poor-white Populists).

Following the debacle of Populism, the frustrated white agrarian
radicals joined the conservatives in disfranchising the Negroes, in the
wan hope that their elimination from the polls would afford whites the
luxury of dividing along class lines. In response, a colorful if profane
parade of racist demagogues did arise throughout the South—men like
Benjamin Tillman and Cole Blease of South Carolina, James Vardaman
and Theodore Bilbo of Mississippi, who viciously baited the poor blacks
in the name of the poor whites. But their reforms were generally minimal
and their reigns short-lived; they betrayed a tendency to sell out to the
conservative business interests, and an unwillingness or inability to crush
their opponents. Subsequently, the Progressive movement struck a responsive chord in the South. But it did so late and timidly, often assuming the form of a kind of "business progressivism" dedicated more to
the modern efficiencies of "good government" and to attracting industry
than to alleviating the distress of the rural poor. When World War I
and the 1920s brought prosperity to the nation, the rural South remained
largely prostrate. When the Great Crash and the Depression hit, the once
proud Southern yeoman hadn't very far to fall.

This, in broad outline, was the Southern legacy that Huey Long in-
herited, and it was packed with social dynamite. Indeed, Long's Louisiana was a somewhat atypical Southern state in this regard, for owing
to idiosyncracies peculiar to its origins, Louisiana had nurtured class
frustrations to an extraordinary degree.

If the Tillmans and Bilboes of other Southern states were for the
most part feckless and ephemeral reformers, it is instructive to note

that Louisiana produced no populist leader of comparable dimensions. Her poor were especially divided, and her conservatives entrenched, owing primarily to two unique attributes of the Pelican State. Louisiana did not differ from her sister Southern states in the degree to which her poor were divided by racial antagonisms. Her Negroes, who constituted approximately one-third of the population, were effectively disfranchised by the constitutions of 1898 and 1921, together with the adoption of the white primary in 1906 (in 1940, Louisiana voter registers listed 702,913 eligible whites and only 897 Negroes—none of whom could vote in the crucial Democratic primary anyway). But she did differ markedly in compounding this typical racial division by the addition of an ethnic and religious barrier that translated into a cultural and geographic one. Approximately half of her population was French Catholic, located in the South; in the Protestant northern parishes Baptists and Methodists were preponderant. This division was frequently apparent when elections or referenda featured the gambling or liquor issues (the southern French parishes enjoyed both pastimes and were contemptuous of the hypocritical piety of the north), and Huey Long ran afoul of it in 1924 when he got caught in a whiplash over the Ku Klux Klan. The striking political volatility of Louisiana's ethnic polarity was commented on by A. J. Liebling:

> Politics is to the conversation of Louisiana what horse racing is to England's. In London, anybody from the Queen to a dustman will talk horses; in Louisiana, anyone from a society woman to a bellhop will talk politics. Louisiana politics is of an intensity and complexity that are matched, in my experience, only in the republic of Lebanon. The balance between the Catholics in southern Louisiana and the Protestants in northern Louisiana is as delicate as that between the Moslems and the Christians in Lebanon and is respected by the same convention of balanced tickets.[1]

Other observers have likened the Gallic flavor of Louisiana's political climate to that of Latin America, thereby reinforcing with the demand for *machismo* the popular Southern delight for what Wilbur Cash called the "hell of a fellow" syndrome in friends-and-neighbors stump politics.

The second unique attribute of Louisiana relevant to the prolonged hegemony of the conservatives was the performance of a cohesive urban machine in New Orleans, then the South's largest city. This city machine originated as the Choctaw Club in 1897, and has been variously referred to as the Choctaws, the New Orleans Ring, and the Old Regulars. Its

[1] A. J. Liebling, *The Earl of Louisiana* (New York: Simon and Schuster, Inc., 1961), p. 18.

strength lay in its cohesiveness as a disciplined and well-financed bloc whose representation in the legislature accurately reflected New Orleans' 20 per cent of the population. The Choctaws represented the interests of New Orleans' conservative commercial leaders and private utilities, in alliance with the old planter elite and the newer, externally owned corporations engaged in extracting lumber, chemicals, and petroleum. This wealthy coalition's opposition to taxation, public regulation, and employer liability laws had been consistent and successful; in light of the aforementioned divisions among the lower classes, Louisiana's conservatives enjoyed an unusual measure of security from the storms of crusading reformists—at least until they collided with Huey Long. But a portentous measure of the social dynamite that was accumulating during these long years of minimal if relatively clean government was reflected in Lousiana's concern for public education: Louisiana ranked last among the states in literacy.

If Louisiana was in these two important respects atypical of Southern states, Huey Long's native Winn Parish similarly manifested patterns of life that contrasted sharply to the stereotyped black belt of porticoed columns and mint juleps. A poor north-central hill parish containing relatively few Negroes, Winn's sentiments had been unionist in 1860, and its delegate had voted against secession in the Louisiana convention of 1861. Huey Long once candidly confessed in the Senate that his forebears had fought for the Confederacy only because the sheriff had dragooned them. When Huey was born, the fires of populism were spreading through the pine hills of Winn Parish, and its persistent strain of agrarian radicalism was to prove enthusiastic for Bryan and congenial to socialist Eugene Debs and even to Big Bill Haywood's militant International Workers of the World ("Wobblies").

The career of Huey Long remains inexplicable without an appreciation of the depths of these roots of alienation. This profound social desperation cannot be invoked simply to justify Long's methods, but critics who unequivocally condemn him without reference to this historical legacy are guilty of ahistorical judgment. In 1935, Huey's eighty-three-year-old father revealed to a northern journalist the dimensions of this abiding disaffection:

> "Didn't Abraham Lincoln free the niggers and not give the planters a dime. Why shouldn't Huey take the money away from the rich and still leave 'em plenty? Abe Lincoln freed the niggers without a price. Why shouldn't the white slaves be freed, and their masters left all they can use?
>
> "Maybe you're surprised to hear talk like that. Well, it was just such talk that my boy was raised under and that I was raised under. My father and my mother favored the Union. Why not? They didn't have slaves. They didn't even have decent land. The rich folks had all the good land

and all the slaves—why, their women didn't even comb their own hair. They'd sooner speak to a nigger than a poor white. They tried to pass a law saying that only them as owned land could vote. And, when the war come, the men that owned ten slaves didn't have to fight.

"There wants to be a revolution, I tell you. I seen this domination of capital, seen it for seventy years. What do these rich folks care for the poor man? They care nothing—not for his pain, his sickness nor his death. And now they're talking again about keeping the poor folks from voting—that same talk. I say there wants to be a revolution." [2]

This was Huey Long's Louisiana. But Long's significance extends far beyond the narrow confines of Louisiana and even of the South, for as a highly visible and dissident U.S. senator during the bitter depression years, he symbolized to millions of desperate Americans the as yet untried possibilities of home-grown radicalism. By 1935 the Great Depression was six years old and showing few signs of abatement. A staggering 10.5 million unemployed testified to the relative impotence of Franklin Roosevelt's first New Deal. Recovery had not been achieved, relief had only held off starvation, reform had been timid and primarily fiscal. The stubborn persistence of the depression and the failure of the first New Deal prompted Minnesota Governor Floyd Olson to blurt: " 'I am not a liberal . . . I am a radical. . . . I am not satisfied with hanging a laurel wreath on burglars and thieves . . . and calling them code authorities or something else.' " [3] Weakened by the years of strain, the American social fabric was tearing apart: law and order were breaking down. When truckers in Minneapolis struck, police provoked an incident and shot sixty-seven people, some in the back. Covering the tragedy was Eric Sevareid, then a young reporter, who wrote: "I understood deep in my bones and blood what fascism was." [4] Union leaders in San Francisco called a general strike, prompting fears of class warfare. Old-age pensionist Dr. Francis Townsend, inflationist radio priest Father Coughlin, and socialist Upton Sinclair peddled their nostrums to an increasingly attentive and disillusioned audience. This was Huey Long's America.

In the pages that follow in Part One, the public Huey Long seeks to explain and justify his extraordinary career. There is much that he omits—much of it at best unflattering and at worst ugly. His contemporary critics were quick to redress the balance—sometimes too quick, too

[2] Forrest Davis, *Huey Long: A Candid Biography* (New York: Dodge Publishing Company, 1935), pp. 48–49.

[3] Donald McCoy, *Angry Voices: Left of Center Politics in the New Deal Era* (Lawrence, Kansas: University of Kansas Press, 1958), p. 55.

[4] Eric Sevareid, *Not So Wild a Dream* (New York: Alfred A. Knopf, Inc., 1946), p. 58.

shortsighted, and overcompensating in their efforts. It is the historians who theoretically have the last word. Yet it is a testimony both to the complexity of the man and to the variety of the American historical tradition that their judgment is neither consensual nor final.

Chronology of the Life of Huey Long

1893	(August 30) Born in Winnfield, Louisiana.
1910	Leaves Winnfield High School as traveling salesman, operating first out of Houston, Texas, and later Memphis, Tennessee.
1912	(January–May) Produce salesman and part-time student at University of Oklahoma in Norman.
1913	Marries Rose McConnell of Shreveport, Louisiana, in Memphis.
1914	Enters Tulane University in New Orleans to study law.
1915	Passes special bar examination and is sworn as a Louisiana lawyer at the age of twenty-one. Begins law practice in Winnfield.
1916	Joins State Senator S. J. Harper in campaign against limited employers' liability.
1917	Defends and wins acquittal for State Senator Harper, whose antiwar radicalism led to his indictment under the Espionage Act. Fails to win appointment as assistant U.S. District Attorney in Shreveport.
1918	Wins runoff election as state railroad commissioner for the northern district at the age of twenty-five.
1919–20	Attacks Standard Oil and supports the gubernatorial candidacy of John M. Parker.
1921–26	Breaks with Governor Parker and becomes chairman of the Public Service Commission. Wins lower telephone, gas, and electric rates, railroad and streetcar fares, and a severance tax on oil.
1924	Loses first gubernatorial campaign in a three-way race dominated by the Klan issue. Reelected to the Public Service Commission.
1926	Supports reelection of U.S. Senator Edwin Broussard, a south Louisiana Creole.
1928	Elected Governor. Delivers Louisiana vote to Democratic Presidential candidate Al Smith.
1929	Impeachment voted by the House and tried in the Senate. "Round Robin" defeats impeachment.
1930	Elected to the U.S. Senate. Begins publishing the *Louisiana Progress*. Green pajamas incident.

1931   Remains in Louisiana as Governor, selects O. K. Allen
as successor, and ousts Lieutenant-Governor Paul Cyr.

1932   Takes Senate oath, proposes Senate resolution on a tax bill
to limit fortunes, and resigns all committee posts when the resolution
is defeated under the direction of Senate Minority Leader
Joe Robinson of Arkansas. Long slate elected in Louisiana.
Campaigns for the nomination and election of Franklin Roosevelt.
Engineers the election of Senator Hattie Carraway of Arkansas.

1933   Breaks with Roosevelt administration and demands redistribution
of the nation's wealth. Sands Point incident. Power base in Louisiana
threatened by revolt in New Orleans. Publishes *Every Man A King*.

1934   Organizes nationwide Share Our Wealth Society.
Returns to Baton Rouge to engineer an extraordinary legislative
program granting dictatorial powers to his regime in Louisiana.
Roosevelt administration channels patronage to anti-Longs
and initiates tax evasion investigations.

1935   Steps up attacks on the Roosevelt administration in Senate speeches
and filibusters, speaking tours and on radio.
Threatens third-party candidacy in opposition to Roosevelt for 1936.
(September) At the age of forty-two is assassinated
by Dr. Carl A. Weiss in Baton Rouge.
My First Days in the White House published posthumously.

HUEY LONG LOOKS AT THE WORLD

1

The Formative Years

In this section we present Huey Long's recollections of his childhood and youth as recorded in his autobiography, Every Man A King.[1] *Long decided to write his autobiography in the fall of 1932, after he had taken his Senate seat and had become a highly controversial national figure. Accordingly, he retired to Baton Rouge and New Orleans and within a year had dictated the entire manuscript, utilizing several secretaries and frequently striding about the room vigorously acting out the episodes being described—a characteristic practice with which his lieutenants and interviewers were familiar. Autobiographies are inherently exercises in self-justification, and those penned by presidential aspirants are even more likely to resemble a campaign tract. But readers can infer from the following passages, some of them remarkably candid and even on rare occasion self-effacing, much about the formative experiences that were to shape Long's fundamental views.*

BOYHOOD IN WINN PARISH

Long was born in 1893 in Winnfield, seat of Winn Parish, Louisiana, the seventh of nine children. Later in his political career he was to make much of his log cabin origins, for the myth of humble beginnings and the virtues of poverty exercised a powerful appeal to Louisiana's depressed yeomanry—and indeed to Americans generally, especially following the crash of 1929. But the following

---

[1] Huey P. Long, *Every Man a King* (New Orleans, La.: National Book Company, 1933; Chicago, Ill.: Quadrangle Books, Inc., 1964). Reprinted by permission of Russell B. Long and Quadrangle Books, Inc. Several of the passages that follow have been abridged for reasons of space.

passages reveal a truer picture of relative prosperity, if measured against the modest standards of the red clay hills and pine barrens of north Louisiana. They also reflect young Huey's staunchly Baptist home environment, his hatred of farm drudgery, his voracious appetite for books, and his early inclinations toward oratory.

Benvenuto Cellini, famed Florentine autobiographer, musician and sculptor, said that when one whose career has been above the ordinary, reached the age of sixty years, he should compile an autobiography for the world.

I am now thirty-nine, some twenty-one years short of that time when, according to Cellini, I should begin to compose such a work. But there is a fable to the effect that Cardinal Mazarin, on his death bed, grieved over the fact that he was near death at the age of fifty-two. A physician is said to have declared that his years of service in the Fronde were four years in one; that, therefore, he was dying at an age past eighty.

If newspapers, magazines and some biographers of this country and other nations find the public so interested in me that they should continue to write and to publish garbled accounts of my career, then perhaps I should write of myself.

In the year 1892 my father, Huey P. Long, and my mother, Caledonia, with their six children moved from Tunica to the community of Winnfield, Louisiana, the Parish Seat of Winn Parish (County) and it was there that I was born August 30, 1893. Land was very cheap at the time my parents settled there and they were able to buy a 320-acre tract, a small part of which was under cultivation. When I was born my parents were living in a comfortable, well-built, four-room log house. A year later we moved into a better house which was built on the same premises.

My earliest and more or less inchoate recollections are that, in the time of my childhood, any person of brawn had some place or opportunity to hew out what was required of him in life. My sympathies were attracted to the persons who had no such physical asset, whose fight for subsistence was one of living from hand to mouth, of which there seem to have been more than a few among the people I knew.

Our community was a kindly one with the philosophy of "live and let live"; no one went hungry or in need of clothes if any one in the neighborhood had things beyond his own immediate requirements. I was frequently sent by my parents with food and clothing of the best kind to some less fortunate family living in the neighborhood. Such people did not need to make their wants known—not even was it necessary that they disclose their identity. If there was a fair sign from which it might be reasonably suspected that someone was in need, we shared with him the best we had.

Among the first of the strange families to have moved into our locality was a Methodist preacher with a number of small children. There were not enough people of his faith to furnish sufficient contribution for his church work. I made frequent trips to their home, sometimes more than once a day, carrying provisions to feed the children.

Years later, when one from this family was among the foremost of the sinister-controlled members of the Legislature undertaking my ruin as Governor I sent someone to him and I said to my messenger:

"Tell him one thing: I am still glad my folks didn't let them starve." But there is and always has been a Providence who understands and who does not forget.

I must have been about eight years old when I saw the first sheriff's sale which I remember. By that time a railroad had been built into the community. A farmer's place was to be auctioned by the sheriff for a debt owed to a store. Before the sale, standing on the steps of the courthouse, this farmer begged the crowd not to bid for his home. He plead that it would be taking it away from his children; that if given time to raise another crop he could pay his debts.

No one in the crowd offered a bid. The creditor remained silent until the sheriff was about ready to declare "no sale," when he took courage and made his bid.

The poor farmer was out; I was horrified. I could not understand. It seemed criminal.

This marked the first sign, in my recollection, of a neighborhood, where the blessings of the Creator were shared one with the other, being transformed into a community yielding to commercial enticements.

A small railroad built a line into Winnfield and located a depot on my father's farm. Soon other railroads entered the same vicinity and Winnfield became a village. Within ten years the town grew to about 3000 inhabitants. One side of my father's farm became part of the business section, and another part of it was occupied by residences.

The surrounding territory soon abounded with sawmills and lumber camps. The sparse farm population increased. But the more remote rural section was never thickly settled and is not now.

I recollect a trip to one of these sawmill camps near my home a few years later when a schoolmate and myself auctioned off a wagon load of books. We had only a banjo and a pair of scissors left in the wagon. We sold them, too.

Returning home that night, after we had calculated our profits, the mule pulling the wagon made a run away going down hill, tearing up the wagon and the harness. Bang went the profits!

The free and easy life and practises of the incoming railroad and sawmill workers rather excited my father, lest his sons might become contaminated by them. With some of the first money which he acquired from the sale of town lots carved from his farm, he bought another farm ten miles back in the country from Winnfield, to which he early announced his intention of moving.

The family home was never moved to this farm; however, we did some of the work there. A few crops of cotton and corn were raised.

I managed to keep as a closed secret the fact that I smoked and chewed tobacco. But when the time came for me to leave town and go to the country farm, I usually managed to smuggle a little along. On one occasion a plug slipped out of my back pocket while I was riding on a spring seat of the wagon. My father picked it up.

"If you stay alive until you are twenty-one, it will be the wonder of this world," he muttered, taking the tobacco away from me.

Practically everbody in the neighborhood, male and female, had done some of the work of planting corn, cotton and potatoes; all had picked cotton; most of them from time to time had worked on the railroad or at the lumber camps and sawmills.

From my earliest recollection I hated the farm work. In the field the rows were long; the sun was hot; there was little companionship. Rising before the sun, we toiled until dark, after which we did nothing except eat supper, listen to the whippoorwills, and go to bed.

Sometimes we split a few rails, or hewed a cross tie or two; occasionally we cut wood or drove a team of mules. The cotton boll-weevil had made its appearance and added to the already uninteresting and unprofitable work. My every sympathy has gone out to those who toil.

At the age of ten, I made my first attempt to run away from home. I got less than fifty miles. I made another effort a few years later, but was caught some twenty miles away from Winnfield.

I had read in the Scriptures of the tears and greetings given for the prodigal son on his return. But when I reached home one of my sisters, in a shrill voice, shouted:

"Come in, tramp!"

While at home I was, under compulsion, a regular attendant of all religious ceremonies. On Sunday morning about nine o'clock we went to Sunday School. Church services immediately followed. On the same Sunday in mid-afternoon I went to the church for the young people's religious society meeting. On Sunday night we returned for more church services. On Wednesday night we attended prayer meeting. We went to every funeral within ten miles. Most of us read the Scripture from cover to cover.

At about the age of thirteen I took up the work of a printer. I mastered the trade fairly well, working in a printing office most of the time while not actually attending school. The compensation was rather good in comparison with what was paid for other work. A book auctioneer, with a large collection of books of all kinds and descriptions, came to Winnfield. He hired me to help in handling the books. I took my pay in books.

A school mate of mine made an arrangement by which he secured some books to auction in nearby and smaller towns. I helped him in some of the towns, with none too great success except to acquire a considerable stock of books. At times we found jobs selling stocks of merchandise at auction.

At the age of fifteen I was sent as a representative in debating from the Winnfield High School to the State High School Rally which was held at the Louisiana State University in Baton Rouge, the Capital of the State. I fared badly, but was given honorable mention.

The following year, April, 1910, I was again sent to the State Rally as debater, declaimer, mile runner and member of the relay team. I made no showing worthy of mention in any of the contests except in debating, in which I won third place and a scholarship to the Louisiana State University.

TRAVELING SALESMAN

Huey's abortive flights from home and farm labor early suggested a streak of stubborn independence and ingenuity—a kind of impudent inventiveness that was to lead to his expulsion from Winnfield High School at the age of sixteen for publishing "a sheet attacking the faculty members every now and then" [2] *(an episode that he omits below). He subsequently spent several years wandering about Louisiana, Texas, Arkansas, Mississippi, Tennessee, and Oklahoma as a "drummer" or traveling salesman, sometimes hobo, and itinerant student of law. In his door-to-door hawking of household supplies, packed foods, produce, patent medicines, and Cottelene cooking oil, the aggressive and gregarious young salesman early developed the essential technique of selling himself. Huey was also a careful observer of the political artistry of Jeff Davis of Arkansas and of James K. Vardaman, Theodore Bilbo, and John Sharp Williams of Mississippi. One of his early promotional cake-baking contests had been won by Miss Rose McConnell of Shreveport; in 1913, at the age of nineteen, Huey won the hand of Miss McConnell.*

Conditions were not very good in the Winnfield community along in 1910.

There were nine children in our family. I was sixteen years old. My parents had been able, with the help the six older children had given, to send them to college until they were practically finished or graduated.

I saw no opportunity to attend the Louisiana State University. The

[2] Charles L. Dufour, *Ten Flags in the Wind* (New York: Harper & Row, Publishers, 1967), pp. 258–59.

scholarship which I had won did not take into account books and living expenses. It would have been difficult to secure enough money.

I secured a position travelling for a large supply house which had a branch office in New Orleans. My job was to sell its products to the merchants and to advertise and solicit orders for it from house to house. Along with the work of soliciting orders from house to house and from merchants, I tacked up signs, distributed pie plates and cook books and occasionally held baking contests in various cities and towns.

I dropped out of the employment of the concern for about four months to attend school at Shreveport, after which I took up the same work.

In the summer of 1911, I secured employment with a packing company as a regular travelling salesman with a salary and expense account. For the first time in my life I felt that I had hit a bed of ease. I was permitted to stop at the best hotels of the day. My territory covered several states in the south. According to the lights and standards of my associates, I had arrived.

On one of my trips back home, I brought a newly invented product, a safety razor. My father undertook to use it. After moistening his face, he stood in front of the looking glass just over the mantel and began to shave. One of my older brothers, a college graduate, was seated on a trunk in the rear of the room. Observing the lather drying and becoming thin, he undertook to advise my father, with a grain of satire.

"Pa," he said, "they say that thing works a little better with lather."

My father paused and looked at my brother.

"I'll just swear," he said, "I have certainly raised smart sons. I'll bet, young man, that the wonder of your life is how pa ever got this far."

The life of a drummer was entirely too easy for me. I turned in a goodly volume of business. I was easily convinced by other drummers that so long as I reported large sales I need not worry as to my expense account or as to the regularity of my work. I found this was not true in my case and that I was working for a strict disciplinarian; after being given a few warnings, which I did not heed, I was summarily discharged.

I undertook to secure my reinstatement without avail whereupon I went back to Houston, Texas, where I stayed for some months. I secured employment at various occupations, but I was not able to get another position as a travelling salesman.

Finally I left Houston for Memphis, Tennessee, but I found no opening for a travelling salesman there, and for several weeks I was without any employment at all. I went from park to depot and depot to railroad yards, sleeping wherever I might be permitted to lay my head and eating what I could get when I could get it. I gave up my effort in Memphis and left for Oklahoma.

Uptown in Oklahoma City was and still stands the office of the Dawson Produce Company. I went there and called for the manager. I met Mr.

K. W. Dawson himself, the owner of the business. He was a very serious but kindly faced gentleman.

I immediately felt at ease and asked to secure some kind of work as a salesman in the vicinity of Norman, Oklahoma, so that I might earn enough money to attend the University there and study law. I was almost penniless at the time but undertook not to disclose it.

Mr. Dawson told me to return the next day. On the following day he told me that there were four towns, including Norman, which were being worked by a salesman whom he could use in the office; that if I wished to make those towns as my territory he thought I could work their trade and attend school all the time necessary to carry on a year's law classes.

I gladly took the job and was given an order book with a price list and the accounts which I was to collect. This occurred January 2, 1912. But how was I to get to Norman?

Snow and sleet covered the ground. The wind was cold and cutting. I surveyed my belongings. I had exactly three nickles.

There was an interurban line which ran half way the route to Norman, from Oklahoma City to Moore. The fare for that first nine miles was fifteen cents. I pondered—whether I should ride the first nine miles for the fifteen cents and walk the remaining nine miles or try to walk the entire eighteen miles, as cold as it was, and have the money when I reached Norman. I took the course of walking the full distance.

I reached there about midnight and walked the streets of the town the balance of the night, spending some time to warm myself at an oil mill where work was being done.

On the morning of January 3, 1912, bright and early, I ventured forth on my new employment. Immediately, I sold one merchant some fifty sacks of potatoes. I finally secured pledges for sufficient orders to account for an entire carload. What luck!

I went to telephone the orders to Mr. Dawson, intending to ask his permission to draw some amount of money on the business. Of course, I placed the call "collect." I had eaten breakfast and had not a cent left.

Word came back that the collect telephone call was declined.

I faced the task of securing twenty-five cents in order to place my telephone call from Norman to Oklahoma City. In my back pocket was a new leather purse which had been sent to me as a Christmas gift. It had been put to no use whatever. It couldn't have been. I found a way to pawn it to a second-hand furniture store, outside the business section of the town, for the necessary amount.

I again placed the telephone call for Mr. Dawson. When he answered I informed him that I had sold a carload of potatoes in Norman at list price.

"I am sorry," he answered, "we are out of potatoes and will be for some time."

I had walked; I had starved; I had disposed of everything of value I had on the face of the earth. So, I planned to leave Norman the best way I could. I would not give up without one more effort. Boldly I went to a bank to see the president and undertook to borrow twenty-five dollars. At least the banker wasn't crazy.

So my plan was made to leave Norman.

I strolled over to the Santa Fe depot.

While there I noticed a well groomed, rather stout looking gentleman, who appeared to be as aimless and purposeless as I was. He seemed unsettled and nervous. He either spoke to me or I to him. One word brought on another. He asked where I was going. I told him I hadn't exactly decided, but that maybe I would go south, or maybe north. Then he said:

"One train is due here any minute."

"I am not thinking about the train," I replied.

"Then, how are you going?" he asked.

"How do most people go that don't ride?" I asked.

"You don't mean you are going to walk?"

"Out of here just like I walked in," I answered.

He introduced himself to me as R. O. Jackson. In the conversation which followed I told him how I had secured employment in Oklahoma City, of walking into the town, of my disappointment in making certain sales which could not be filled, of my inability to stay there long, and of my decision to leave.

He reached into his pocket and pulled out several bills. He offered to hand me one of twenty dollars.

"I do not want you to give me twenty dollars or anything else," I said. "The chances are, however, that whatever you hand me will be a gift. If I can make it here at all, I can do it on five dollars. If you will lend me five dollars, and I can't pay it back, then you can feel that I at least saved you fifteen."

He handed me the five dollars.

My new friend and creditor did not leave me after lending me the money. On the following morning, when I approached the mercantile establishments of Norman, I was frequently informed that Jackson had been to one or the other asking that they give as much of their business as possible to the Dawson Produce Company. I met Mr. Jackson on the street the following morning.

"What are you going to do for law books?" he asked me.

"Go without any until I can get some money to buy them," I replied.

"My brother-in-law owns the drug store here that handles the law books. He will credit you."

I was at the University from January until May, 1912, where I spent the happiest days of my life. I attended my law classes regularly and I earned, on the average, nearly $100.00 per month for my work as a salesman.

My previous experience did not make much of a mark on me. I spent my money as I made it. What I did not spend, I either loaned or gave away to other boys at the University more in need than myself.

I left that school at the end of its session in the spring of 1912, expecting to return that autumn. I secured a job with a manufacturing house of Kansas City, Missouri. I was one of the regular salesmen for the concern.

Eventually, other salesmen were placed under me—men doing work similar to that which I had done in the early days with the supply company.

I was soon located in Memphis, Tennessee, with headquarters at the Gayoso Hotel. My territory embraced parts of Texas, Oklahoma, Louisiana, Arkansas, Tennessee, Illinois, Kentucky, Mississippi, and Alabama.

I had begun to help certain others. I could not see a way to return to the University of Oklahoma, a fact which gave me much grief and heartache.

During Christmas week, 1912, I came back to my home in Louisiana on a month's vacation. I spent much of my time in Shreveport. I invited Miss Rose McConnell, whom I had met while attending school in Shreveport, to go with me to the Grand Opera House to see the opera "Lohengrin."

A few days later I was arrested and charged with having shot at some one, but at a time during the hours when I had been at the Grand Opera House. Miss McConnell had kept the stubs torn off the theatre tickets. We located all the people who had been near us at the show and I was released.

We were married the following year in Memphis, Tennessee. I was nineteen years old.

SMALL TOWN LAWYER

Young Long's ambition was reinforced by a supreme self-confidence. In 1914 he borrowed $400 from "a brother" (the brother was Julius Long, with whom he had broken bitterly by 1933) to attend Tulane Law School. After only one year of cramming, he brazenly requested and passed an extraordinary oral examination, and was admitted to the Lousiana Bar in 1915 at the age of twenty-one. His initial law partnership in Winnfield was also with his older brother Julius (and is also not mentioned below); their incompatibility led to its dissolution within two months, and Huey hung out his modest shingle on his own. Huey also sat out the

*World War. In addition to claiming an exemption as a husband
and father, he ingeniously claimed additional immunity from the
draft as a public official: a notary public! (The first claim was allowed; the second was not.) When later attacked politically for his
evasion of military service, he was consistently to reply, "I wasn't
mad at nobody"—and to argue, with greater plausibility, that the
vast war expenditures had settled nothing but the enrichment of
bankers and munitions makers.*

Late in the summer of 1914, when war clouds had gathered in
Europe, I spent a final few weeks on the road with the Chattanooga
Medicine Company at a better rate of pay, and in October entered Tulane University at New Orleans as a law student. I undertook to carry
the work of a three-year law course in one year in order that I might
be admitted to the bar in the following spring. I had a few hundred dollars and a brother had promised to lend me $400.00 more.

My wife and I settled in a dingy two room apartment in the city of
New Orleans. I attended such classes as the hours would permit, studying
many other subjects without the help of class instruction.

I entered a contest to become one of the school's debaters, and was
chosen by the University to debate against a girls' college. That was the
year, I think the only year, when that girls' college won the debating
contest from Tulane.

I studied law as much as from sixteen to twenty hours each day. My
weight fell to 112 pounds. While I passed such of the examinations as
I was permitted to take at Tulane, is was not possible under the scho-
lastic rules of the University for me to take the other examinations so
that I might secure a diploma.

My money gave out completely during the last months of the spring.
I faced the alternative of becoming a lawyer very quickly or of abandon-
ing the effort.

I went to Chief Justice Frank A. Monroe, of the Supreme Court of
Louisiana, in New Orleans.

"My name is Long. I am a special student at Tulane University," I
said to the Judge.

"All right, Mr. Long, what can I do for you?"

"Judge, I don't know that you can do anything for me, but I want to
give you the facts about my situation and get your advice on what I
should do and if possible, your help."

The old Chief Justice appeared responsive. I felt perfectly at ease.

"Under your rules here I cannot take an examination for the bar until
the last part of June. I would like to wait until June if I could. I am
married. I have no money. I have borrowed to get to where I am now.
I want to know if it's at all possible for the court to give one an examination other than on the day set by the rules."

"This court can do anything that a majority of its members want to do," he replied. Then he continued: "The only difficulty I can see for you is in getting the bar committee to examine you. Looks to me like they ought to be reasonable."

"Well, Judge, if it's not asking too much, just how would you advise me to go about getting the bar committee."

"Why, just go to them like you came to me. If you are well enough up on your subjects they can examine you orally. We'll try them out. Let me know how you make it."

I sought a meeting of the bar committee for the next day, and was able to arrange it. I was passed by the bar committee, whereupon Chief Justice Monroe assembled a majority of the court, gave the necessary examination, and on the 15th day of May, 1915, at the age of 21, I was sworn in and declared a full-fledged lawyer in the State of Louisiana.

I arrived at my old home town of Winnfield some few days after I had been admitted to the bar, ready for the practice of law. My first few months' effort netted me no returns. I gave up the office I had occupied.

With no money and apparently with no chance of earning any through the practice of law, I undertook to secure employment as a travelling salesman. I couldn't secure a position. I had no law books except a copy of the Civil Code, a volume of the Code of Practice and a "formulary."

I found a small ante-room, located over the Bank of Winnfield. It was about eight feet wide by ten feet long. It had no electric lights and only one window in it. The bank trusted me for the rent of that ante-room at $4.00 a month. I secured a white pine top table, placed my three law books on it, had painted a fifty-cent tin sign, and again undertook to herald to the world:

"Huey P. Long, Lawyer."

A shoe store opened on the street immediately next to the bank. The proprietor promised that, whenever I was wanted at the telephone, he would call me. . . .

I managed for several months to pick up a little "chip and whet-stone" practice. The bank from which I was renting my office pressed me pretty hard for the $4.00 per month rent. It was hard to get. . . .

I had bought a typewriter and was in arrears trying to pay for it at the rate of $10.00 a month. I had bought the revised statutes of the State, a filing cabinet, an oak table and typewriter desk, on all of which my payments amounted to an additional $20.00 per month. I still occupied the ante-room, had no telephone and worked at night by the light of a kerosene lamp. . . .

My wife being very economical, we lived modestly for a few dollars per month. No children had been born to us up to that time, but we were very happy.

2
Louisiana Kingfish

Given young Long's discernible neo-Populistic sympathies, his pronounced ambition and aggressive personality and the close linkage between the law and politics, it seems inevitable that he should have sought elective office. And given the considerable degree to which Louisiana politics was responsive and indeed subservient to the wishes of what Long increasingly denounced as "the vested interests"—the Standard Oil Company and gas and shipping interests, comfortably allied with the New Orleans Ring and the traditionally conservative merchant and planter élite—it also seems inevitable that Huey and the interests would clash. What seems far from inevitable is that the impertinent and impecunious young challenger should survive the encounter—much less triumph. The selections that follow are abridged from Every Man A King.

A TASTE FOR POLITICS

When the struggling young Winnfield attorney took a widow's apparently hopeless case against a bank and won it, the poor people of Winn Parish began to bring their grievances to him. Long's professional and financial interest in liberalizing workmen's compensation laws led him into politics at the age of twenty-two. Allied with his friend S. J. Harper, a state senator and incorrigible radical who opposed the war and demanded conscription of wealth not men, Long successfully broke the niggardly $300 maximum which the heavily lobbied Legislature had placed upon damages obtainable for negligence in the injury or death of a workman. The following year he sought an appointment as assistant United States attorney at Shreveport, but his populistic reputation prompted political opposition from the conservative corporate interests that killed the appointment. In one of his most revealing self-appraisals, Long confessed that "once disappointed over a political undertaking, I could never cast it from my mind."

I had begun a state-wide agitation against a new law of the State which had severely restricted the right of recovery for injury or death incurred in the course of work. I created quite a sentiment against the law.

The State Legislature met in May, 1916. My friend, S. J. Harper, of Winnfield, was a member of the State Senate. I prepared for him certain amendments which he was to offer in the Committee on Capital and Labor, of which he was a member.

It was my first time to have seen a legislature in session. The formalities, mannerisms, kow-towing and easily discernible insincerities surrounding all of the affairs of the session were, to my mind (untrained to such a scene), disgusting.

I was twenty-two. . . .

In the course of a few days a meeting of the Committee on Capital and Labor of the State Senate was assembled in the evening to consider, among other things, the Harper amendment which I had prepared. Upon my asking to be recognized I was generally ordered to sit down.

One time when I rose the committee chairman asked,

"Whom do you represent?"

"Several thousand common laborers," I said.

"Are they paying you anything?"

"No," I replied.

"They seem to have good sense."

The attendants guffawed.

Several speeches were made condemning my activities against the law. I was referred to as an impostor by one or two lawyers and members of the Senate, but still I could not secure recognition to speak.

One lawyer there told a story of a fly alighting on the hub of a wagon passing through a sand bed which said to itself:

"See what a dust I am raising!"

He referred to my having been admitted to the bar of the State for only one year, and urged ignoring such contemptuous furor as I had undertaken to create.

At about the hour of midnight a motion was made that consideration of the amendments be terminated and that the committee adjourn.

I had stood for about all the legislative practices that my system could tolerate. Neither the rulings and orders of the chair nor anything else could have hushed me at the time. Without being recognized I rose at the foot of the table and began to speak. I was not interrupted. I said:

> For twenty years has the Louisiana Legislature been dominated by the henchmen and attorneys of the interests. Those seeking reforms have, from necessity, bowed their heads in regret and shame when witnessing the victories of these corrupting influences at this capitol. But, gentlemen, with all this, not until 1914 did they possess the brazen audac-

ity to command the General Assembly of Louisiana to pass unanimously a law by which a laborer's family should not receive over an average sum of $300.00 for a life upon whom they depend for education and support, though it be lost while in the honest discharge of duty. . . .

Yet, there are those here representing the combined corporations, who declare that they merely seek justice. What a subterfuge! Exposure seems to be an irresistible converter. There are hours when the infidel invokes God and the anarchist calls on the government. There are times when the people cling to that which they have repudiated. Can it be that these gentlemen, after exposure seems imminent, will now attempt to invoke the term "justice" after their continued practices of fraud and deceit? We are afraid of such conversions.

Most of the amendments proposed by Senator Harper were lost on the vote of the committee, but enough sentiment was aroused that many of them were adopted following debate on the floor of the Senate. . . .

An opportunity seemed to appear to make it possible for me to move to the City of Shreveport, when a vacancy occurred in the United States Attorney's office there. I undertook to secure the position of Assistant United States Attorney. I received such assurances as to convince me that the position was practically mine for the asking. Later, a severe opposition developed from all the corporations of my territory, which I could not overcome.

Probably that was my evil day. Once disappointed over a political undertaking, I could never cast it from my mind. I awaited the opportunity of a political contest.

RAILROAD COMMISSIONER

By 1918, at the age of twenty-four, both Long's political ambition (he had early announced to his bride his firm intention to become President of the United States) and the essence of his neo-populistic creed were fixed. The latter is reflected in his letter to the New Orleans Item *(below) and the former in his announcement as a candidate for the office of Railroad Commissioner. The three-man commission had been a largely moribund regulatory body. But, shortly to be transformed into a Public Service Commission of widely enhanced regulatory powers, its potential as a launching platform for an aspiring politician was promising. Probably a shrewd appreciation of this promise rather than the lack of a statutory minimum age tempted Long to launch his political career with the Railroad Commission. His early campaign innovations, his personal vendetta against Standard Oil, his mercurial political alliances, and his frenetic battles for political survival and for genuine socioeconomic change are all harbingers of a calculated and mete-*

oric political career that was to lead him to the Louisiana State House, the U.S. Senate, and boldly toward the Presidency.

My legal and political opposition to the vested interests took on larger proportions from month to month. I was being called to different parts of the State to handle cases in the Courts.

But "save the mark" when we ran into a battle against one of these corporations before a State board. We didn't have the chance of a snowball in a fire.

I had concluded to wage a fight on a wide scale to reform both the personnel and the conduct of certain State departments. Somehow, in my youthful enthusiasm, I felt perfectly equal to the task. Had I known then the hill I had picked to climb, it is certain that my plans to free these departments from corporate influences would have been less ambitious.

What a fight lay ahead! Always my cases in Court were on the side of the small man—the under-dog. I had never taken a suit against a poor man and have not done so to this day.

I find in the newspaper files the following letter which appeared in the columns of the New Orleans *Item* and other papers of the State, on March 1, 1918, viz:

THINKS WEALTH SHOULD BE MORE EVENLY DISTRIBUTED

The Editor of the Item:

A conservative estimate is that about sixty-five or seventy per cent of the entire wealth of the United States is owned by two per cent of the people. Sixty-eight per cent of the whole people living in the United States own but two per cent of its wealth. From the year 1890 to 1910, the wealth of this nation trebled, yet the masses owned less in 1910 than they did in 1890 and a greater per cent of the people lived in mortgaged and rented homes in 1900 than in 1890, and more lived in rented and mortgaged homes in 1910 than did in 1900. Reports from the Committee on Industrial Relations, appointed by the President, showed that wealth is fast concentrating in the hands of the few.

But the greatest cause for industrial unrest is that of education. Authorities on education tell us that eighty out of every one hundred people in the United States never enter high school; only fourteen out of every thousand get a college education; 690 out of every thousand never finish the fourth grade in school. Does such a condition give the ordinary man his proper return of the nation's prosperity? What do you think of such a game of life, so brutally and cruelly unfair, with the dice so loaded that the child of today must enter it with only fourteen chances out of a thousand in his favor of getting a college education and with 986 chances against his securing the lucky draw? How can this Nation prosper with the ordinary child having only twenty chances in a thousand of securing the first part of the game?

This is the condition, north, east, south and west; with wealth concentrating, classes becoming defined, there is not the opportunity for Christian uplift and education and cannot be until there is more economic reform. This is the problem that the good people of this country must consider.

HUEY P. LONG.

I was twenty-four years of age.

Through a careful perusal of the State Constitution I found that there was no minimum age limit prescribed for a Railroad Commissioner. I was, therefore, eligible for election. Five candidates, including myself, entered the race for Railroad Commissioner from the North Louisiana District in the summer of 1918.

My headquarters were established in the small residence of my father-in-law in Shreveport, from which my wife, with the help of the family and friends in the neighborhood, mailed out literature and answered letters. Although our first child was only one year old my wife conducted my campaign "headquarters" with courage and efficiency.

The motor car was a new thing in our country. Its appearance was generally considered to be resented among the country population but I paid no attention to this supposed prejudice. I borrowed sufficient money to buy an automobile in which to travel over the district.

Soon, however, my funds ran out. Politics involving personally running for office was something new to me. I went to the office of O. K. Allen. He was the Tax Assessor of the Parish.

"Oscar," I began, "I haven't a penny in the world that I can get my hands on to continue this race. I don't see that I can go any further."

"How much money have you got?"

"Not a penny. I was afraid my gasoline would give out before I could reach Winnfield. If it had I would have had to beg for some."

"Well," he said, "I can get some money."

"Get me five hundred dollars if you can."

He negotiated his own note at the bank and brought me back the money in cash. I left the town and renewed my work.

I canvassed the farmers in person and spent most of my time at night tacking up my campaign posters in the neighborhood being canvassed. Occasionally, so intense was my campaign, I called people from their beds at all hours of the night to talk politics.

Nothing in my campaigning seemed to please farmers more or cause them to recollect me nearly so favorably as to call them from their beds at night. All over the neighborhoods flew the news of my working through the nights.

I ran second—some two thousand votes behind the incumbent in the first primary. A second primary was ordered and was soon on in full force.

The final reports of that contest gave me a majority of 636 votes. My opponent congratulated me upon my victory.

I thus became Railroad Commissioner just as I entered the age of twenty-five.

Immediately following the second primary I announced a change of residence from Winnfield to Shreveport.

I had done certain legal work for some of my Winnfield friends connected with the oil business in Caddo Parish, of which Shreveport is the parish seat. They paid me in oil stock. I bought additional stock from some of them.

Several companies in which I was interested were very successful. We finally had a very large concern which gave promise of becoming an even larger affair.

It was just at this time the big companies threatened to begin pipeline embargoes, designed to freeze out small companies and independent operators.

We feared the worst for our company.

More than one hundred other independent oil concerns with thousands of stockholders, were in the area affected by this pipeline embargo. They had all been encouraged to develop the field to the fullest extent. The pipelines of the oil trust were paying $1.55 per barrel for the oil and begging for more of it.

Like a flash, however, all the independents were told they would take no more of their oil. I had gone to sleep one night with transactions all ready to be closed for options and equities I had acquired which meant I might some day be mentioned among the millionaires, to awake in the morning to read that nothing I had was of value because the three pipeline companies said so.

A meeting was held at the Shreveport Chamber of Commerce, attended by officials of the Standard Oil Company and the other pipeline companies allied in the embargo.

The faces of the Standard Oil group bore expressions of self-content. About these men there was that undefinable something that betokens freedom from money cares and anxiety as to the future. But the faces of the men in the independent group told a different story. Care, and in some cases, desperation, was written in every line.

Some of the other big companies had not at that time issued any announcement that they were going to proceed to an embargo. An officer of one of them arose.

"I think maybe we can work this thing out," said the pipeline officer, "provided we all stop drilling any more wells. My company has not said it will refuse to take this oil."

"But you are going to," the Standard Oil vice-president authoritatively announced.

The official of the other pipeline company subsided.

"And this a free country," I spoke for the first time. I continued: "You've done this before and got by with it, but this time, go do it and see when you hear the last of it."

I left the meeting.

The following days I had occasion to learn considerably more of the courses pursued and the results from such oil controversies. Elderly oil operators informed me that nothing was ever gained fighting the big companies. . . .

With the State faced by an oil embargo and "freeze out," I undertook to bring the large oil companies operating pipelines before the Railroad Commission for regulation. Louisiana had a law that gave us a measure of control over them.

I was not successful in securing much action from my two associates, except that in a meeting held at Shreveport, several independent oil operators were allowed to come before our body to make certain representations of facts about conditions existing in the operation of pipelines.

The oil trust officials did not even appear. They seemed to know their ground. Nothing said at the meeting was disputed. It could not have been.

I prepared a condensed statement of findings together with a set of recommendations based upon the presentations made to the Commission by the independent oil operators.

My ultimate hope was to force an extra session of the Legislature, or if not that, to force the oil question as an issue in the state-wide political campaign soon to start.

To a meeting of the Railroad Commission held in the old Capitol, at Baton Rouge, on March 25, 1919, I took several prepared copies of these proposed findings, making no mention of this fact until the Commission had gone into executive session.

Then I presented my report and argued for its adoption.

One commissioner seemed to be willing to sign. The Chairman hesitated. He read and re-read from portions of the proposed findings.

The old Capitol building is situated on a high bluff immediately overlooking the Mississippi River. When the argument had reached its height I looked out of the window and saw an oil tanker steaming up the river. I pointed to it.

"Look at that, Shelby," I said. "There now is a ship coming up the river loaded with Mexican crude to go in the tanks where they will not let us put our oil."

Chairman Shelby Taylor took one look at the ship. He reached for a pen and signed the document. Michel put his name on it.

I handed the paper to the Secretary, who engrossed it as a Commission document. I had the copies of the findings which I had in my possession certified by the Secretary, some of which I handed to the newspapers that night. Next day it was given sensational publicity.

News that the Commission had issued such a finding swept through the City of Baton Rouge the next morning like a hurricane.

Adjacent to the Capital City was located its large refinery and oil tank farms, the largest in the world.

Lawyers and agents representing the Standard Oil Company flocked to the City at an early hour of the morning following the Commission's findings to see what could be done to remedy the situation. In the meantime the Commission had gone into session to hear other cases.

The Chairman lived and practiced law in Baton Rouge; he appeared to be ill at ease. He stormed at the Secretary as we sat behind the table listening to the evidence and arguments in other cases.

"Where is that document? I've been made a fool of; hand it to me and I will tear it up," I heard him say in muffled tones.

I intervened, exhibiting a number of certified copies.

"This document is issued," I said, "and I have plenty of copies; I have given plenty of others to the press."

Governor Pleasant declined to call any extra session to deal with the oil question though sentiment favored it.

I issued several statements but the Governor was adamant.

With a new Governor to be elected in January, 1920, an opening campaign meeting for the preceding July 4th, was scheduled at Hot Wells, a health resort in the center of the State. All candidates for Governor were invited to speak.

I was permitted to speak on the oil trust fight at this meeting.

A newspaper, unfriendly to me, carried, in its report of the meeting:

"LONG WAS THE SENSATION"

"When he concluded, John R. Hunter, of Alexandria, who presided over the meeting, referred to the Long speech as being 'as hot as this boiling water that bubbles up from Hot Wells at 116 degrees. . . .'

"He recited the history of the Standard Oil at Pine Island and at Chrichton, charged that they had driven oil prices down and frozen out the little fellows until they got control.

"'It was weak-backed Democrats like Pleasant that drove the Third District Democrats from the Democratic Party' he charged. 'Thank God, he opposed me when I was running for Railroad Commissioner.'

"Mr. Long said that if there ever was an institution that stood convicted before the people, that it is Standard Oil. 'This octopus is among the world's greatest criminals. It was thrown out of Texas following its raid in Spindle Top; it was ousted from Kansas; it was forced to terms in Oklahoma by the famous Oklahoma pipe line bill.' "

The 1919–1920 campaign finally dwindled to two candidates—Frank P. Stubbs and John M. Parker.

A meeting was arranged between Mr. Parker and myself when he reached Shreveport in the early part of November, where he was to speak the next day. I urged that he should renew his declarations on the oil question in somewhat more specific language and rather assured him that if he did so, I would come to his support in the campaign.

I went over some of the hardships imposed on the independent oil men and farmers as a result of the freeze-out.

"I know how to sympathize with you fellows," Parker said. He looked very straight at me and continued:

"You know, once I had a patent that some big outfit decided to take away from me, and when I started to get into a fight with them I went to a lawyer and was told that I might win it, but that it would cost me more than I would ever get out of it."

He made sufficient pronouncement the next day to satisfy my mind. I declared in his favor.

There was no time to lose in North Louisiana. Because of our lack of newspaper support in some sections, I had many thousands of circulars printed for distribution. I took the stump for a period of approximately seventy days and went to many places where no other campaign orator had ever reached, traveling at times by horse-back to fill appointments.

We managed to break what our opponents called the "solid North Louisiana vote." It gave a slight majority for Parker. He was elected.

Governor Parker immediately addressed me a few letters, taking occasion to thank me for the support which I had given to his candidacy.

Before his inauguration, however, I was shelved.

It was here I saw occur a phenomenon that has frequently presented itself in the after years. Those of us, zealous for reform and who had exhausted ourselves in the election, hied back to our work to give attention to our several neglected affairs. The crowd of wiseacres, skilled at flattery and repartee, surrounded our newly elected governor. Soon he was convinced that his insurmountable virtue alone had wrought the victory; before long he was made to see how much bigger his majority might have been but for the "hindrance" of such "objectionables" as myself.

The elements we had defeated, always in his easy view, broke into ecstasies of delight at which they had so lately found to be his words of wisdom. They had felt a divine spark. When the slaves of the campaign had the time to visit him, the element we had expected to oust were needed to introduce us to our late candidate.

He made his own program with the help of Standard Oil lawyers, who had been called in to write some of the laws affecting that Corporation. He appeared to desire only such legislation as was agreed to in compromise on all sides.

Cain became his own judge.

But the independent oil interests and I fostered our legislation none the less. The Governor had made too many promises to oppose us in the open, for the time being.

His floor leader, however, announced the Governor's opposition to the passage of our pipeline bill when it came up for a vote in the Lower House, in spite of which we won with the scant margin of two votes.

The bill went through the Senate, though considerably emasculated —as a result of the Governor's efforts.

We feared, and our enemies thought, that it had been so weakened that the pipeline companies could not be held as common carriers.

Some years later, however, as an attorney before the Supreme Court, I succeeded in getting a decision holding these lines to be common carriers under that statute.

As a result of the fight over this pipeline legislation Governor Parker and I became openly hostile. He called a public hearing at which he presided, and requested me to explain certain statements I had made and caused to be published. I faced him with pledges he had made.

Though I do not presume to give the reason for Governor Parker's reticence, since that day he has never dared to offer himself for an office in Louisiana, and we have been bitter enemies. . . .

The office of Railroad Commissioner which I held was a constitutional office.

While I was out of the State, a supporter of the Parker administration introduced an ordinance, the effect of which was to take me off of the Railroad Commission. I drew amendments to save my right to continue as a Commissioner. We brought the amendments to a vote at the most propitious time. My status as a member of the old Railroad and of the newly named Public Service Commission was thus preserved.

But the constitutional convention adjourned in a furor. Even former Governor Pleasant, whom Governor Parker had appointed a delegate to the convention, denounced the members in a speech which he made on the floor of the convention for having allowed the lobbyists and attorneys of the Standard Oil Company to dominate their official conduct.

"I was at a conference at the Governor's Mansion," the former governor said. "We discussed the three per cent severance tax and practically everyone there was in agreement for it to be written into the constitution. All of a sudden Governor Parker rang for the treasurer of the Standard Oil Company to come to the Mansion, and upon his coming there and peremptorily announcing that his company would not stand for the three per cent law, the Governor informed us that that ended the matter; that he could not tolerate the three per cent severance tax provision in the constitution."

With its adjournment, the constitutional convention issued a call for a special session of the Legislature to meet on the first Tuesday of September, 1921. When that Legislature met, a draft of a new law on the severance taxes was to be submitted.

I issued a document to the members of the Legislature, which is a part of the court records of the District Court of East Baton Rouge Parish, Louisiana, which read in part:

> As a means of forcing upon the State legislation injurious to the people but highly profitable and beneficial to the Standard Oil trust and its allied corporate monopolies, you have seen an administration trade in offices which belong to the people and barter them away in a manner unbecoming an ancient ruler of a Turkish domain. Better to have taken the gold hoarded in the Standard Oil vaults at 26 Broadway and deliberately purchase the votes with which the administration has ruled this State for nearly two years than to have brow-beaten, bulldozed and intimidated the Legislature for the benefit of the corporate interests through the free use of the peoples' patronage.
>
> Bold and amazing is the Governor's cry that he has no bill to submit to you, for the reason that it is at 26 Broadway for its final polish. Are you, law makers of Louisiana, to return to your people as fallen chattels who have been counted at the behest of an administration which loudly proclaims the visible control vested in the hands of the corporate interests by an administration which has crept into office through false promises and under pretenses which have shamed the best of our citizens?

A storm broke loose in the Legislature, in which I was severely condemned and threatened with impeachment or prosecution but at the conclusion of which I issued another circular, headed:

"THEIR SINS HAVE FOUND THEM"

I followed later with a third circular.

I issued other statements to the newspapers, some replying to an attack made on me.

I had scarcely returned to my home in Shreveport, when I was telephoned by the Sheriff of our Parish:

"Huey, the Governor has had them issue warrants for your arrest for libel. Say nothing about it. Come to my office to see me."

No news of the matter had reached anyone up to that time.

"Of course, Huey," the Sheriff said, when I called at his office, "I am not going to arrest you. You take these warrants and papers and go on to Baton Rouge as soon as you can and make bond. I will say nothing about it." . . .

Action was announced to result in specific process to bring me to impeachment. A caucus was called, composed of the members of the House of Representatives, either to start process to impeach or to address me out of office as Public Service Commissioner, also including the names of the other two members of the Commission.

The caucus of the members formally assembled at night. The air was heavy and the reek of tobacco would have resurrected Carrie Nation.

Nerves were worn and tempers were out of bounds. It was a gathering in which loyalty was at a premium.

My opposition was in the majority, but a few clever parliamentary strategists aiding me kept the caucus in confusion.

Eventually, I suggested a motion that the three members of the Public Service Commission be requested to forthwith submit their resignations and to thereafter reappear before the people for reelection. Some legislators seized upon the suggestion as being a fair and quick solution.

I immediately had it stated from the floor that I was there and then personally ready to tender my resignation and make my appearance before the people for reelection. One member shouted:

"Sure he will, but he is the only one that can be reelected!"

The opposition forces began to react.

We got a break. The floor leader of the House for the Parker administration arose.

"I am no Huey Long man, but apparently you are not willing for anything to be done here that is fair. I am taking my hat and walking out of this damned session."

Near pandemonium reigned. Any kind of a yell would result in a general confusion. Someone gave the yell.

That ended the impeachment effort in my career for eight years.

Before the legislature could adjourn I drafted a recall law for the State. It was passed.

I was soon to stand trial on the two criminal charges in the district court of East Baton Rouge Parish. . . .

The trial in Baton Rouge was heard.

"Mr. Long," the judge said to me, "I think under the circumstances we all understand it to be impetuousness that persuades you to make some of the statements you have made. The sentence of this court is that on the first charge you serve thirty days in prison, but I will suspend that; and on the second charge my sentence is that you pay us $1.00 or serve one hour."

He left the entire amount of the costs, amounting to a large sum of money, to be paid by the State.

"Judge," I answered, "I am not going to pay that dollar."

"Well, some of us will have to pay it," answered the judge smilingly.

I had noticed that the judge had failed to add the words "during good behavior" to his suspension of sentence.

Judge Brunot declared a recess of court for five minutes and came down from the bench. Of two of the defense counsel he asked 25¢ each, which they gave him. He then took 50¢ out of his own pocket and handed the dollar to the Sheriff. Resuming the bench, he said:

"Mr. Sheriff, Mr. Long's fine is paid. Adjourn court."

When, a few days later, I started the fight all over again and reiterated what I had been saying about the Standard Oil Company and the administration, I heard that Judge Brunot was asked to call me back to court on the suspended 30-day matter. According to report, Judge Brunot became angered and said:

"I've tried to save Governor Parker's face—now don't try it again."

THE LESSONS OF DEFEAT

Long's burgeoning political reputation generated a momentum that led inexorably toward the governor's chair. In 1921 he became chairman of the Public Service Commission and served simultaneously as its chief counsel, flamboyantly arguing and usually winning his cases against rising telephone and electricity rates, railroad and streetcar fares, and oil and gas pipeline restrictions. But in his first gubernatorial race in 1924, he got caught between a pincers. In a three-man race in which the Ku Klux Klan was the predominant issue, Long's opponents were a Catholic lawyer from the Southern French parishes who vigorously opposed the Klan and a Protestant from Baton Rouge who supported antimasking demands but who enjoyed Klan support as a lesser evil. Left swinging in the middle, Long campaigned for what he called the "real issues": better roads, toll-free bridges and schools, free textbooks and lower taxes, and against the Standard Oil "octopus." Long carried northern Louisiana but polled so poorly in New Orleans that he failed to make the runoff. Even so, Huey's third place showing had been surprisingly strong. Subsequent rumors of his retirement from politics to his Shreveport law practice were decidedly premature.

Perhaps I can qualify as a product of the melting pot for in my veins there flows the blood of English, Dutch, Welch, Irish, Scotch and French forebears. An eminent ethnologist has been at great pains to prove that such an admixture produces one capable of conflict.

I proceeded promptly against the Standard Oil Company, having issued Commission process to compel it to bring its books and records before our body. Litigation began. It was in process when matters were suspended for the summer vacation of the courts. Before they reconvened in the fall I had become a candidate for Governor. A writ of injunction had been issued out of the Court in Baton Rouge to stop our hearings. I took the chance of contempt, ignored the injunction, proceeded with hearings and applied for a writ to the Supreme Court. I was upheld.

On my thirtieth birthday, August 30, 1923, I announced my candidacy for Governor in the primary election to be held in January, 1924.

I had neither newspaper nor organized political support, other than my own scattered faction.

Neither could I get favorable or complimentary mention by any of the newspapers, which gave me less than no credit for anything I had done up to that time. They warned against the wild activities with which the people might be afflicted should I become the Governor. . . .

I pursued my campaign for Governor.

We issued many . . . circulars which I handed out and which Mrs. Long and our children mailed from my home and my office helpers mailed from my law office in Shreveport. Campaign posters were tacked up with my own hands, for I had been a sign tacker in the old days and that experience served me in good stead.

I drove my automobile and usually travelled alone, my car loaded with campaign literature and buttons which I handed out at my meetings before and after speaking. . . .

Of my two opponents, one was the Lieutenant Governor serving under, and the other had been an appointee of, the same governor.

It had been arranged for the three of us to appear on the stump at the same meeting in Lafayette Square in New Orleans on Armistice Day.

I had planned a stroke for that day. I thought it would surely turn the tide of the campaign.

With the two on the platform with me, I planned to tell the following, which I originated:

> A merchant finding business slackening, went into producing and selling eggs. He picked the guinea that was the most dependable laying fowl, but when his premises became covered with the guineas their cackle and cluck was such that he was unable to stand their constant racket. He therefore concluded to breed a cross between the guinea and some fowl not possessed of the objectionable cackle. So he took two eggs from the nest of a guinea; one of which he put under a turkey, the other of which he put under a setting hen, expecting both to hatch, one with a cross between the guinea and the turkey, the other a cross between the guinea and the hen, trusting that through the cross breed of one or the other, he would develop a fowl with the laying qualities of the guinea and minus its cackle and cluck.
>
> When the products of the hatch grew to full size, they were guineas, still with the cackle and cluck.
>
> Now, ladies and gentlemen, gaze at my two opponents on this platform; both come from the political nest of John M. Parker. One of them has been put in the incubator of the New Orleans Ring, the other has been put in the nest of the Sullivan Ring. Both Parker eggs are to hatch. One is supposed to breed a cross to lose the cackle of Parker and the other is supposed to breed a cross to lose the Parker strut. But, ladies and gentlemen, before the day of inauguration shall have arrived, from the hatch of these candidates you will have nothing but two men with the same cackle, cluck and strut as you had during the last four years.

Both of the opposing candidates, who at no time had appeared on the platform with me, learned that I had planned some kind of faux pas for the occasion in Lafayette Square.

The largest crowd in the history of the campaign assembled there to hear us; but, at the eleventh hour, both opponents sent in the report that illness, accident or something else prevented their appearance.

I went through with my illustration, but without the two candidates there the loss of its effect failed to give me the hoped momentum.

During the last part of the campaign, there appeared a possibility of my being in the second primary. I had carefully surveyed the State. I was hoping to enter the second primary, as I had when I ran for Railroad Commissioner, by reason of a heavy country vote and in places where my strength was least suspected.

On the night preceding the election, a heavy downpour of rain fell in every part of the State.

The Ku Klux Klan issue was injected.

One of my opponents drew almost solid Klan support, and my other opponent a solid anti-Klan endorsement. The State, aroused and divided into bitter religious conflict, cleverly manipulated by the corporations and newspapers, left me out of the running in many places.

There was no need of full returns for me to know of my defeat. I knew it when the first box was reported. Some one said to me, late in the afternoon.

"Have you heard about the first box?"

"No," I said. "What is it?"

"It's the Clay box. 61 votes cast there and you got 60 of them."

"I'm beat," I replied. "There should have been 100 for me and 1 against me. Forty per cent of my country vote is lost in that box. It will be that great in the others."

It was a case of

> "Rise and shine,
> Stand up and take it!"

The vote was, in round numbers, Fuqua 81,000, Bouanchaud 84,000, Long 74,000. I carried the country over both opponents, but ran too bad a third in New Orleans to be second.

I settled down to my law office in Shreveport. There was considerable private litigation awaiting attention. I was seriously in need of money. I immediately delved into the preparation and trial of lawsuits, sometimes as many as two to three in one day. . . .

Following my removal as chairman of the Public Service Commission, I was provided with more time to pursue my private law practice. It had grown by leaps and bounds. I worked through the nights to take advantage of the opportunities.

I pause here to say that my wife and children paid a rather dear price for the fights I made against the entrenched powers of the State. With the exception of some few big cases, I had generally represented only the poorer class of clients. My fees were many but small. It required continuous work to earn them.

I had persisted in a course to take no business that might require me to act against any poor man.

We now had three brilliant children who had learned almost by the time they could walk to fold and mail literature for campaigns. The eldest of my children was a little girl named Rose, after her mother. The next child was a boy, whom we named Russell Billiu after my wife's favorite cousin. The youngest child was another boy named Palmer Reed, who was born the day I was indicted in Baton Rouge and given the name of two of my lawyers in the case.

If the loyalty of a wife and children could have elevated anyone in public life, I had that for complete success. The thing that hurt me at heart in losing a political campaign was the disappointment of our children, who could not seem to understand how the people could fail to elect me.

When the millionaires and corporations of Louisiana fell out with each other, I was able to accept highly remunerative employment from one of the powerful to fight several others which were even more powerful. Then I made some big fees with which I built a modern home in the best residential section of the City of Shreveport at a cost of $40,000.00.

My family was happy and content in their new surroundings. Encouraged by the peace and quiet of a less active political life, I had considered settling down entirely to my law business and pursuing no further political ambitions.

While carrying on my law practice at home, I had also formed a partnership in the State of Arkansas. I devoted a considerable part of my time to practice in the southern part of that State.

Further cause for my attitude toward having less to do with politics came with the death of Governor Henry L. Fuqua, who was succeeded by Lieutenant Governor O. H. Simpson. Governor Simpson had supported the re-election of Senator Broussard. It was known that he would be a candidate to succeed himself.

GOVERNOR HUEY P. LONG

It is extremely doubtful that Long ever entertained any serious "disinclination" to continue his pursuit of a political career. Keenly aware of his poor showing in the southern French parishes in 1924, he shrewdly championed the reelection in 1926 of Senator Edwin

S. Broussard, an archconservative Catholic and a wet running against a dry Protestant from the north, by stumping not only in the north, where Broussard was weak and Long's influence was greatest, but also in the south, where Long needed the exposure. The passages below only begin to hint at the white heat generated by the bitter class warfare of 1928. Long's temporary alliance in 1928 with dissident factions of the New Orleans machine suggests a political flexibility that his evangelical rhetoric disguised. The rich political metaphors and biting sarcasm of 1928 adorned an epic battle of the dispossessed dirt farmers against the regnant conservative coalition. The latter sought first to stop Huey's drive for the governor's chair and, failing that, to impeach him.

My disinclination to enter a second race for Governor soon melted away, and I found myself actively campaigning as a candidate. A legion of political supporters counted heavily upon my making the campaign of 1928, the issues which I had urged four years before became so much the topic of Louisiana's political circles, that it was practically impossible for me not to be moved into the sea of that fight.

I designated an organization force in charge of Mr. Harvey E. Ellis, at Covington, Louisiana. Then I sought to secure some kind of organization in the City of New Orleans and some newspaper support. Colonel Robert E. Ewing, at that time the Publisher of the *Daily States* of New Orleans and of the Shreveport *Times* in Shreveport, who was aligned with Colonel John P. Sullivan in New Orleans, early appeared as about ready to espouse my candidacy. . . .

Eventually, Sullivan announced his support for me. Colonel Ewing was soon to follow. We wanted the support of Ewing's newspaper in New Orleans. It developed that to get Ewing we would have to take Sullivan first. Our forces argued pro and con on whether we would lose more to take Sullivan than we would gain in getting Ewing. The campaign manager was adamant against taking Sullivan to get Ewing or anyone else.

I finally settled the issue to try to get everybody.

Immediately upon Sullivan announcing for me, my campaign manager, Mr. Ellis, publicly resigned as my campaign manager, issuing a blistering statement that he would not tolerate the Sullivan support. He declared that Sullivan's name was a synonym for vice of various forms, particularly gambling.

I little dreamed at the time that final returns of the election would show the percentage of my votes in the area affected by Sullivan's organization and Ewing's newspapers to be less than I had received in the campaign four years before when I ran without political organization or newspaper help.

On July 8, 1927, a political conclave was held in the City of Alexandria, composed of all groups opposed to my becoming Governor, for the purpose of drafting some candidate possessing outstanding qualifications, the principal requirement being his probable ability to beat me. It was declared that Governor Simpson was not strong enough to make the grade, and that another and stronger man must be had. With considerable glamor, newspaper headlines, trumpeteering and barbecues, all participants unanimously went on record as calling for the candidacy of Congressman Riley J. Wilson to save the State from Huey P. Long.

Mr. Wilson, like myself, had been born in the Parish of Winn, and raised a country boy. He had moved to the eastern part of our parish where he taught school, became judge, ran for and was elected to Congress. He was then serving his fourteenth consecutive year. His friends claimed he had put forth great effort to secure flood control, which was at that time quite a lively issue among the people of the State. It was announced that his candidacy would largely be based upon what he had done and what he proposed to do in the work of flood control.

Our forces waited about one month after this conclave in Alexandria and advertised a meeting to be held in the same city to open my campaign for Governor. Our rally was attended by an even larger crowd than the meeting of our opposition.

The newspapers and interests behind the calling of the Alexandria gathering against us had generally announced that the meeting would be composed of men of affairs in the business and politics of the State. They heralded their gathering as a meeting of "the better element."

We thereupon paraded throughout the State the announcement of our meeting to be held in Alexandria with a display of banners reading:

"EVERY MAN A KING, BUT NO ONE WEARS A CROWN"

*   *   *

In answering the clamor that Congressman Wilson should be elected Governor by reason of his flood relief work, I said:

"So they seek to elect the gentleman because of his flood record! What is that flood record? Why he has been in Congress for fourteen years and this year (1927) the water went fourteen feet higher than ever before, giving him a flood record of one foot of high water to the year, if that's what he's claiming credit for."

The satire and ridicule of the meeting spread throughout the State and almost destroyed the Wilson candidacy. It was months before it could be revived. For some time it appeared that Governor Simpson would be the second candidate in the race.

It was in the speech that I delivered under the historic oak where Evangeline waited for her lover Gabriel, as described by Longfellow, that I said:

And it is here under this oak where Evangeline waited for her lover, Gabriel, who never came. This oak is an immortal spot, made so by Longfellow's poem, but Evangeline is not the only one who has waited here in disappointment.

Where are the schools that you have waited for your children to have, that have never come? Where are the roads and the highways that you send your money to build, that are no nearer now than ever before? Where are the institutions to care for the sick and disabled? Evangeline wept bitter tears in her disappointment, but it lasted through only one lifetime. Your tears in this country, around this oak, have lasted for generations. Give me the chance to dry the eyes of those who still weep here!

My political opposition pointed out early in the campaign that even if I were elected Governor the Legislature would be 3 to 1 of men opposed to me.

"Those men will never stand for what Huey Long is advocating. They will impeach him before he is Governor a year," they said frequently. . . .

In the first primary election, occurring January 20, 1928, the vote was as follows: Long 126,842; Wilson 81,747; Simpson 80,326.

I had defeated both of my opponents together in the country outside New Orleans by 7,518 votes. Each of them had defeated me in New Orleans, Congressman Wilson leading me in that City by 20,425 and Governor Simpson leading me by 4,505.

The Sullivan-Ewing support in New Orleans meant little. . . .

My running mate for Lieutenant Governor was Dr. Paul N. Cyr, of Jeanerette. He was [also] elected.

All three of the candidates for governor, however, Wilson, Simpson and I, declared in favor of letting the final contracts for the free bridges over Lake Pontchartrain. . . .

I did not wait to become Governor, but asked Governor Simpson to begin the operation of free ferries parallel to the toll bridge immediately. Governor Simpson was later to become part of my administration. He ordered the free ferries. The bridge company went into the hands of a receiver soon after I became Governor. It is in such a situation today. Its possible $8.40 charge has since fallen to 60¢.

IMPEACHMENT AND THE ROUND ROBIN

Long had reached the State House largely by following a consistent policy of violating the traditional rules and procedures of the political game. He had fundamentally transformed the old Railroad Commission, and in the campaign of 1928 he had ignored the polite decorum of political gentility by inundating his opponents with humiliating ridicule. As governor he became his *own floor leader, often openly bullying recalcitrant legislators in their own traditional sanctum. When the legislature adjourned after eight months, Governor Long could point to a considerable achievement. He had passed a $30,000,000 highway bond to sustain his road and bridge building program, piped cheaper natural gas to New Orleans, repealed the tobacco tax, and increased severance taxes on the extractive "foreign" corporations. He had ingeniously circumvented the constitutional ban on state aid to parochial schools by distributing free textbooks directly to all school children rather than through their schools—thereby especially cementing his class appeal in Catholic southern Louisiana. His progressive and free-spending program was doubtless resented by conservatives, and his tax of five cents a barrel on refined oil especially angered the powerful oil lobby, but his program was far from a radical one. Yet during the special legislative session called by the overconfident young governor in 1929, this resentment boiled into demands for impeachment. The anti-Longs desperately sought to stop Huey before he could firmly root his power in the masses of voters. They had a case of sorts against the high-handed governor, but they pressed it with incredible sloppiness and produced a rambling and often trivial indictment that betrayed the primacy of their political motives. And in a political contest none could match the adroitness and ruthlessness of Huey Long.*

I faced a very queer and difficult situation in the first session of the legislature. There were 100 members of the House of Representatives and 39 members of the Senate. Of that number, only 18 members of the House and only 9 members of the Senate had supported me for Governor.

To pass any legislation I had to recruit my support from legislators who had not favored me for Governor.

The first test came in the election of the Speaker. My candidate was John B. Fournet, who won by a vote of 72 to 27. In the Senate, Senator Philip H. Gilbert was our candidate for President Pro Tempore. He was also elected.

My program for the legislature was to supply additional funds to the schools of the State, and to furnish the children with free school books. To secure revenues for that purpose it was necessary to change the severance taxes on oil, gas, timber and other natural resources to a quantity basis, resulting in a considerable increase from the corporations pursuing such businesses. Coupled with such was a tax on the business of manufacturing carbon black in the State.

We avoided complications in the free school book law. The Constitution of the State prevented any State donations to private or sectarian schools. I drew a law providing that the books should be furnished children, thereby enabling us to provide all children attending schools with the text books required.

Our highway system had so deteriorated that some of our roads were nearly impassable. The Department owed more than five million dollars, and had no money to improve old roads or build new ones. We proposed a Constitutional amendment (which had to be submitted to the people for a vote) to secure funds for the debts of our predecessors and to begin a program of paved highways and free bridges in the State.

We sought to increase the appropriations for the schools for the blind and deaf and dumb; also for the two hospitals for mental diseases and our two general charity hospitals. The school for the blind had been conducted in an old building which had been abandoned as unfit for use as a public schoolhouse in the '90's; the patients furnished treatment for mental diseases had been held in cells or locked beds at night and chained to hoes and plow stocks to work in the day time. The charity hospitals had been forced to allow some of their patients to lie on the bare floor.

We also proposed legislation needed to strengthen the hand of the administration, such as giving the Governor the power to remove the old and appoint new boards to control the levees and manage the State Board of Health.

We were faced by an opposition composed of good parliamentarians and clever strategists. In the House they introduced bills in great number and persuaded other members of the legislature, men who were inclined to be friendly to us, to introduce bills to cover their pet schemes.

Eventually we were faced with a clogged calendar and were unable to force consideration of our important proposals. Every effort we devised failed to clear the way. We met on several occasions to devise plans to extricate ourselves from the dilemma. At one of them a little French representative stammered out excitedly:

"What would happen if you passed all those bills?"

I thought a moment and said:

"Well, it would take just as long to pass them, wouldn't it?"

"No," he shouted. "Why you don't move to pass every bill quick as you reach it? No man can complain because you pass his bill whether he speak or not!"

I saw the light. After a little discussion I said:

"Tomorrow morning as fast as a number is read on a bill, allow as little talk as possible and let the Speaker recognize our floor leader and let him move the final passage and previous question. You can clear the calendar in a day in that way. I will veto every bill after it is passed that I don't want."

The next morning the legislature opened early. The first numbered bill was called. Our floor leader rose.

"I move to final passage of the bill and move the previous question."

The bill was passed instantly. With only occasional speaking every man's bill was passed. The calendar was cleared by noon. The opposition had been unable to figure a way to prevent it.

In the rush of so many bills passing, one member of the opposition, somewhat intoxicated, sought to halt the proceedings. He rose and shouted:

"Mr. Speaker! A point of order!"

"The pint is well taken," replied the chair. "Sit down!"

I later vetoed the objectionable bills by the score. . . .

The opposition called a mass meeting in the Capital City to start the fireworks for my impeachment. It was held March 26, 1929. Headlines of the *Times-Picayune,* on its front page of March 27, 1929, give a synopsis of that story, to-wit:

6000 AT MEETING CALL FOR INQUIRY INTO LONG'S ACTS

PROTEST GATHERING AGAINST TAX TURNS TO
SCAN MISDEEDS

*   *   *

The first and most prominently displayed cause for urging my impeachment by this mass meeting was stated:

1. That for the purpose of satisfying a personal grudge and getting personal revenge for a real or imaginary personal grievance against the oil industry of Louisiana, and in pursuance of his boast often shamelessly publicly announced, he has proposed and used the power of his great office to have enacted a so-called occupational tax on oil refineries and other manufacturing industries of the State, etc.

In other words, I had dared to propose to tax the Standard Oil Company!

Further along in the resolution were pronouncements of such statements as:

13. That he has attempted to intimidate and browbeat capital honestly and worthily invested, etc.

That was an answer to my program to shift taxes from the small man to the flourishing corporate interests operating in the State, so that the wealth gathered from the top might be used to build up the citizenship from the bottom.

When the resolution had reached the "Be it resolved" part, among other things the following was contained:

Be it further resolved, That we condemn as being vicious, dangerous
and utterly without merit, any and all systems of taxation, whether they
be called an occupational, a license or a manufacture tax, which directly
or indirectly seek to impose tax burdens upon industries within the State
of Louisiana.

From the above it appeared that the opposition element was about
ready to tax nobody but the one-horse farmer and small business man
in the State. . . .

Some speakers declared me too weak and unlearned to give the courage
and talent necessary to the Executive Department of the State, while
others pictured me as a dictator, with scheming motives and designs.
Charges in the legislature were not entirely similar to those urged by
the mass meeting. On the contrary, the following were the principal
ones.

1. That I had carried a pistol at times, particularly during the Dreher-
LeBoeuf hanging; this, notwithstanding the fact that the laws and Constitution of the State of Louisiana not only make the Governor the
chief peace officer of the State but make him the head of the National
Guard.

2. That I had illegally paroled a convict by the name of Elmer Dun-
nington; this, in the face of the fact that the Attorney General, Percy
Saint, and the Lieutenant Governor, Paul N. Cyr, my political enemies,
had signed and recommended in writing the granting of the parole and
it had passed through my office almost as a matter of form.

3. That as Governor, I had bought some law books, to-wit: Reports
of the United States Supreme Court; statutes of the United States and
Reports of the Supreme Court of the State of Louisiana and Revised
Statutes of the State of Louisiana. It appeared to be the view that the
Governor need not consult the statutes of the United States, nor the
decisions of any courts.

4. That I had torn down the old mansion; this, notwithstanding the
fact that the Board of Liquidation, by unanimous vote, and the Legislature of the State, by an overwhelming majority vote, had authorized
the building of a new mansion on the old mansion site. The Attorney
General had taken the position that authority to build a new mansion
on the ground whereon sat the old mansion did not authorize tearing
down the old building.

5. That in using the militia to raid gambling houses and to seize
their funds and to otherwise maintain law and order, I had acted
without authority.

6. That when the Legislature allowed me $6,000.00 to entertain the
Governors of the States, either all the money was not spent for entertainment or else that part of the same might have been spent for liquor; this,
notwithstanding the fact that I held a receipt for the expenditures made

in the full amount from the member of the entertainment committee placed in charge of the matter, and that certain additional costs had been paid by friends and people anxious to have the best of entertainment.

7. That one Battling Bozeman had been asked by me to kill a member of the Legislature; on this charge the testimony of the said Bozeman was accepted without allowing any testimony to be introduced to the contrary. Yet the opposition did not allow that charge to be voted upon in its own controlled House of Representatives because of its ridiculousness.

8. That a publisher of a newspaper had a brother who was in the hospital for the mentally sick (which brother was subsequently cured), and that I had told the newspaper publisher that I was going to tell the public about it; this, notwithstanding the fact that all persons in public hospitals of the State are enrolled on several records subject to the public's general inspection.

9. That during the Mardi Gras season in New Orleans, I had attended a Little Theatre where some actresses hired for the show danced scantily clad, and that some of the persons had taken a drink of liquor during the performance.

10. That I had fired some people and appointed others in their places, among whom was a telephone operator who failed to secure a telephone connection soon enough to satisfy my extreme haste.

11. That a cousin of mine had been hired and paid money to act as a chauffeur.

12. That I had walked into a committee of the Legislature and asked it to adjourn, and that upon the chairman refusing to do so, I persuaded the members to adjourn and leave any way.

13. That I had undertaken to impose my views upon the Legislature, the condition being that the Legislature could operate better without the Governor.

14. That I had recommended that the Highway Commission pay for some culverts which had been built, which some thought to be defective; this, notwithstanding the fact that the culverts had been paid for before I became Governor of the State and the Highway Commission under me had held up some other money belonging to the contractors until they made some deduction on the same. The culverts are in use to this date.

15. That members of the Legislature who helped put through programs of the administration, were favored by patronage, but that those who voted the other way were not favored so well.

16. That when visitors from the City of Shreveport (where they refused to hand out the free school books), called upon me that I used some "cuss words" in expressing the way I felt over their actions.

The foregoing include a great many things upon which even the

House of Representatives did not vote impeachment. It likewise includes everything upon which they did vote to impeach me.

Be that as it may, the law of impeachment is such that if the legislative body impeaches a man for walking the streets and the Senate will vote guilty on the charge, it is an impeachment nonetheless. . . .

The quest for votes went on. It was apparent that quick action was necessary to hold my friends together.

There were thirty-nine members of the Senate; fourteen of them could prevent impeachment. It took twenty-six votes in the Senate to find me guilty on the charges. I waited until the week-end. Nearly every member of the Senate had gone to his home. Baton Rouge was quiet and deserted.

The opposition was busy in New Orleans making up a slate of appointments for the "New Governor" when I was impeached. They had already begun to wrangle over the spoils. To hold some of their men in line they had promised the same job to more than one.

The hour had arrived when I had built my power to strike to the maximum.

I had prepared a document, generally referred to as a "round robin," containing, among other things, the following:

> Therefore, we, the members of the Louisiana State Senate, do respectfully announce and petition:
> 1. That by reason of the legal irregularities and the circumstances bearing upon the procedure as above outlined, we cannot conscientiously and will not approve the impeachment proceedings and charges preferred against the Governor by the present extra session of the Legislature, or to be preferred under the purported and illegal continuance of said session.

I kept my plans to myself.

Suddenly I arranged for an automobile to be at the premises of each of fifteen Senators whom I telephoned and asked to come immediately to Baton Rouge. All of them came. I asked them to sign the "round robin."

Some of them signed without quibble. With some of them I argued and discussed the law until I had secured the signatures of thirteen Senators. I needed but one more to have more than one-third of the membership of the Senate.

The fourteenth Senator reached my office a short time before midnight. He read the document which I had drawn. He was unequivocally against impeachment but was not convinced on the propriety of the round robin.

"When you sign this," I said, "I have one member more than the one-third."

"But," he rejoined, "you are asking me to say here that regardless of what may be shown, I will not vote to impeach?"

"You are a lawyer," I answered. "I am asking you as a lawyer to say that charges which, in law amount to nothing, cannot be the basis of impeaching me. None of these charges, even if true, can legally be the basis of an impeachment."

"I admit that, but is this not a funny way to do it?"

"Haven't you filed many a demurrer to an indictment?" I asked.

"Yes," he answered.

"Didn't your demurrer to the court say that even though your client was guilty of all that which he was charged with, still he should not be tried on a defective charge?"

"That is right," he answered.

"Now let me talk to you from a practical standpoint. I am exhausted; I have not a dime financially. This fight has cost me all I had; all I can rake, scrape and borrow. It is taking one thousand dollars a day to get the truth to the people. How long can we stand it?"

"Is all that necessary?" he asked.

"It is necessary for you. If you were to vote to free me from this impeachment, it would be dangerous unless your people have been given the facts so that they noted the propriety of your vote," I answered.

But still my friend hesitated. We argued back and forth, hour after hour. Soon the sun would be throwing its light across the earth. He said,

"What would you think if I asked my law partner for his advice on the law in this case?"

"Fine," I answered.

Immediately we called over the telephone to his law partner in New Orleans. He agreed to leave immediately for Baton Rouge. We awaited his arrival. He came just at good daylight.

Again we went over the proposition. The law partner read the petition and left with the Senator whose signature I was then requesting. Within about one hour they returned.

"Governor," said the law partner, "this is the right thing to do."

The fourteenth senator's name was signed to the round robin.

Later in the day, a fifteenth member affixed his signature. I had one more than necessary. We tried to keep that document's existence a closed secret.

I had the assurance of a few other members of the Senate that they agreed on the law, but considered it best not to sign the resolution. Nevertheless I continued my speaking tours and the distribution of circulars throughout the State.

The people were becoming aroused to a white heat. In crowds of ten to fifteen thousand a vote would be taken, never more than one or two failing to hold their hand up in my favor. . . .

Eventually the day for the trial of the impeachment charges came. My attorneys filed demurrers and answers denying all charges. . . .

We prepared during the night a condensed resolution along the lines of the round robin. The same fifteen Senators who had previously signed that paper signed the resolution.

Coupled with that resolution was a motion for the Court of Impeachment to adjourn sine die. This later document was also commonly called the "round robin." . . .

Upon the "round robin" being filed, the Senate took a short recess, but upon reconvening thirty-nine out of the thirty-nine voted to adjourn sine die.

I sent a crew of carpenters into the Senate Chambers where they began to tear down what I had termed the scaffolding arrangement made for my trial.

The newspapers, ever vicious over my victory in the impeachment, never ceased to call attention to any favor I did one of those fifteen men.

"Theirs is the earth and the fullness thereof," the papers proclaimed.

It became a matter of considerable mirth among the fifteen senators and myself.

On one occasion one of these senators, a full blooded Frenchman with a great sense of humor, Hugo Dore, called to see me in my bedroom in New Orleans.

"Governor," he said, "we want to get a little road gravelled leading out east of Mamou."

"My gracious, Hugo!" I exclaimed. "Won't you ever get through asking for roads for that country? There isn't room to plow there now, we've got so much pavement and gravel in that country."

"Now, Governor," shot back the senator, "don't get too strong now; remember what we've done for you."

Several of our friends seated in the room laughed at his remark.

"GOVERNOR–UNITED STATES SENATOR-ELECT"

The laughter masked a grim determination, an old one considerably hardened by the bitter battle for survival. "I used to try to get things done by saying 'please,'" Long reportedly observed. "That didn't work and now I am a dynamiter. I dynamite 'em out of my path." [1] *While still sitting as Governor, Long went after the Senate seat of incumbent Joseph E. Ransdell with patented Long dynamite. He ridiculed the goateed Ransdell as "Old Feather Duster." In response to the almost unanimous opposition of the "lyin'*

[1] Forrest Davis, *Huey Long: A Candid Biography* (New York: Dodge Publishing Company, 1935), p. 119.

newspapers," he created his own weekly, the Louisiana Progress, *which was often delivered along with his innumerable circulars in State Highway trucks and police patrol cars. His campaign was financed in part by a system of "deducts" from the paychecks of state employees—a practice not new to Louisiana politics, but openly systematized by Long. Further, he brilliantly capitalized on the political potential of radio by launching folksy and entertaining diatribes against his opponents, and he pioneered as well in the employment of the sound truck. The colorless Ransdell was overwhelmed and the Constitutional League of Louisiana, the conservative instrument of opposition, promptly folded. Finally, Huey mopped up by removing troublesome Lieutenant Governor Paul Cyr, with whom he had broken, replacing him with a trusted ally. This he accomplished through a characteristically bizarre countermaneuver that blocked Cyr's bold attempt to declare himself governor in light of Long's elevation to the Senate.*

When the 1930 Regular Session of the Legislature passed into history, I immediately announced that I would carry my program before the people as a candidate for the United States Senate. I made no secret of the fact that if the people saw fit to stand with me in the election, I would expect them to back up the processes necessary to bring about a fulfillment of administration purposes; but that, should the people see fit to express themselves as not favoring me, that I would accept that verdict and allow [Lt. Gov.] Cyr to take the post of Governor.

A newspaper said:

"Huey Long has piled all his chips on the table to bet on one throw of the dice. Win this time and we are through with him."

It was the battle of Louisiana's history. For once the public press was united—all against me.

Our opposition undertook to form a coalition of practically every political element in the City of New Orleans to overcome whatever lead I might have in the country outside of that city. . . .

While the campaign between Senator Ransdell and myself occupied a period of approximately seven weeks, in bitterness and intensity it exceeded any campaign this State has ever known. Copies of the *Louisiana Progress* to fight the unanimous press opposition were printed by the hundred thousand, then by the quarter million and finally by as many as one million copies to the issue.

Every parish in the State was combed by the opposition with a list of speakers that invaded the most isolated communities. I delayed my course of taking the rostrum until speakers of the opposition had fairly well covered the State. Then I began a tour, covering only the parish seats, taking my time, compared to other campaigns, making only from three to five speeches a day. When I had covered the State, however, I had spoken to practically every voter within its borders.

It was in that campaign that I invented our sound truck,—the first portable appliance of its kind ever used in a political campaign. With its aid, I took my time in my speeches and spoke for as long as was necessary to explain clearly and succinctly each and every matter and transaction connected with affairs of the State. . . .

The results of the election between Ransdell and myself were overwhelmingly in my favor.

While I lost the City of New Orleans by 4,600 votes, we carried all the adjoining parishes and overcame the scant city lead to elect two candidates for Congress. I carried the State by over 38,000. Senator Ransdell immediately wired his congratulations.

On Wednesday, following my election, the Constitutional League of Louisiana was announced as deceased. . . .

The extra session of the Legislature of 1930, comprised of the same men who had sought to bring about my impeachment, submitted to the people for adoption the following:

1. A new State capitol at a cost of $5,000,000.

2. A $75,000,000 road and free bridge program, to be directed by my administration. . . .

3. A bill to refinance the debts of the city of New Orleans.

4. An increase in the gasoline tax of one cent, half of which was to be applied to the benefit of the public schools, and the other half to pay the interest and maturities of bonds issued by previous Governors for the port of New Orleans, for which they had provided no means of payment, as well as to give additional support to the Port of Lake Charles.

5. Both houses of the Legislature adopted a resolution formally declaring that the impeachment charges which had been brought against me in the preceding year were at an end and dismissed. This was passed almost unanimously. . . .

And thus the extra session of the Legislature of 1930 adjourned with Huey P. Long, Governor and United States Senator-elect, endorsed and successful in everything he had ever advocated. All enjoyed peace, harmony and good will, except the exiled who were left to their own devices.

The depression then afflicting the nation was fought by a united front in our State. . . .

The time came when I could have claimed my compensation as Senator, March 4, 1931, but I had requested the Secretary of the Senate not to send me either salary check or expense allowance; and I would not claim my office there until I had practically served out my term as Governor.

The Lieutenant Governor, Paul N. Cyr, began to clamor that, with my election to the Senate, I had vacated the office of Governor. He drove to my old home in Shreveport and with some acclaim, took the oath of office as Governor, thereby occasioning some momentary confusion. I was in New Orleans at the time. Hurrying back to Baton Rouge, I placed a few guards around the State house and the Mansion. I ordered that Cyr should be arrested as an impostor if he appeared upon the premises.

Soon thereafter he filed suit in the district court at Shreveport, claiming title to the office.

When Cyr took the oath to the governor's office, I claimed he had vacated the office of Lieutenant Governor. My friend, Senator Alvin O. King, was President pro tempore of the Senate. Under the constitution of Louisiana, when the office of Lieutenant Governor becomes vacant, the President pro tempore of the Senate succeeds to it.

With Brother Cyr suspended in mid-air about the Governor's chair, Senator King took the oath of office as Lieutenant Governor and took the executive seat.

At last I was through with Mr. Cyr as Lieutenant Governor. I had only to beat him in a lawsuit over the Governor's office to put him out altogether. What a pleasant scene to contemplate!

3
On the National Scene:
Every Man A King

Aware that his freedom of maneuver as a senator would largely depend upon the security of his power base in Louisiana, Governor–Senator-elect Long unfurled a full slate of nine candidates for the January, 1932, state office primary. The ticket was headed by Oscar K. Allen of Winn Parish, a supporter of Long since Huey's political debut in 1918. Allen was a Long lieutenant of such ironclad loyality—or supine obeisance, as anti-Long critics claimed—that great mirth was subsequently made of the apocryphal story told by Huey's younger brother, Earl, that a leaf one day blew through a State House window onto "O.K." Allen's desk, and he signed it. Huey's ticket swept the state, and in September, he engineered the election of another loyal lieutenant, Congressman John H. Overton, as his junior U.S. senator. Although elected to the Senate in November of 1930, Long was not sworn in until January 5, 1932. Since the first session of the 72nd Congress did not convene until December 7, 1931, Long was technically only one month late in assuming his new post. To critics who charged that Louisiana was not being fully represented in the Senate, Long replied that Senators Hiram Johnson and Robert LaFollette had similarly delayed their trips to Washington—and that in the case of Old Feather Duster Ransdell, the seat had been vacant for a long time anyway.

The freshman senator from Louisiana was ill disposed to play the deferential role of the model freshman senator. He immediately seized the initiative in his new national forum with a two-pronged verbal assault, first against the inflated fortunes of the Mellons, Rockefellers, Morgans, and Baruchs, then against the miseries of depressed America. He played to the bellowing galleries and delighted newsmen in flaying plutocrats and in ridiculing with an impish wit the more conservative of his staid senior colleagues. "'I do not talk one way in the cloakroom and another way out here,'" Long soberly affirmed. "'I do not talk one way back there in the hills of Louisiana and another way here in the Senate.'"[1]

[1] Howard W. Odum, *Southern Regions of the United States* (Chapel Hill: University of North Carolina Press, 1936), pp. 531–32.

As the Depression proved resistant to the reforms of Franklin Roosevelt's first New Deal, Long's swelling "thunder on the left" alarmed the New Dealers, whose ranks he eventually deserted in disgust with their unwillingness to support his radical formula for redistributing the national wealth. When an assassin's bullet cut him down in September of 1935, the enigmatic Long had attracted the devotion of millions of the dispossessed, but he had also generated widespread fear and even hatred. This section traces his meteoric career as a senator and presidential aspirant by focusing on his speeches and personal interviews as expressive of his motives and intentions.

AMERICA'S CRISIS AND AMERICA'S DREAM

In April of 1932, Long delivered on the Senate floor the following speech, entitled "Doom of America's Dream." [2] *The indictment by a Southern Democrat of President Hoover's impotent measures against the Depression was standard political fare. But Long sought the root cause of the Depression in a statistical analysis of the degree and extent of corporate monopoly and maldistribution of wealth. Frustrated by the ponderous seniority system and by the unwillingness of either Hoover Republicans or Senate Democrats to support his proposal to share the wealth, Huey resigned all of his new committee seats (Naval affairs, Manufactures, Commerce, and Interoceanic Canals) in protest. His support for Roosevelt's nomination at the Chicago Democratic convention that summer was crucial, and he campaigned effectively in the northern plains states for Roosevelt's election in the fall, hoping that the new leadership would prove more congenial to his vision of "America's Dream."*

America's Crisis

If this Congress adjourns and does not provide a law for the effective starting of a redistribution of wealth in the United States you need not be worried about the amount of deficit that there is going to be in the National Treasury. If we adjourn here with this tax bill before us, with a bill passed as a result of it or with this bill passed, without providing a means for the redistribution of wealth in the United States to-day, and allow this snowball to go downhill for two or three more years as it is now, and allow this panic to be exploited as it is now being exploited

[2] Abridged from the *Congressional Record*, 72d Cong., 2d sess., Vol. 76 (Washington, D.C.: Government Printing Office, 1933), pp. 4673–75.

to concentrate every business enterprise in this country, you do not need to worry about the Federal Government nor the Budget of the Federal Government. You will have a problem before you that is a great deal bigger than any problem of the Budget of the Federal Government.

I have letters which I have received to-day, which I intended to read to the Senate. One man, a peaceable citizen, has undertaken to make a living as long as he could, and finally went into a business prohibited by law because it was the only thing out of which he could make a living for his wife and children. He is now in the Federal penitentiary. Another letter is from a widow with a 19-year-old son that she is undertaking to send to college, living in a college town; and he can not continue his work in the university because she can not find the funds even to buy the books. Yet we are sitting here talking about balancing the Budget.

The Unblessed Coalition

Who is thinking about those people? Who is thinking about this condition? Who is doing anything about it? . . . Have Rockefeller and Morgan and Baruch sent in their ill-fated recommendations and demands that were so effective in other administrations? . . .

We are told that there never was a ruling class that abdicated. A great deal of speculation is made over who is the leader and who are the party leaders of this Nation, who are the leaders of Congress. I have been here long enough to say that if I had any legislation in the United States Congress to-day, I would a whole lot rather know that it had the sanction and approval of Morgan and Rockefeller and Baruch than to know that it had the sanction and approval of every party leader in both Houses of Congress. They are here to fight the tax on the importation of oil. They are here to fight the tax on stock exchanges.

We have a cotton exchange and a stock exchange in the city of New Orleans, just as they have a stock exchange and a cotton exchange in the city of New York, and I am not afraid to tell you that there is not a more nefarious enterprise that ever operated on the face of the globe than the stock exchanges and cotton exchanges in the city of New York and in the city of New Orleans. They have lived for years out of the miseries and the slim profits that might have meant some convenience and comfort to the people of this country, and there is no tax on the living face of the globe that can be more justly and properly assessed than a tax on the stock exchange and a tax on the cotton exchange. I am not politically afraid for them to know that I have expressed exactly those sentiments on the floor of the Senate. It does not make any difference to me whether they like it or not.

Now, these men are fighting the inheritance tax and the surtax. The newspapers tell us that this is a great effort to soak the rich. Soak the rich—the "soak the rich campaign." It is no campaign to soak the rich,

Mr. President. It is a campaign to save the rich. It is a campaign the success of which they will wish for when it is too late, if it fails, more than anyone else on earth will wish for it—a campaign for surtaxes to insure a redistribution of wealth and of income, a campaign for inheritance taxes to insure a redistribution of wealth and of income.

*　　*　　*

Evidently we do not realize that there is a crisis. Apparently we do not. We do not have to go very far to find it out. Mr. Herbert Hoover, in his speech in Indianapolis the other day, said that we were now in the midst of the greatest crisis in the history of the world. If Mr. Hoover can be believed, neither disunion, rebellion, war, nor pestilence compares with the condition that faces the American people to-day. . . . Mr. Hoover went on to say that a different means of taxation had to be found for this country; that we had to find a means of taxation that would take the taxes off the small man. That is what Mr. Hoover said: . . . that we had to formulate a tax policy that would take the taxes off the farmers and home owners of this country; and in the same speech —which evidently was not censored as most of them probably will be hereafter and probably have been heretofore—he went on and said that the remedy was by the distribution wealth.

But now every power of the administration which can be brought from the White House is exerted against anything being done which means the distribution of wealth among the people of this country.

The Light of America's Dream Is Fading

The great and grand dream of America that all men are created free and equal, endowed with the inalienable right of life and liberty and the pursuit of happiness—this great dream of America, this great light, and this great hope—has almost gone out of sight in this day and time, and everybody knows it; and there is a mere candle flicker here and yonder to take the place of what the great dream of America was supposed to be.

Another Slave Owner

The people of this country have fought and have struggled, trying, by one process and the other, to bring about the change that would save the American country to the ideal and purposes of America. They are met with the Democratic Party at one time and the Republican Party at another time, and both of them at another time, and nothing can be squeezed through these party organizations that goes far enough to bring the American people to a condition where they have such a thing as a liveable country. We swapped the tyrant 3,000 miles away for a handful of financial slaveowning overlords who make the tyrant of Great Britain seem mild.

Much talk is indulged in to the effect that the great fortunes of the United States are sacred, that they have been built up by the honest and individual initiative, that the funds were honorably acquired by men of genius far-visioned in thought. The fact that those fortunes have been acquired and that those who have built them for the financial masters have become impoverished is a sufficient proof that they have not been regularly and honorably acquired in this country.

Even if they had been that would not alter the case. I find that the Morgan and Rockefeller groups alone held, together, 341 directorships in 112 banks, railroad, insurance, and other corporations, and one of this group made an after-dinner speech in which he said that a newspaper report had asserted that 12 men in the United States controlled the business of the Nation, and in the same speech to this group he said, "And I am one of the 12 and you the balance, and this statement is correct."

Twelve men! If we only had that passing remark, which, by the way, was deleted from the newspaper report which finally went out, although we have plenty of authority that the statement was made; if we did not have other figures to show it, we probably might not pay so much attention to that passing remark.

You want to enforce the law, you want to balance the Budget? I tell you that if in any country I live in, despite every physical and intellectual effort I could put forth, I should see my children starving and my wife starving, its laws against robbing and against stealing and against bootlegging would not amount to any more to me than they would to any other man when it came to a matter of facing the time of starvation.

Whoever tries to guard the existence of these fortunes becomes a statesman of high repute. He is welcome in the party counsels. Whoever undertakes to provide for the distribution of these fortunes is welcome in no counsel.

They pass laws under which people may be put in jail for utterances made in war times and other times, but you can not stifle or keep from growing, as poverty and starvation and hunger increase in this country, the spirit of the American people, if there is going to be any spirit in America at all.

Let All Enjoy Our Wealth If the Country Is To Be Saved

Unless we provide for the redistribution of wealth in this country, the country is doomed; there is going to be no country left here very long. That may sound a little bit extravagant, but I tell you that we are not going to have this good little America here long if we do not take care to redistribute the wealth of this country.

*   *   *

Who Owns America?

I have here the statistics showing the concentration of American industries.

Iron ore: 50 to 75 percent owned by the United States Steel Corporation.

Steel: 40 per cent of the mill capacity owned by the United States Steel Corporation.

Nickel: 90 per cent owned by the International Nickel Co.

Aluminum: 100 per cent owned by the Aluminum Trust.

Telephone: 80 per cent owned by the American Telephone & Telegraph Co. It is more than that, as they would state if they understood the subsidizing contract which that company requires every little independent telephone company to sign in order to get long-distance connections. If that were stated, it would be found that the telephone industry in the United States is 100 per cent in the hands of the American Telephone & Telegraph Co.

Telegraph: 75 percent in the Western Union.

Parlor car: Pullman Co., 100 per cent monopoly.

Agricultural machinery: The International Harvester Co. has 50 per cent.

Shoe machinery: The United Shoe Machinery Co. has a monopoly.

Sewing machines: The Singer Sewing Machine Co. controls that field.

Radio: The Radio Corporation, 100 per cent.

Sugar: The American Sugar Refining Co., 100 per cent.

Anthracite coal: Eight companies, 80 per cent of the United States tonnage.

Sulphur: Two companies own the world's deposits.

Oil: To show how conservative this report is, it states that 33 per cent of the oil is controlled by five companies, when, as a matter of fact, they own 105 per cent, if you can get that much out of the total quantity of oil produced. That which they do not own they have absolute dominion over and manipulate the oil tariffs and the importations of the foreign group in such a manner that no independent man can stay in the oil business in this country to-day in competition with the Standard Oil Co.

Meat packing: Two companies, 50 per cent.

Electrical equipment: Two companies, 50 per cent.

Railroad rolling stock: Two companies, monopoly.

Chemicals: Three companies, monopoly.

Matches: Two companies, monopoly.

Rubber: Four companies, Monopoly.

Moving pictures: Three companies, monopoly.

Aviation: Three companies, monopoly.

Electric power: Four groups, monopoly.

Insurance: Ten companies, 66 per cent of the insurance in force.

Banking: 1 per cent of the banks control 99 per cent of the banking resources of the United States.

That is the concentration that has occurred in this country.

The statistics further show that only 2 per cent of the people ever pay income taxes. Mr. Mellon points out that that is a grave condition; that the law has been miraculously at fault in failing to collect an income tax against a larger percentage of the people.

It is not the law that is at fault. That is not the trouble at all. It is the infernal fact that 98 per cent of the people of the United States have nothing, rather than it being the fault of the fact that only 2 per cent of them pay any income tax.

*   *   *

Over 2,000,000 Earn Less Than 504 Plutocrats

I have the statistics here. Here is how the income is being distributed. In 1929 there were 504 supermillionaires at the top of the heap who had an aggregate net income of $1,185,000,000. That is 504 people. These 504 persons could have purchased with their net income the entire wheat and cotton crops of 1930. In other words, there were 504 men who made more money in that year than all the wheat farmers and all the cotton farmers in this great land of democracy. Out of the two chief crops, 1,300,000 wheat farmers and 1,032,000 cotton farmers—2,300,000 farmers raising wheat and cotton—made less than those 504 men.

From the official statistics we find that $538,664,187 was the net income of the 85 largest income-tax payers in 1929. The 421,000 workers in the clothing industry received in wages $475,000,000. Those 85 men could have paid the entire wages of the clothing industry of the Nation and have had $100,000,000 left. Yes; there has got to be relief from this condition.

Mr. Gompers was termed a socialist when he said:

> Hundreds of thousands of our fellow men, through the ever-increasing extensions and improvements in modern methods of production, are rendered superfluous. We must find employment for our wretched brothers and sisters by reducing hours of labor or we will be overwhelmed and destroyed.

*   *   *

But O Mr. President, if we could simply let the people enjoy the wealth and the accumulations and the earnings and the income and the machinery and the contrivances that we have. If, with the invention of every machine, we could secure the education of every man; if with increased production of every kind there could be less toil, more hours of pleasure and recreation; if there could be a happy and contented people enjoying what the Almighty has made it possible to provide; if there could be people clothed with the materials that we have to clothe them with to-day, and no place to put them; if the people could be fed with the food that we have to feed them with, and no place to put it; if the people could be sheltered in the homes we have to-day that the Federal land bank has taken away from them because they can not pay the interest on the mortgages—if that could be done, if we could distribute this surplus wealth, while leaving these rich people all the luxuries they can possibly use, what a different world this would be.

THE TREASON OF THE DEMOCRATS

Long received little more support for his wealth-sharing proposal from President Roosevelt's administration than he had from that of Hoover. Although he voted for many of the New Deal reforms, he remained a constant critic on the left when debating economic policies. His impatience with Roosevelt soon combined with his political ambition to estrange him from the President, and he constantly needled his fellow Democratic congressmen with charges of hypocrisy and even treason. The following two passages are typical of Long's extemporaneous Senate rhetoric. In the first, he chastises his fellow Democrats for having defaulted on the people's mandate; his allusion to the "big, masterful [man] of finance right next to Louisiana" is directed at Senate majority leader Joseph Robinson of Arkansas, whom Long delighted in ridiculing. The second speech further demonstrates Long's artful harassment of powerful senior Democrats; here he provokes the ire of sixty-one-year-old Senator Henry Ashurst of Arizona in a debate over prison parole. Long's contrast of the harsh justice accorded Louisiana "niggers" to the unpunished sins of Postmaster General Farley is richly revealing.

What have we done? Congress may sit here and twiddle its thumbs, as it has done ever since I have been here. I say that advisedly; I say that Congress has sat here, to my certain knowledge ever since I have been here, and fiddled while Rome has burned—the Democratic Party and the Republican Party.

I hear the Democratic leaders get up and decry Hoover and make a whole lot of "hurrally" as to how terrible Hoover was, and yet the Democratic leaders on this side of the Chamber supported Hoover in everything he tried to do. When we had enough votes on the other side of the Chamber of the progressive Republicans to have undone this damnable cataclysm, the Democratic leaders were following in the tracks of Hoover and doing what Hoover said to do. They did later get up and blame Hoover, but they were the greatest disciples Hoover ever had; there was not anybody on the other side of the Chamber who could hold a candle to them. They were doing everything they could and you could not break them loose. I merely listened to them when I heard those songs they sang of Herbert Hoover and Hooverism, when I know from the record that every dadgummed one of them followed Hoover's tracks and were the most useful disciples he had. You cannot expect anything from them when they get out that old claptrap and sing the songs and dance the dances of politics. Their record shows that they sat here and helped send this country to hell with Herbert Hoover in the saddle. Poor old Hoover was less to blame than they were.

Now we come along here and we are going to change leaders. I had something to do with changing the leaders. The leaders on this side of the Chamber did not have anything to do with it, Mr. President, but I did. [Laughter in the galleries.]

The PRESIDING OFFICER. The Chair will request the occupants of the galleries to maintain order.

Mr. LONG. I had something to do with changing these leaders, to try to get some liberality in the Democratic Party, to give us a chance to break loose. I had something to do with it in a material way, because I went out and helped raise the sinews of war, the nickels and dimes and dollars that we had to have to finance a little campaign to nominate a man to start with; and I helped get the votes that went into the convention. I helped get the votes right in the States that were dominated by big, masterful men of finance right next to Louisiana [laughter], to take them into the Chicago convention and vote them for the nomination of Franklin Delano Roosevelt.

Why were we making all this fight? Because Mr. Roosevelt came out with a statement over his signature in which he said that he was in favor of the distribution of wealth among the people of this country so that the starving could be fed in the land of plenty, and because he had advocated taking it from the top and supporting the Government and distributing it to those at the bottom.

We have had an election—an election on beautiful principles and on beautiful platforms. What do platforms mean? I said to my friend the junior Senator from Washington [Mr. BONE], when he was speaking, that in the army they shoot a traitor. When are we going to decide that a party can be a traitor? When are we going to decide that a party is held to the same obligation after signing up for a year's service as we hold a private or officer of the United States Army to? [3]

---

[3] From the *Congressional Record*, 73d Cong., 2d sess., Vol. 78 (Washington, D.C.: Government Printing Office, 1934), p. 5986.

Mr. President, I merely wish to say to my friend from Arizona that I am very mindful of his comprehensive knowledge of this question [of prison parole], and also of his good intentions and his good-heartedness; but, since so much is being said by my friend from Michigan and the Senator from Arizona, I want to say that I cannot help but have a charity for people in the penitentiary when I know so many others who ought to be in the penitentiary in this day and time, when I know that most of those who have observed the ordinary course of government feel as John Wesley felt, who, when they were carrying some man through the streets to hang him, said, "But for the grace of God, there goes John Wesley."

Mr. ASHURST. Was not that John Bunyan?

Mr. LONG. No.

Mr. VANDENBERG. It was John Wesley.

Mr. LONG. Now both Senators are in argument, but that is all right.

Mr. ASHURST. Mr. President—

Mr. LONG. Just a moment. Those of us who have observed law enforcement since prohibition and since it has been repealed have come to find out that the matter of law, I regret to say, is, to a large extent, who you are and where you are and how you are. If I may do so, I will at a later time take up many provisions of the Constitution and the laws of this country, and I will show open and admitted violation of the criminal statutes, while men are held in the penitentiaries for minor infractions of some law and are pointed out as despicable characters, threatening the safety of the people. All the people in the "pen" are not gangsters; the gangsters are only a smaller part of them. In Louisiana we have practically no such thing as gang warfare. There was not a bank robber in the city of New Orleans or in the State whom we did not capture, and none of them have been pardoned and none of them have been paroled. But most of the people in the penitentiary are very much like the 10 niggers whom they captured in Richmond Parish, I think it was, in Louisiana, who killed one $2 yearling and barbecued the yearling, and the 10 niggers were sent to the penitentiary for one $2 yearling. Yet we do not take up a case, of which we all have knowledge, of one using the Government printing facilities or stamps.

Go to the penitentiary and I will guarantee it will be found that many postmasters are in the "pen" right now who did not steal over 50 cents' worth of stamps or over $5 worth; but, nonetheless, we, gentlemen of the Senate—and I acknowledge, let me say, that I am a part of the body corporate—have allowed one of our illustrious men flagrantly to violate the law to the extent of many thousand dollars and yet extol him as one of eminent virtue and capacity, to be emulated by our sons and our daughters. So while we are discussing these poor devils who are in the "pen" think rather charitably, gentlemen of the Senate, lest somebody might accuse us of not enforcing the law against our elders in this Government.

Mr. ROBINSON. Mr. President—

The PRESIDING OFFICER. Does the Senator from Arizona yield to the Senator from Arkansas?

Mr. ASHURST. I yield.

Mr. ROBINSON. I do not think that the repetition of the insinuations that a high Government officer has stolen stamps should be passed unnoticed. I understand the Senator from Arizona expects to make some comment upon the subject.

Mr. ASHURST. Yes.

Mr. ROBINSON. But I do not feel that the Senator from Louisiana has any justification for that statement. I feel that he is offensive to everyone in the Senate, except himself, when he makes that statement, and generally to people who believe in decency in government.

Mr. ASHURST. Mr. President, I did not seek a controversy with the Senator from Louisiana; I do not seek it now; and I doubt if I shall be forgiven for consuming the Senate's time at this juncture—

Mr. LONG. Mr. President, will the Senator yield?

Mr. ASHURST. Certainly.

Mr. LONG. I want to state that I have not during this morning hour used the words "stolen stamps." Of course, that is the only definition that might be given to it, but I wanted to be very judicial and courteous in my remarks this morning. The Senator from Arkansas puts that interpretation on the matter, and, of course, I agree that he is probably justified in it.

Mr. ROBINSON. Mr. President, that is just the point I am making. The Senator from Louisiana uses language such as he did employ, and then he is surprised if anyone takes offense at it.

Mr. LONG. Mr. President, will the Senator from Arizona yield?

Mr. ASHURST. I yield.

Mr. LONG. Do I understand it now to be said that it is not true that Mr. Farley printed some special stamps for his friends?

Mr. ROBINSON. If the Senator understands the English language he must understand me to say that when he charges that Mr. Farley stole stamps it is untrue in every sense of the word, and the Senator from Louisiana knows it is untrue.

Mr. LONG. I have stated the facts.

*   *   *

Mr. ASHURST. The gravamen of the Senator's speech was that he made an insinuation, if not a direct charge, against absent persons who, under our rules and under the Constitution, are unable to reply. I want the Senator from Louisiana to understand that I am not adopting the attitude of a censor; I am not trying to correct somebody else; possibly I need correction as much as any Senator here; but, in view of the Senator's charge, I feel a disposition this morning to say that if we walk on the seacoast after a storm at sea has subsided, particularly if the storm was of such violence as to agitate the ocean to an unusual depth and send huge billows upon the shore, we discover curious denizens of the deep from the world of cold and dreadful night below the ocean's surface, that have been upthrust and cast ashore by the fury of the storm. We find wriggling on the beach, crustacea, such as crawfish, shrimps, mudcrabs, and lobsters; among the fish we find the grunt, puffer, pike, topknot, toadfish, jellyfish, kingfish, starfish, sawfish, stingray, and, indeed, too great a variety of types to admit of a complete definition.

When the sea is calm and tranquil these creatures seldom appear to human vision. Only some unusual agitation brings them from obscurity to conspicuousness.

Mr. President, the same physical principle operates on mankind when the distress of depression, the fury of financial panic and storm, and the terror of economic uncertainty agitates a people. We then are no longer the assured, free-swimming, self-reliant folk we seemed to be when the waters of life were smooth and placid. This law of physics is not peculiar to the American race alone. To all tribes of men, when confronted with any insecurity, whether it be economic, environmental, social, or philosophical, there come dangerous thoughts, feelings, and fears, and thus some men usually called "odd fish," are forced to the surface from the swamps of anonymity.

Many of such men thus projected to conspicuousness are excellent men who believe that they know how to reach the pot of gold at the rainbow's end; how to obtain a living in this practical, brass-tack, workaday world without giving any equivalent therefor; or how to break economic laws and avoid any penalty.

Thus, in these agitated and distressful days, we must expect to encounter whimsical, droll, eccentric, and erratic persons who occupy the stage for a time, and they, at least, divert us, interest us, entertain us, and, I am bound in fairness to add, they sometimes instruct us. Their fatal error is that they refuse to face the fact that only iron sacrifice can rescue a nation from a depression; they never realize that no easy way to achieve success has ever been, or ever will be discovered. It was ordained at the beginning of time that success shall be difficult. No one will ever circumvent destiny on that point, for she has resolved that, in obtaining success, man shall be put upon his mettle until the end of the film. In these recurrent depressions and times of poignant distress, wise and well-balanced men are sometimes confused and saddened and lose track of the simplicity of the rules of life. Moreover, we have complicated our existence to the point where it not only stupefies the ordinary man but defies the comprehension of the wisest man.

In such a whirligig epoch as the present many persons, in normal times sensible, become overwrought and unjustly suspect and defame such of their fellow citizens as do not subscribe to their particular reforms or gyrations.

Therefore, the suspiciousness of the Senator from Louisiana and his intolerant attitude toward and his denunciations of his colleagues, are quite understandable.

Such strictures, reproaches, and intemperate speeches from the Senator from Louisiana are really the wailings of an apostle of despair. He has lost control of himself. He is trying to play billiards with elliptical billiard balls and a spiral cue. He has adopted the apothegm of the French dramatist, Beaumarchais: "Calumniate, calumniate, caluminate; something is sure to stick."

*   *   *

It is not for me to pass judgment upon the Senator from Louisiana. He has as much right to pass judgment upon me as I have to appraise him. An attitude of censoriousness is the one attitude the Senator never tolerates and never forgives any of its Members, but I will venture the suggestion that if the Senator from Louisiana should look [at himself] objectively, as he doubtless will some day, for he is of an inquiring mind, he will distinctly perceive a man frequently disrespectful of the rights and feelings of others, exalting himself with an unwarranted sense of superiority over others less gifted and less fortunate than himself; a man too often taking undue advantage of his privileged position here; a man of reckless abandon in speech and relentless in his forays upon those who disagree with him.

*   *   *

Mr. LONG. . . . I desire to acknowledge my gratitude of the special preparation which my friend from Arizona made with regard to me. I would not have given him a chance to read this marvelously concocted written preparation had I not by accident run into the discussion between himself and the Senator from Michigan [Mr. VANDENBERG]. I believe he has me to thank for having brought about the occasion by which his efforts in preparing this eloquent address were not sniped out in some other experiences which might not have given the Senator from Arizona the opportunity to read his carefully prepared statement. I thank the Senator from Arizona for this.

The Senator, however, has his facts a little wrong. He says that during these days of depression, as in the case of all storms, various things are washed up on the sands and on the shores; and he says that among other things washed up, I believe, are the catfish, the crawfish, the kingfish, the barracuda, and other kinds of fish. The kingfish is even a more vicious species of marine life than the barracuda itself, so I am told; but the Senator from Arizona overlooks one thing. There is another species that is washed up on the shores in large numbers, and that is the tadpole. That is the animal that I now wish to bring to the attention of the Senator from Arizona.

The tadpole is a form of life which, during these depressions, goes out and promises one thing and then comes in and does another. That species is far more numerous than the kingfish, the whale, the crawfish, the turtle, or any other form of marine life. If it may please my friend the Senator from Arizona, I shall be glad to have him call to mind that, undertaking to avoid some of the descriptions which he has seen fit to give to the Senate, I have taken the words of our illustrious President for all the course I have followed here; not that he was the first to have made the statement, but I have taken the words of our illustrious President wherein he said that the people of the United States are entitled to share in a redistribution of wealth. Therefore I have used that as my landmark since the political campaign of 1932 ended.

For the benefit of the Senator from Arizona, however, I will state that I am advocating what I advocated at the age of 21. It did not have much support in this body during those days, I am sure. It had little support when I came here. However, it has been advocated by the present President of the United States, and by the ex-President of the United States, and they are all going to be "exes" until they cease that promise or some of them see fit to keep it.[4]

[4] Abridged from the *Congressional Record*, 74th Cong., 1st sess., Vol. 79 (Washington, D.C.: Government Printing Office, 1935), pp. 9363–66.

LOUISIANA'S ACCOMPLISHMENTS

Long's break with Roosevelt and administration leaders led him publicly to attack their program and to direct toward them his characteristic derision. The President became Prince Franklin, Knight of the Nourmahal (after Vincent Astor's yacht, which frequently bore Roosevelt). The Secretary of Agriculture became Lord Corn Wallace; Harold Ickes, the Chicago Cinch Bug; Hugh Johnson, Sitting Bull. In retaliation, Roosevelt directed Postmaster General Farley to channel federal patronage to the anti-Longs and subsequently arranged for Harold Ickes to curtail $10,000,000 worth of PWA projects in Louisiana. Further, Roosevelt directed the Bureau of Internal Revenue to initiate a tax investigation which led to the indictment of several prominent Long aides for tax evasion. In addition, the Senate began investigating the clouded circumstances of the election of Long's junior colleague, Senator John Overton. In February of 1933, Long addressed the Senate in an attempt to blunt the charges of fiscal and electoral irregularity in Louisiana *by pointing to Louisiana's dramatic transformation under his leadership into a model of a share-our-wealth society.*[5]

Mr. President, I do not conceive that the administration of Gov. O. K. Allen, of Louisiana, and of myself as Governor of Louisiana are appropriate objects of inquiry on the part of the Senate. . . . But so much has been printed about these administrations of mine and my successor as governors that I am required to answer, hoping that some of the facts which I mention here may gain their way into the publications of this country to answer what was testified in the hearing and printed, but which was not, I contend, relevant.

Mr. President, I wish to say that when I became the Governor of Louisiana in 1928 the State was committed to a penitentiary losing some years to around a million dollars a year. At the conclusion of my administration and during the administration of Governor Allen that penitentiary, which had been losing a million dollars a year, is on a self-sustaining basis, and perhaps a paying and profitable basis.

I wish to say, Mr. President, that that penitentiary, along with the other penitentiaries of the United States, was investigated by a committee sent out by the N. E. A. newspaper services, and they reported on the penitentiary systems of the 48 States. When they reached Louisiana they stated that the penitentiary of Louisiana was the most ideal, from every standpoint, among all the penitentiaries of the United States. That was printed throughout the world in all newspapers, except in the newspapers of the State of Louisiana.

Mr. President, the next thing which I hope will find its way into print to counteract what has been printed as a result of this hearing, under privilege, is that when I became the governor of that State, Louisiana was at the bottom of the list as the most illiterate State in the United States, according to statistics of the census of the United States. When I left the governor's office, we had opened up night schools to educate the illiterate people who were 20 years old and older. We sent them to school when they were 20 years old, 40 years old, or 70 years old, and when I retired from the governor's office in 1932 to become a Member of the Senate, illiteracy in that State had been reduced to such a point that Louisiana was among the States recognized for the education of the people, from the top to the bottom, regardless of age. The educational system had been so improved that the illiterates had been reduced from 238,000 by 150,000 adults being educated in night schools.

Mr. President, that is not all I wish to say in order that my State and my administration may not be stabbed unfairly in this proceeding. There

[5] From the *Congressional Record*, 72d Cong., 2d sess., Vol. 76 (Washington, D.C.: Government Printing Office, 1933), pp. 4673–75.

was an improvement among the Louisiana colleges. The Louisiana State University, particularly, was rated by the Intercollegiate Association of State Universities as a third-rate college, and when I retired from the office of governor of the State of Louisiana it was rated as an A No. 1 university of the United States, as good as Harvard, Yale, Johns Hopkins, or any other university.

Criticism has been made in the record of the committee hearing of the fact that I built a medical college for the Louisiana State University. That is true. In 1905 a law had been passed providing that a medical college should be built. I completed that work, under that act, in 1931 or 1932, but I wish to say that, regardless of the criticism that has been put into the record, that medical college only a few days ago was given the highest rating that can be given by the American Medical Association to a medical college.

Then, Mr. President, a great deal has been said about the highway work that has been done in Louisiana. When I became governor of that State we had just a few miles, perhaps 30 or 40 miles, of paved highways. Up until this day, as a result of what was done under my work as governor and under Gov. O. K. Allen, the State of Louisiana has about 2,000 miles of paved highways and about 9,000 or 10,000 miles of farmers' gravel road. The State of Louisiana stands out to-day when its program is completed, particularly, as the best State in America and the best community of the world for highways to accommodate its citizens, and no one has to go any further than the United States Bureau of Public Roads to find it out.

* * *

In the matter of education, in order that the facts regarding my State may be known, we adopted the free school-book system in Louisiana, and under my administration I gave the schools, out of the State treasury, $1,000,000 more than ever had been given them before, and Governor Allen has increased my allotment even in these hard times by appropriating out of the treasury $1,500,000 a year to the school children more than I appropriated when I was governor, and I appropriated $1,000,000 more than my predecessor.

* * *

Not only that, Mr. President, but in Louisiana those waterways, which are streams in Nebraska and Michigan, are rivers. By the time they get to our part of the country, that which one may step across in Minnesota, is a mile wide in its ordinary stages. At flood stages it may be 10 miles wide. That means that we have to build a bridge by dumping out a certain length and then making a bridge that is 2 miles in length for a river 2 miles wide. That is what we have done down there in Louisiana that we are being criticized for and investigated because a man was elected on a ticket we happened to favor.

We are building to-day a bridge across the Mississippi River that has been promised the people for 40 years. We are undertaking to start to build another bridge at Baton Rouge. We are building a big, but not so long bridge over the Red River at Shreveport. We have already built a bridge over the Red River at Moncla. We are building another one at Moncla. We are building another one at Alexandria, La., and another one over the Black River at Jonesville. We are building another one over the Ouachita River at Sterlington; another one over the Ouachita River at Monroe—that one has been completed, however. We are building another one over the Ouachita River at Harrisonburg, La.

We have built bridges and are building bridges the like of which can not be found in the length or breadth of this country, under soil conditions such as no other State has had to contend with. We have built the best in the world, we have built the strongest in the world, we have built them at the least cost, and yet all the condemnation that could be poured upon the State and upon her governors has been brought forth in this irrelevant fashion.

*   *   *

Taxes on Those Able to Pay

But where did the money come from? Mr. President, we put a severance tax on oil. That is where a part of it came from. We put a manufacturers' tax on carbon black. That is where some more of the money came from. We put a tax on the sales of tobacco. That is where some of the money comes from. We put a tax on malt. That is where some of the money comes from. But, Mr. President, under Governor Allen we did the terrible thing of voting a corporation franchise tax to get $1,000,000 or so, and the still worse thing of voting a tax on the manufacturer of electrical power and energy, which gives our State 2 per cent of the gross receipts derived from the manufacture of electricity and does not permit or allow it to be charged on the bills of the customers consuming it.

We also put a tax upon the natural gas severed from the soil of one-fifth of 1 cent per thousand cubic feet. As a result we have lowered the taxes on the little man, we have collected from the corporations, who should have paid and who are willing, I think, now to pay. They can not help themselves if they are not willing. Also, we have lowered the taxes on the little man. We have put the taxes on the corporation franchises. We have put the taxes on electricity, which taxes we have not allowed to be charged upon the bills of the consumers. We have put the taxes upon the elements and interests that could best bear the taxes. We have taken the State out of illiteracy. We have raised the standards of its colleges. We have reformed the penitentiary to where it is on a self-sustaining basis. We have gone into the hospitals, where they were taking care of

1,600 patients a day in one hospital, and improved conditions so that to-day they are taking care of 3,800 patients in the same hospital. Where the death rate before I became governor was 4.1 per cent, the death rate has been reduced to 2.7 per cent, a reduction of 1.4 per cent that has been made in the death rate at that hospital.

Justice for a State

Mr. President, I wish to say further, because I want my State to have the credit, that I am merely undertaking to erase the kind of publicity we have been given. We have built there a home for epileptics. There was no such thing in existence before I became governor of that State. When I became Governor of Louisiana our hospitals and asylums were treating the mentally sick, some of them in chairs in which they were locked, in strait-jackets; some of them had chains tied around their hands locking them to plow handles. We have abolished these barbarous practices in Louisiana under my administration and the administration of Governor Allen. There are three insane asylums in the world rated first class to-day that America knows of, and one of those is in the State of Louisiana.

Mr. President, with this statement I am not going to discuss the matter further unless occasion should arise. I am prepared, however, to discuss the matter in such other and further detail as may be made necessary. I wish to say only this further word. We have undertaken to keep our State from receiving that kind of unfair and unfavorable publicity. It is a known and open fact that certain of the newspapers of that State have tried to break the credit of that State. They have sent over their wires and printed in their publications every line of misinformation that could possibly be spread. The State has a balanced budget; it has every finished picture; its university, which had 1,500 students, has now between 4,000 and 5,000 students. We have built everything modern that a State could have. We have come out of it with a State that has less taxes, Mr. President, than any State in America to-day, taking it from one side of the country to the other, that has anything like the improvements that we have in the State of Louisiana with the property we have.

So, Mr. President, I want to thank the Members of the Senate for their attention and hope these remarks will be justified but, at least, will suffice.

SHARE OUR WEALTH

Long's answer to Roosevelt's opposition and his solution to "America's Crisis" was to transform his share-the-wealth proposal in 1934 into a full-blown Share Our Wealth movement. He had first introduced his proposal in the Senate as early as March, 1932. By

1935 he had organized over 27,000 Share Our Wealth clubs and claimed a membership of 4,684,000 and a mailing list of 7,500,000. Every state was represented, although the heaviest concentrations were in the South and in the north central states, where Huey had campaigned so successfully for Roosevelt in 1932. The circular reprinted below, addressed "To Members and Well-Wishers of the Share Our Wealth Society," contains a strong indictment of Roosevelt and the New Deal and an eight-point outline of Long's wealth-sharing program.[6] In essence a soak-the-rich proposal, it contained something for almost everybody but the rich: farmers, urbanites, the aged, veterans, workers, and high school graduates. Critics damned it as a visionary and irresponsible economic nostrum. But General Hugh Johnson, unleashed by Roosevelt to attack Senator Long, inadvertently testified to its political potency: " 'Who is going to attempt to tell any man he ought not to have $5,000 a year, if Huey can get it for him—or even why they shouldn't be a King? The fact is that nobody is answering Huey in language anybody can understand. He is getting away with it without a contest.' "[7]

To Members and Well-Wishers of the Share Our Wealth Society:

For 20 years I have been in the battle to provide that, so long as America has, or can produce, an abundance of the things which make life comfortable and happy, that none should own so much of the things which he does not need and cannot use as to deprive the balance of the people of a reasonable proportion of the necessities and conveniences of life. The whole line of my political thought has always been that America must face the time when the whole country would shoulder the obligation which it owes to every child born on earth—that is, a fair chance to life, liberty, and happiness.

I had been in the United States Senate only a few days when I began my effort to make the battle for a distribution of wealth among all the people a national issue for the coming elections. On July 2, 1932, pursuant to a promise made, I heard Franklin Delano Roosevelt, accepting the nomination of the Democratic Party at the Chicago convention for President of the United States, use the following words:

> Throughout the Nation, men and women, forgotten in the political philosophy of the Government for the last years, look to us here for guidance and for a more equitable opportunity to share in the distribution of the national wealth.

[6] Abridged from the *Congressional Record*, 74th Cong., 1st sess., Vol. 79 (Washington, D.C.: Government Printing Office, 1935), pp. 8040–43.

[7] Allan P. Sindler, *Huey Long's Louisiana* (Baltimore: The Johns Hopkins Press, 1956), pp. 84–85.

It therefore seemed that all we had to do was to elect our candidate and that then my object in public life would be accomplished.

But a few nights before the Presidential election I listened to Mr. Herbert Hoover deliver his speech in Madison Square Garden, and he used these words:

> My conception of America is a land where men and women may walk in ordered liberty, where they may enjoy the advantages of wealth, not concentrated in the hands of a few, but diffused through the lives of all.

So it seems that so popular had become the demand for a redistribution of wealth in America that Mr. Hoover had been compelled to somewhat yield to that for which Mr. Roosevelt had previously declared without reservation.

It is not out of place for me to say that the support which I brought to Mr. Roosevelt to secure his nomination and election as President—and without which it was hardly probable he would ever have been nominated—was on the assurances which I had that he would take the proper stand for the redistribution of wealth in the campaign. He did that much in the campaign; but after his election, what then? I need not tell you the story. We have not time to cry over our disappointments, over promises which others did not keep, and over pledges which were broken.

We have not a moment to lose.

It was after my disappointment over the Roosevelt policy, after he became President, that I saw the light. I soon began to understand that, regardless of what we had been promised, our only chance of securing the fulfillment of such pledges was to organize the men and the women of the United States so that they were a force capable of action, and capable of requiring such a policy from the lawmakers and from the President after they took office. That was the beginning of the Share Our Wealth Society movement.

Let me say to the members and well-wishers that in this movement, the principles of which have received the endorsement of every leader of this time, and of other times, I am not concerned over my personal position or political fortune; I am only interested in the success of the cause; and on any day or at any time when, by our going for any person or for any party, we can better, or more surely or more quickly secure home, comfort, education, and happiness for our people, that there is no ambition of mine which will stand in the way. But there can be no minimum of success until every child in this land is fed, clothed, and housed comfortably and made happy with opportunity for education and a chance in life.

Even after the present President of the United States had thrown down the pledge which he had made time after time, and rather indicated the desire, instead, to have all the common people of America fed from a half-starvation dole, while the plutocrats of the United States were allowed to wax richer and richer, even after that, I made the public proposition that if he would return to his promise and carry out the pledge given to the people and to me that, regardless of all that had passed, I would again support his administration to the limit of my ability.

Of course, however, I was not blind; I had long since come to the understanding that he was chained to other purposes and to other interests which made impossible his keeping the words which he uttered to the people.

I delayed using this form of call to the members and well-wishers of the Share Our Wealth Society until we had progressed so far as to convince me that we could succeed either before or in the next national election of November 1936. Until I became certain that the spirit of the people could be aroused throughout the United States, and that, without any money—because I have none, except such little as I am given—the people could be persuaded to perfect organizations throughout the counties and communities of the country, I did not want to give false hopes to any of those engaged with me in this noble work. But I have seen and checked back enough, based upon the experiences which I have had in my public career, to know that we can, with much more ease, win the present fight, either between now and the next national campaign, or else in the next national campaign—I say with much more ease than many other battles which I have won in the past but which did not mean near so much.

We now have enough societies and enough members, to say nothing of the well-wishers, who—if they will put their shoulders to the wheel and give us one-half of the time which they do not need for anything else—can force the principles of the Share Our Wealth Society to the forefront, to where no person participating in national affairs can ignore them further.

Now, here is what I ask the officers and members and well-wishers of all the Share Our Wealth Societies to do—two things, to wit:

First. If you have a Share Our Wealth Society in your neighborhood—or, if you have not one, organize one—meet regularly, and let all members, men and women, go to work as quickly and as hard as they can to get every person in the neighborhood to become a member and to go out with them to get more members for the society. If members do not want to go into the society already organized in their community, let them organize another society. We must have them as members in the movement, so that, by having their cooperation, on short notice we can all act as one person for the one object and purpose of providing that in the land of plenty there shall be comfort for all. The organized 600 families who control the wealth of America have been able to keep the 125,000,000 people in bondage because they have never once known how to effectually strike for their fair demands.

Second. Get a number of members of the Share Our Wealth Society to immediately go into all other neighborhoods of your county and into the neighborhoods of the adjoining counties, so as to get the people in the other communities and in the other counties to organize more Share Our Wealth Societies there; that will mean we can soon get about the work of perfecting a complete, unified organization that will not only hear promises but will compel the fulfillment of pledges made to the people.

It is impossible for the United States to preserve itself as a republic or as a democracy when 600 families own more of this Nation's wealth—in fact, twice as much—as all the balance of the people put together. Ninety-six percent of our people live below the poverty line, while 4 percent own 87 percent of the wealth. America can have enough for all to live in comfort and still permit millionaires to own more than they can ever spend and to have more than they can ever use; but America cannot allow the multimillionaires and the billionaires, a mere handful of them, to own everything unless we are willing to inflict starvation upon 125,000,000 people.

* * *

Here is the whole sum and substance of the share-our-wealth movement:

1. Every family to be furnished by the Government a homestead allowance, free of debt, of not less than one-third the average family wealth of the country, which means, at the lowest, that every family shall have the reasonable comforts of life up to a value of from $5,000 to $6,000. No person to have a fortune of more than 100 to 300 times the average family fortune, which means that the limit to fortunes is between $1,500,000 and $5,000,000, with annual capital levy taxes imposed on all above $1,000,000.

2. The yearly income of every family shall be not less than one-third of the average family income, which means that, according to the estimates of the statisticians of the United States Government and Wall Street, no family's annual income would be less than from $2,000 to $2,500. No yearly income shall be allowed to any person larger than from 100 to 300 times the size of the average family income, which means that no person would be allowed to earn in any year more than from $600,000 to $1,800,000, all to be subject to present income-tax laws.

3. To limit or regulate the hours of work to such an extent as to prevent overproduction; the most modern and efficient machinery would be encouraged, so that as much would be produced as possible so as to satisfy all demands of the people, but to also allow the maximum time to the workers for recreation, convenience, education, and luxuries of life.

4. An old-age pension to the persons of 60.

5. To balance agricultural production with what can be consumed according to the laws of God, which includes the preserving and storage of surplus commodities to be paid for and held by the Government for the emergencies when such are needed. Please bear in mind, however, that when the people of America have had money to buy things they needed, we have never had a surplus of any commodity. This plan of God does not call for destroying any of the things raised to eat or wear, nor does it countenance wholesale destruction of hogs, cattle, or milk.

6. To pay the veterans of our wars what we owe them and to care for their disabled.

7. Education and training for all children to be equal in opportunity in all schools, colleges, universities, and other institutions for training in the professions and vocations of life; to be regulated on the capacity of children to learn, and not on the ability of parents to pay the costs. Training for life's work to be as much universal and thorough for all walks in life as has been the training in the arts of killing.

8. The raising of revenue and taxes for the support of this program to come from the reduction of swollen fortunes from the top, as well as for the support of public works to give employment whenever there may be any slackening necessary in private enterprise.

I now ask those who read this circular to help us at once in this work of giving life and happiness to our people—not a starvation dole upon which someone may live in misery from week to week. Before this miserable system of wreckage has destroyed the life germ of respect and culture in our American people let us save what was here, merely by having none too poor and none too rich. The theory of the Share Our Wealth Society is to have enough for all, but not to have one with so much that less than enough remains for the balance of the people.

Please, therefore, let me ask you who read this document—please help this work before it is too late for us to be of help to our people. We ask you now, (1) help to get your neighbor into the work of this society and (2) help get other Share Our Wealth societies started in your county and in adjoining counties and get them to go out to organize other societies.

To print and mail out this circular costs about 60 cents per hundred, or $6 per thousand. Anyone who reads this who wants more circulars of this kind to use in the work, can get them for that price by sending the money to me, and I will pay the printer for him. Better still, if you can have this circular reprinted in your own town or city.

Let everyone who feels he wishes to help in our work start right out and go ahead. One man or woman is as important as any other. Take up the fight! Do not wait for someone else to tell you what to do. There are no high lights in this effort. We have no State managers and no city managers. Everyone can take up the work, and as many societies can be organized as there are people to organize them. One is the same as another. The reward and compensation is the salvation of humanity. Fear no opposition. "He who falls in this fight falls in the radiance of the future!"

Yours sincerely,

HUEY P. LONG,
United States Senator, Washington, D.C.

To: HUEY P. LONG
U. S. Senator,
Washington, D. C.

This is to inform you that a Share Our Wealth Society has been organized here with_____members. Address and officers are as follows:

Post office:_____ State:_____
President:_____
Address:_____
Secretary:_____
Address:_____

(Allied Printing Trades Council, Union Label, Baltimore, 5.)

THE IRRELEVANCE OF RACE

Critics early labeled Huey Long a demagogue, and it is true that his flamboyant political style resembled the emotional appeals of the South's familiar Tillmans and Bilboes. But as was acknowledged by Wilbur Cash, a contemporary of Long's and author of The Mind of the South, *Huey Long "was the first Southern demagogue largely to leave aside nigger-baiting and address himself to the irritations bred in the common white by his economic and social status."* [8] *This is not to suggest that Long's racial views differed in any fundamental way from those of the typical Southern white. But he regarded the race question as a settled one, and essentially irrelevant to his class program. In the interview that follows, Roy Wilkins, then editor of* The Crisis, *the journal of the National Association for the Advancement of Colored People, questioned Long in 1935 concerning his racial views.* [9]

[8] Wilbur Cash, *The Mind of the South* (New York: Alfred A. Knopf, Inc., 1941), pp. 291–92.

[9] From *The Crisis*, XLII (February, 1935), 41, 52. Reprinted by permission of The Crisis Publishing Co., Inc.

Contrary to my expectations, I had no difficulty getting an interview with Senator Huey P. Long, the Kingfish, Dictator of the State of Louisiana, aspirant to the Presidency in 1936. I reasoned that nothing more serious could happen than a refusal to see me, especially since the location was New York and not Baton Rouge or New Orleans, so up to the twenty-fifth floor of the Hotel New Yorker I took myself.

Two things I wanted to know, if the Kingfish would talk: what was he going to do about the lynching which had been staged the day before in Franklinton, La.: and what hope did his "share-the-wealth" program hold out for Negro Americans?

It is a certainty that I am not as important as a German naval captain and since Huey had received that worthy some years ago in green pajamas, I could not complain when he received me in maroon silk pajamas.

It developed that in calling at 9:30 I had arrived just about as the senator was rising. After a bit he came into the room barefooted and bawling for breakfast to be ordered. He shook hands with all of us present, hesitating not a bit when he came to the only Negro. The dictator's hair was tousled; sleep was in his eyes; the pajamas added the only bright note. All men, I thought, dictators or not, look pretty much the same in the morning. After an hour and a quarter of waiting my turn came.

Through a sitting room, past a bathroom and into the bedroom of the "Dictator of the Delta." There he was, barefoot still, in pajamas still, bending over his bed on which were spread nine or ten shirts from which he was trying to make a selection.

"Sit down," he invited, plunging right in, "you know I came up here to see a show, to get a little fun away from the senate, but I haven't done a thing but see newspapermen."

"Well, Senator, I would like to ask you just a few questions," I began.

"Sure. Let me tell you about the nigras," he interrupted. In the first two minutes I found out Huey does all the talking and that he uses "nigger," "nigra," and occasionally "colored," but mostly "nigger."

"One of them newspapers (he hates newspapers) yesterday tried to put me on the spot about niggers voting. You saw it? Why, say, I ain't gonna get into that fight. They don't vote in the South—you from the South?— well, they don't vote down there, so why should I go into that? I have been able to do a hell of a lot of things down there because I am Huey Long—they know I'm square; a lot of guys would have been murdered politically for what I've been able to do quietly for the niggers. But do you think I could get away with niggers voting? No sirree! These newspapers are trying to jam me!"

"But, Senator—" I tried to edge in. No use. The flood continued while he shook out some tooth powder and hunted his toothbrush:

"Lissen here. My educational program is for everybody, whites and blacks. I can't have my people ignorant. Louisiana had a high illiteracy rate, couldn't read or write. I mean whites couldn't either, but there were more among the niggers. (I thought of the figures for education in Louisiana and thought to say a word, but no one could stem that tide of words from him; anyway I was here for an interview, not for an argument.) When I became governor I said 'this has gotta stop.' I gave 'em school books free at the state's expense. I started free schools, day and night, so they could learn to read and write and figger.

"Maybe you think that was easy in the case of the niggers. There are plenty of ignorant white people with hatred in their hearts from the war between the states. They did not want the niggers to go to school. That was tough on me. They said their niggers had to work. So what did I do? I opened night schools. They kept on hollering and I simply had to put my foot down. I said (beating his breast) 'I'm the governor and I say the ignorant in this state have to learn, blacks as well as whites.' And they learned."

"Yes, but—" I made another effort. He merely took another swipe with his toothbrush and drove on, cocking a shrewd eye at me as I stood at the door of the green and black bathroom:

"Now, young man, you can see some things without me writing them down. I'm not working for equality or anything like that. I figger when you teach niggers to read and write and figger they can kinda look out for themselves—you know, people can't cheat them like they did before. You know they cheat them, don't you? (Did I?) Why, (and here he grew confidential, drawing a diagram on the dresser with his toothbrush handle) down home we have plantations ten miles long and five miles wide. They have a system that's lawful but bad for the niggers. Maybe when a nigger tenant got through working at the end of the year he had enough to buy the baby a rattle for Christmas and maybe not. That ain't right. I taught 'em to figger. They got to look out for themselves. Maybe you think it didn't raise hell among the landlords. . . ."

He paused to read a telegram and answer the telephone (incidentally in very correct English) and I managed to get in a question:

"How about lynching, Senator? About the Costigan-Wagner bill in congress and that lynching down there yesterday in—"

He ducked the Costigan-Wagner bill, but of course, everyone knows he is against it. He cut me off on the Franklinton lynching and hastened in with his "pat" explanation:

"You mean down in Washington parish (county)? Oh, that? That one slipped up on us. Too bad, but those slips will happen. You know while I was governor there were no lynchings and since this man (Gov. Allen) has been in he hasn't had any. (There have been 7 lynchings in Louisiana in the last two years.) This one slipped up. I can't do nothing about it. No sir. Can't do the dead nigra no good. Why, if I tried to go after those lynchers it might cause a hundred more niggers to be killed. You wouldn't want that, would you?"

"But you control Louisiana," I persisted, "you could—"

"Yeah, but it's not that simple. I told you there are some things even Huey Long can't get away with. We'll just have to watch out for the next one. Anyway that nigger was guilty of coldblooded murder."

"But your own supreme court had just granted him a new trial."

"Sure we got a law which allows a reversal on technical points. This nigger got hold of a smart lawyer somewhere and proved a technicality. He was guilty as hell. But we'll catch the next lynching."

Quickly and positively changing the subject he ran on:

"Now about 'the share-the-wealth.' I say niggers have got to have homes and security like anybody else. (I thought: security and lynching?) I stand on that. They say to me: 'Do you mean niggers have to have a home?' I say: 'yes, a nigger is entitled to a home.' Who'll disagree with that? It's fair."

Sitting down opposite me now with his legs crossed, wriggling his toes, talking now quietly, now oratorically, but always amiably, the senator switched to another topic. He was courtesy itself (except for that word "nigger" which he certainly does not regard as offensive) and he was evidently trying earnestly to put over what he considered his "good points" on the Negro question.

"Why down in Louisiana," he continued, "the whites have decided nigras have got to have public health care. Got to give 'em clinics and hospitals. Got to keep 'em healthy. That's fair and it's good sense. I said to them: 'you wouldn't want a colored woman (one of his few uses of the word "colored") watching over your children if she had pyorrhea, would you?' They see the point. The same goes for other diseases. We got hospitals and clinics down there to care for niggers just like everybody else."

"In your article," he concluded, as he called for a long distance call to New Orleans and moved to select some underwear, "don't say I'm working for niggers. I'm not. I'm for the poor man—all poor men. Black and white, they all gotta have a chance. They gotta have a home, a job and a decent education for their children. 'Every Man a King'— that's my slogan. That means every man, niggers long with the rest, but not specially for niggers. . . .

"Come to see me in Washington. Drop in any time. Share the wealth, yessir—Hello, New Orleans? Goodday—hello, hello. . . ."

With a wave of his naked arm in farewell (he had taken off his pajama coat) the Kingfish sent me on my way.

In the hall his secretary said a little proudly, as if to prove something: "Well, you got your interview, didn't you?"

What about Kingfish Long and Negroes? What can they expect from him? Draw your own conclusions from the above. I have not attempted to polish it off. It is pretty much as he said it. No smooth, Ph.D.

language. No oily phrases like: "I admire the Negro race because it has made the greatest progress, etc., etc." No special promises.

He dodges the hard questions on lynching and the vote, and is vague on the easy ones.

My guess is that Huey is a hard, ambitious, practical politician. He is far shrewder than he is given credit for being. My further guess is that he wouldn't hesitate to throw Negroes to the wolves if it became necessary; neither would he hesitate to carry them along if the good they did him was greater than the harm. He will walk a tight rope and go along as far as he can. He told New York newspapermen he welcomed Negroes in the share-the-wealth clubs in the North where they could vote, but down South? Down South they can't vote: they are no good to him. So he lets them strictly alone. After all, Huey comes first.

Anyway, menace or benefactor, he is the most colorful character I have interviewed in the twelve years I've been in the business.

SUI GENERIS

Public fascination with Huey Long was reflected in a vigorous national debate by 1935 over his appropriate label. Was he a Southern demagogue, a dictator, a fascist, a democrat, a Karl Marx of the hillbillies? Long once tired of listening to such a discussion by a group of visiting correspondents in New Orleans and blurted, "Oh, hell, say that I'm sui generis *and leave it at that." One such journalist, Forrest Davis, interviewed Long in preparation for writing a biography of the Kingfish. In a portion of the interview reprinted below, Davis, whose biography was hostile to the Senator, recollected Long's explication of his political views in a folksy vernacular.[10] Long's open expression of his presidential ambitions and his contempt for the two-party system are particularly revealing.*

While we were talking about the Senator's personality, his likes and dislikes and his vagaries, he followed the idiom of his native hills. He was a Louisiana Will Rogers, falling, as if naturally, into back-country locutions and figures of speech. But when we got around to the nub of the interview, his justification for the Louisiana dictatorship and his political methods, his understanding of democracy, his thoughts on recovery and generalizations on politics, he used clichés more sophisticated. . . . The later, more significant section of the interview exposed the Senator's rounded attitude on the political developments of his time. It disclosed a mind clear, agile and plausible. . . .

[10] Abridged from Forrest Davis, *Huey Long: A Candid Biography* (New York: Dodge Publishing Company, 1935), pp. 33–42.

The Kingfish scoffed at the charge that he is a Fascist and that the end result of his rise to power would be inevitably one-man, one-party rule in the interest of the owning classes. He confessed to only a hazy idea of European Fascism.

"I don't have any time for those people," he said. "I believe in democracy, old-fashioned American democracy; only we've got to change it around some. This thing we've got now up there," motioning toward the White House end of Pennsylvania Avenue, "ain't democracy. Killin' millions of pigs, plowin' under cotton and wheat while the pore go hungry and naked in the midst of plenty. Playin' politics with the needs of the people while the favored rich go on pilin' up bigger surpluses than ever. That ain't democracy, that's St. Vitus dance government; it's more like Fascism than what we've got in Loozyanna.

"Did you ever hear of a dictator that widened the base of the suffrage in his State? That's what I did. I repealed the poll tax, which had been put on there by the old aristocracy to keep the little fellow from voting, and I made it possible for three hundred thousand more people in my State to go to the polls."

When I was in Louisiana Governor Allen advised me that he was merely a puppet in the hands of his friend, Long. The Governor said: "I'm mighty proud to be Long's lieutenant. All the brains and energy that go into running this State come from him. He is the greatest man of his day and generation." I repeated the remarks of the Governor to the Senator.

The quotation displeased him.

"Did he say all THAT?" he mocked. "Why, Oscar; I wish the so-and-so would mind what he says. He causes me a hell of a lot of grief down there when he goes astray.

"But I ain't the dictator of Loozyanna. I have my ideas, my program and my organization down there. I mess around with what goes on a good bit. Things get out of hand when I don't. The government of Loozyanna is loose. The Governor hasn't got the power he ought to have. There's a lot of commissions and State departments independent of the Governor. It takes someone to keep the thing kind of centralized. The way I look at it, I'm responsible for the Long organization, and the Long organization is responsible to the people for running the State.

"But I don't order them around. The way it is is this: they come to me with their problems; they say 'how about this, Huey' and 'won't you take hold and help out with this.' The same with the legislature. They look to somebody to get up the program for them; they're committed to the general program and so we get through with it without squandering the State's time and money."

"The principle of leadership," I interjected.

"That's correct," said Huey, "they look to me for leadership."

"Your enemies in Louisiana condemn your political methods," I said.

"They call you the most brazen spoilsman since Andrew Jackson, accuse you of building up an arrogant, corrupt machine, of stealing votes and denying freedom of political expression."

The Kingfish's eyes clouded.

"They always say that; that bunch of has-beens and ex-es. When they ran the State the people never had a chance. They passed the offices and the plums and the graft around, and the people couldn't get anywheres near the trough. When I got into politics I was just an ignorant boy from the country. All the political tricks I learned, I learned from them when they were trying to keep Huey P. Long out.

"The corruption in that State was terrible. I found out that the State penitentiary was losing a million dollars a year. I couldn't break up the graft there. The State was buyin' the same mules and the same seed over and over again. As fast as I canned a crook and put in an honest man they'd corrupt him. 'Don't be a fool,' they'd say, 'here's a chance to make five or ten thousand a year over your salary if you go along with us.' I finally had to fire the whole damn crowd, and now the penitentiary is on a payin' basis, not costin' the taxpayers a cent. The same way in the Highway Commission. Loozyanna was swallowed up by dust and mired hub-deep in winter. We had no roads, but the Highway Commission was spendin' millions a year just the same. The year I took office as Governor, 1928, we faced a deficit of $5,000,000 at the end of the year even if we didn't repair or build a single road the whole year. The same all over the State government.

"They had a system of looting of many years' standing. It all descended to us from the Loozyanna lottery. The State was run by an oligarchy of a few families. All of them lived off the people. They would have a toll ferry here, a toll bridge yonder; some had property they rented to gambling joints and bawdy houses; the political families worked in with the big corporations, and their members had fancy jobs with the corporations preyin' on the State.

"They just naturally hate to see that broken up and the State run in the interest of the people.

"I've beat 'em, beat 'em, beat 'em and they kick that I've got a good organization. If I didn't have a good organization they could get back in power and suppress Huey P. Long and what he's done for the State of Loozyanna. You can't have an organization without jobs. I didn't invent that idea. Jim Farley and his Tammany pals in New York City know a thing or two about that idea.

"But I don't like that part. The job end of it is only a headache. If I had my way I wouldn't have a ward leader in Loozyanna. I'd get up a program and go to the people naked, without organization, and say, 'Here's what I'll do for you if you put me in.' But if I did that, the old gang would have all the ward leaders on their side, and the people wouldn't have a chance to express their will."

"What," I asked, "is your theory of democracy?"

"The rule of the people," the Senator replied. "My theory is that a leader gets up a program and then he goes out and explains it, patiently and more patiently, until they get it. He asks for a mandate, and if they give it to him he goes ahead with the program in spite of hell and high water. He don't tolerate no opposition from the old-gang politicians, the legislatures, the courts, the corporations or anybody.

"That is the best politics. Get the people to endorse your program and then put it through."

. . . I asked if the Senator's definition of democratic processes did not express, in essence, Hitler's formula for organizing the power of the State. The Kingfish was elaborately uninterested in speculating about similarities between himself and *Der Fuehrer*.

"It's the rule of the people, ain't it?" he demanded.

"Some people say you are a demagogue." I countered.

The Kingfish was scornful.

"The people that say that think anybody who presumes to talk for the people is a demagogue. There are all kinds of demagogues. Some deceive the people in the interests of the lords and masters of creation, the Rockefellers and the Morgans. Some of them deceive the people in their own interest. I would describe a demagogue as a politician who don't keep his promises. On that basis, I'm the first man to have power in Loozyanna who ain't a demagogue. I kept every promise I ever have made to the people of Loozyanna. None of them ex-es and bellyachers that have been fightin' me down there ever kept his promises when he was in office. It was an unheard-of thing in Loozyanna until Huey P. Long got in.

"If I was a demagogue, would I want to educate the people, old and young? When I got in I found Loozyanna at the bottom of the list in illiterates. I gave 'em night schools and buses to take the old folks to and fro." The Kingfish himself wrote a textbook, I was told in Louisiana, smoothing the path to literacy in fifteen easy lessons.

"If I was a demagogue and wanted to keep the people in ignorance, would I be buildin' up my university? I got fifty-five hundred students out there now and if I stay in power another four years I'll have fifteen thousand."

*   *   *

"Have you faith," I asked, "that the abundance of this country will be distributed in our time?"

He regarded the question as slightly naïve. He had no doubt of it.

"If I don't do it, somebody else will," he said with finality.

The talk turned to his announced candidacy for President. He hedged about his plans for 1936, although accepting as a certainty the prospect that he would run either in that year or 1940. "No man," he laid it down emphatically, "has ever been President of the U-nited States more than two terms. You know that; everyone knows that. But when I, g in, I'm going to abolish the Electoral College, have universal suffrage, and I defy any sonofabitch to get me out under four terms."

I asked about the chance of his becoming the candidate of a third party.

"I don't know that there will be a third party," he said. "It may be there won't be any number one and two parties. I may break up the Democratic and Republican parties before another year is out. What would you say if I had a majority of the voters signed up in every Congressional district in the country only to vote for a Share-Our-Wealth candidate? Where would the candidates be? They'd be out for Share-Our-Wealth, wouldn't they?"

"Do you include the Senators who would be running for re-election next year?" I asked.

"I include them that we call Senators for want of a better word.

"You are going to see in this country something you have never seen before. I am going to organize the country like I organized Loozy-anna. I am going to have twenty-five men to a precinct, organizing all over the country. Right from the ground up, we're going at it. I've got organizers out all over the country now, speakin' from sound trucks and linin' up the voters. Because you don't read about it in the papers, don't think Huey P. Long ain't organizin' the U-nited States.

"We ain't dependin' on anybody else, or any political party. We're buildin' up a Long organization like we did in Loozyanna. Politicians ain't worth a goddam."

The Senator was coursing the carpet, tracing figures in the air, responding to newer visions of power.

"Where do you think the old parties are goin' to get off when they find that Huey P. Long has got a majority of the voters in this country organized?"

The Senator's face was flushed, lids lowered over his eyes. He was entranced.

"I got millions of voters signed up now to the Share-Our-Wealth clubs; and when a man signs up for that it ain't like these other things that's goin' around. He signs up there, with Share-Our-Wealth, because he wants a five-thousand-dollar homestead, and a car and a radio, and twenty-five hundred dollars cash comin' in to the family every year, and a pension in his withered old age and to have the children educated, according to their deserts and ability, right up through the university without cost to him.

"The people that sign up are goin' to fight to get that," said the Senator.

"But will they get it?" I interrupted.

"Ask anybody in Loozyanna if Huey P. Long ever made a promise he didn't keep," he fired back.

PART TWO

HUEY LONG VIEWED BY HIS CONTEMPORARIES

Long's assassination in 1935 denied him the opportunity to keep that promise, thereby casting into the realm of speculation our attempt to assess the full meaning of his remarkable career. But so controversial was the volatile Kingfish and so desperate were the times that his contemporaries formed sharply contrasting views of his intentions and significance. This section reflects the range and depth of contemporary opinion, which tended to be widely polarized, for few remained indifferent to the fundamental challenges that he posed.

4

The Rev. Gerald L. K. Smith: The People's Choice

Long's chief lieutenant in the Share Our Wealth crusade was the Reverend Gerald L. K. Smith. A Wisconsin-born radical of LaFollette persuasions, Smith had been pastor of a wealthy Shreveport congregation, but resigned (with the conservative congregation's enthusiastic encouragement) to devote his full attention to organizing the Share Our Wealth Society. Invited by the editors of a liberal magazine, The New Republic, *to defend Huey Long and his program, Smith conceded that Long displayed the "surface manners" of a demagogue. But he insisted that Huey's ability to deliver on his promises distinguished him as a statesman—indeed, as a "superman." On balance, the assessments of Long published during his lifetime are critical, for both liberals and conservatives feared his radicalism. Here Smith seeks to speak for the devoted but largely inarticulate masses of Long supporters, whose only voices were their votes.*[1]

Nine years ago, Louisiana was a feudal state. Until that time it was ruled by the feudal lords in New Orleans and on the big plantations: the cotton kings, lumber kings, rice kings, oil kings, sugar kings, molasses kings, banana kings, etc. The state was just a "mainland" of the territory. The common people in New Orleans were ruled, domineered over and bulldozed by a political organization known as the Old Regulars. The great mass of people in the city and the country worked like slaves or else lived in an isolation that excluded opportunity. Labor unions were very weak and the assembly of workers was prohibited in most industrial centers. It was not uncommon for labor organizers to be beaten or assassinated.

The great corporations ruled the state and pushed the tax burden onto the poor. The Chambers of Commerce spent money in the North urging industry to come South for cheap labor. Illiteracy was as common as peonage. The commissary plan was in force in mills and on plantations; it kept the workers from receiving cash and left them always in debt to the employer. The highway system was a series of muddy lanes with antique ferries and narrow bridges with high toll charges. Great forests sold for a dollar an acre, to be "slaughtered" and removed with nothing left to enrich the lives of stranded cut-over population. Families north of New Orleans were forced to pay an $8 toll to cross Lake Pontchartrain into New Orleans and return.

Of course, we had our grand and glorious aristocracy, plantation mansions, the annual Mardi Gras festival, horse races, and those staunch defenders of the old South, the newspapers. Of course, the old Louisiana aristocracy, with its lords, dukes and duchesses, had to be preserved, regardless of what happened to the people. State institutions constituted a disgrace. The insane were strapped, put into stocks and beaten. The penitentiary was an abyss of misery, hunger and graft. The State University had 1,500 students with a "C" rating. Most of the young people were too poor to attend Tulane, the only big university in the state. Ten thousand aristocrats ruled the state while 2,000,000 common peo-

[1] Gerald L. K. Smith, "Or Superman?," *The New Republic* (February 13, 1935), pp. 14–15. Smith later drifted into the ranks of ultra-right-wing racist organizations that proliferated in response to the postwar civil rights movement. Critics who viewed Long as essentially a fascist have cited Smith's subsequent activities as corroborating evidence of Long's allegedly fascist leanings. While Smith's subsequent career should not be ignored, it should also be noted that right-wing critics of Roosevelt have employed similar *ad hominem* logic in alluding to the flirtations with communism of some of the New Dealers.

ple wallowed in slavery with no representation in the affairs of the state. Half of the children were not in school. Great sections of the adult population could not read or write. Little consideration was given to Negro education. Professional training was available only to the sons of the privileged.

Huey Long grew up in the pine woods of Winn Parish. He had witnessed the sale of trees worth $10 each for $1 an acre. He was sensitive to injustice. He knew the difficulty of receiving a higher education. He seemed to have an intuitive appreciation of ideal social conditions. At the age of twenty, his Share the Wealth ideal was fixed in his mind. Shortly after, he announced his ambition to become Governor. He was ridiculed, patronized and pitied. True enough, he was a mustang—rough, wild, vigorous, and at the same time mysteriously intelligent. At thirty, he was the best lawyer in Louisiana. He had the surface manners of a demagogue, but the depth of a statesman. This dual nature accounts for many of his victories. He wins like a demagogue and delivers like a statesman. His capacity for work was unlimited. He waded through mud, drove along dusty highways, and soon became the poor man's best friend. After fifteen hours of hard work, he could recover completely with three hours of sleep. He recognized the value of entertainment in leading these sad, enslaved people out of bondage. He is Louisiana's greatest humorist. It was his wedge, but behind that wedge was a deep sympathy and a tender understanding of the needs of his people.

In 1928 he was elected Governor. He had promised many things that even his staunchest admirers questioned his ability to deliver. He moved to Baton Rouge, tore down the old Governor's mansion, built a new one, built a new capitol, built new university buildings, refused to entertain socially, attended no banquets, snubbed the elite and opened the mansion to the muddy feet of his comrades. He offended the sensibilities of the tender sons and daughters of privilege. He whipped bankers into line, he struck blow after blow at peonage, he gave orders to the Standard Oil Company, the bank trust and the feudal lords. Society matrons, lottery kings, gamblers, exclusive clubs and—not to be forgotten—leading clergymen with sensitive flocks joined hands to impeach this "wild," "horrible," "terrible," "bad" man. The war was on. Impeachment proceedings failed. State senators, representatives and appointees began to obey like humble servants—not in fear, but quite as anxious parents obey a great physician who prescribes for a sick child. He was recognized by friend and foe as the smartest man in Louisiana.

Severance taxes were levied on oil, gas, lumber and other natural resources, which made possible free schoolbooks for all children, black and white, rich and poor, in public and private schools. Telephone rates were cut, gas rates were cut, electric rates were cut; night schools were opened up and 149,000 adults were taught to read and write. Then came free ferries, new free bridges, 5,000 miles of paved and improved roads (six years ago, we had only seventeen miles of pavement in Louisiana); a free medical school was built, as fine as any in the country. Free school buses were introduced, the assembly of workers for organization was guaranteed, new advantages were created for the deaf, the blind, the widows, the orphans and the insane, the penitentiary was modernized, traveling libraries were introduced and improved highways were forced through impassable swamps. Recently poll taxes were abolished, giving the franchise to 300,000 who had never voted. Legislation has been passed, removing all small homes and farms from the tax roll. This means that 95 percent of the Negro population will pay no taxes and 70 percent of the total population will be tax free. This transfers the tax burden from the worker to those who profit by his labor.

This was not easy to accomplish. Numerous attempts have been made to assassinate Huey Long, vigorous plots have been made to assassinate his character. These plotters have at all times enjoyed the coöperation of the Louisiana newspapers. We who hold mass meetings in the interest of our movement are threatened, guns are drawn on us and every conceivable hazard is put in our way by hirelings. Prior to the last legislature, when word was received that the tax burden was to be completely shifted from the little man to the big man, the newspapers actually appealed to and encouraged violence. They promoted mass meetings in the state capital and encouraged armed men to come to Baton Rouge, and expressed the implied hope that Huey Long would be killed. Although these meetings had the support of the combined press of the state, they fell flat in the presence of the sincerity of Governor Allen and Senator Long. The moratorium bill protected homes and farms and personal property against sheriff sales.

In the midst of all this, Huey Long was elected to the United States Senate, and began to preach in Washington what he had been practising in Louisiana. He made the first real speech and introduced the first real bill for the actual redistribution of wealth.

On February 3, 1934, he founded the Share Our Wealth Society and called on the American people to organize in order to accomplish the following objectives:

1. Limitation of poverty to a minimum of a $5,000 family estate.
2. Limitation of wealth to a maximum of 10,000,000.
3. Free higher education for all, with a mental test instead of the tuition test. If men in the army can be fed, boarded and clothed while we teach them how to kill, we can do as much for our best minds while they are being trained to live.
4. Employment for all by the shortening of hours.
5. Full compensation for veterans.

6. Old-age pensions.
7. Great national development programs to absorb the unemployed.

This program of work was strengthened by Senator Long's activity in connection with bank legislation, the Frazier-Lempke farm moratorium bill and numerous other pieces of legislation favorable to veterans and workers.

Our newspapers have given out the report that Senator Long is our dictator. The fact of the case is that the power to govern in Louisiana has been transferred from the feudal lords and their servile newspapers to the common people who elected a man to lead them and are standing by him. At the close of the Legislature this summer, long stories were written about Huey Long's puppet Governor and Legislature. The facts are these: At the close of the Legislature, the program was submitted to the people for a referendum and by a vote of 7 to 1 every major thing accomplished by the Legislature was approved.

Demagogues do not decide to educate their people. They thrive on ignorance. They may promise the same things that Huey Long promises, but they never deliver them. He keeps all of his campaign promises. We, who follow him, adore him and consider ourselves flattered when he asks our help. He never lies to us. He never uses the fall-guy method of protecting himself. He takes the blame for our mistakes.

The Share Our Wealth Society numbers 326,000 in Louisiana. We have passed the 3,000,000 mark in America. We do not fear an attack. Those who attack us become our best friends when they discover their mistake. Our plan can be understood and described easily. Therefore, we do not depend on the press. We do not create a state of mind, we merely discover and recognize a state of mind that has been created by conditions. Millions of people have joined us just because of what has been passed to them by word of mouth.

Huey Long is the greatest headline writer I have ever seen. His circulars attract, bite, sting and convince. It is difficult to imagine what would happen in America if every human being were to read one Huey Long circular on the same day. As a mass-meeting speaker, his equal has never been known in America. His knowledge of national and international affairs, as well as local affairs, is uncanny. He seems to be equally at home with all subjects, such as shipping, railroads, banking, Biblical literature, psychology, merchandising, utilities, sports, Oriental affairs, international treaties, South American affairs, world history, the Constitution of the United States, the Napoleonic Code, construction, higher education, flood control, cotton, lumber, sugar, rice, alphabetical relief agencies. Besides this, I am convinced that he is the greatest political strategist alive. Huey Long is a superman. I actually believe that he can do as much in one day as any ten men I know. He abstains from alcohol, he uses no tobacco; he is strong, youthful and enthusiastic. Hostile communities and individuals move toward him like an avalanche once they see him and hear him speak. His greatest recommendation is that we who know him best, love him most.

5

Raymond Gram Swing: Forerunner of American Fascism

American liberals in the 1930s were hyperconscious of the growth of fascism in Europe, and tended to judge Huey Long with a wary eye to Hitler and Mussolini. Typical of this fearful concern is the following report, which was published in a liberal weekly, The Nation, *early in 1935, and later the same year was included in a book entitled* Forerunners of American Fascism.[1] *The author, Raymond Gram Swing, wrote the report in Baton Rouge after having observed Senator Long ram through the Louisiana legislature a series of bills clearly designed not only to further his class reforms, but also to cripple and punish his opponents and to consolidate his control of state and local patronage to a degree unprecedented in American politics. Swing acknowledges that Long seemed to lack a systematic commitment to fascist ideology, but his explicit analogy of Hitler and the Nazis remains a central analytical model.[2]*

The state legislature is in session for the fourth time this year. The summons went out Friday for a meeting Sunday night, December 16, which anywhere else would trumpet an emergency. Here it meant simply a new maneuver by Huey Long. More patronage is to be grabbed for the Long machine, though there isn't much left to grab. More Long enemies are to be punished. But the purpose of the session is also to create diversion. Seymour Weiss, unofficial treasurer of the Long organization, president of the Dock Board, and nationally known hotel man, was indicted on Thursday. The federal investigators who trapped Al Capone have dug up evidence for charges that Weiss evaded paying income tax on $176,972 in the years 1929–33. Everyone on Thursday was talking about Weiss, the second of the inner four of the Long ma-

[1] Raymond Gram Swing, *Forerunners of American Fascism* (New York: Julian Messner, Inc., 1935).

[2] Abridged from Raymond Gram Swing, "The Menace of Huey Long," *The Nation* (January 9, 16, and 23, 1935), pp. 36–39, 69–71, 98–100.

chine to be tangled in the federal net. So far eight men have been involved in charges of evading the tax on more than a million dollars of income in the four years of Huey Long's rule. New Orleans was humming with gossip on Thursday. But by Friday night everyone was talking of the special session. As if to create a further diversion, Huey Long, United States Senator, clashed on Saturday with Captain "Biff" Jones, football coach at Louisiana State University. The Senator wanted to give his favorite football players a "pep" talk between halves of the Oregon game. The coach refused, exchanged hot words with the Senator, resigned. By Monday not only was the Weiss indictment off the front page; the Jones incident was outranking the special session in the newspapers.

The legislators meet Sunday night in the new $5,000,000 Huey Long Statehouse, a fine building with a thirty-story tower, which went up in a year. Everyone is happy, as though coming to a party. There is much hand-shaking and back-slapping. Only the insiders, back from a caucus in the governor's mansion, know what Huey Long is up to. These legislators are much like those in other states. Here and there is an outstanding fellow, but most are good-hearted, representative small-town citizens. One ten-gallon hat from an upstate parish . . . is on parade. The lofty, overdecorated assembly hall of the lower house is noisy with the buzz of talk. The galleries are crowded. A few women sit in members' seats, but they are only wives, privileged on an opening session. (Huey, bitterly opposed by the society women of New Orleans, is no feminist. To my question, "How does he stand on feminism?" a close colleague replied: "He is perfectly normal on that. I never heard him discuss it.") The session begins; everyone stands in silence for a prayer, beseeching God's guidance during the work of serving the people of Louisiana. It is an earnest prayer; one feels for a moment that Huey's people actually believe they are there for public service. The prayer ended, roll call is taken by electricity; members press buttons on their desks, a light shines beside each name on a huge board behind the Speaker's dais. Then all is confusion again, as thirty-five bills are read by title into the microphone and resound through the hall over the din of a hundred conversations.

Huey Long is ubiquitous. Now at the Speaker's chair for whispered consultation, now on the floor, he speaks to this man and that, then in the aisles, laughing, shouting, gesticulating. His loud voice is easily heard over the din. He is in a boisterous humor. As United States Senator he has no business there, no official status. The technicality occurs to no one. Why should it? This is Huey's Statehouse, Huey's legislature, Huey's state, his and his alone. The business proceeds; Long answers a question from the floor, he grins and waves his arms, he struts and grimaces with eyes protruding, face flushed. He is like a young father on a romp in the nursery. Anyone can see how much fun it is being dictator. Six years ago a Louisiana legislature nearly impeached him. Now see where he is: he has more power in one state than ever a man in American history; he is stronger than a king. He revels in his triumph, and most of the members appear to enjoy it too. The last of the bills is read. Only a few members have risen to ask questions or to protest against the hurry. The opposition still does not know what is hidden in the bills; it wants them printed before the committee meeting in the morning. Huey halts in the aisles to promise he will see to it. The meeting adjourns, and the legislators rush out to the gala chocolate-marble lobby to continue their fraternizing.

Let us follow the course of the thirty-five bills in the Committee of Ways and Means, which met Monday morning at nine o'clock. This committee has seventeen members, fifteen of them Huey's, only two from the opposition. All house bills, whatever their contents, now go to this committee, which meets on the tenth floor of the Statehouse tower. Here, one would assume, the real work of legislation is done. Here bills should be studied, analyzed, modified. Here should emerge the conflicts of interest and principle later to be fought out in debates of the house, and subsequently carried to the state at election time.

At five minutes before nine Huey arrives noisily with his bodyguard. He looks well-groomed in a brown suit. But everything about this man is exaggerated; his voice is too loud, his color too flushed, his gestures too sweeping, his sudden moments of earnestness too fanatical, his commands too noisy. No man could well be more bereft of dignity.

"This is no way to run a legislature," he shouts on finding he is almost first on the scene. "Nine o'clock, and nobody here!" One of his bodyguard slips out; members begin scrambling in, taking their places around the committee table. Roll is called promptly at nine (and one thinks how Mussolini made the trains run on time). The night before, Huey dominated the legislature, but it still was managed by its own officials. This morning, without formality, he takes full charge. A United States Senator, he has no right before the committee unless invited to address it. But this is dictatorship. Huey stands at the side of the chairman. "Before I explain these bills," he begins with unctuous humor, "I want to hear any comments by opponents." The bills had come from the printers just in time for the meeting, so the opponents had had no time to read them. The leading member of the opposition, a handsome young man of twenty-three, scowls and mutters a complaint. Huey grins. The chairman hands up Bill No. 1 and Huey glances over it.

"This bill," he begins conversationally, still reading, "is just a formality. The last legislature passed a liquor law—" He then tells in a few words what the bill provides. Someone whispers in his ear. "Oh yes, the bill also—" A member moves a favorable report, the gavel smashes down, the bill is approved. Huey is handed Bill No. 2, an income-tax measure. He explains it in a sentence; it is reported favorably. Bill No.

3 is a patronage grab giving the state machine the appointment of thirty employees in the tax collector's office in New Orleans. Huey again is solemnly humorous. "This is a very charitable law. It gives the gentlemen down in New Orleans the advantage of the best talent available. It relieves the heart of Mr. Montgomery [the tax collector] of a heavy burden."

"Has he requested the change?" speaks up twenty-three-year-old Representative Williamson.

"Not yet," says Huey; "we just anticipated that."

"Do you think he will like it?" asks Williamson.

"He will have to like it." The bill is approved at once. Three bills are out of the way in an elapsed time of six minutes. The same rate is maintained throughout. Huey stands there the entire time, the chairman's only function being to call for a vote, bring down his gavel, announce that the measure is approved, Representative Williamson and usually the second opposition member, voting no. Such questions as are raised are addressed to Huey and he answers them. One or two of the members interject remarks but Huey talks them into silence. He is running the show. Only one committee man makes a short speech, as by a special dispensation.

The object of much of the legislation is patronage grabbing. One bill takes from the city attorneys the right to name more than three assistants. New Orleans has ten. Hereafter this patronage goes to the Long machine through the Attorney General. Another bill transfers to the state the naming of all but five deputy sheriffs in any parish. Another requires all police and firemen to hold a warrant issued by the state. Huey promises that the state will not exercise discretionary power in issuing warrants, but the promise is not written into the bill. So the state gets control over every local police force and fire station after having taken over the appointment of police and fire chiefs in the last session.

The most important bill of the day provides for new schools of dentistry and pharmacy at Louisiana State University. Loyola University in New Orleans already has a dental college; Loyola also operates a radio station which did not give Huey all the time he wanted during the last campaign. Loyola will now feel the competition of a wealthy new dental school and Louisianna will have improved dental facilities. Instead of three free chairs in the Charity Hospital, there will be seventy-five. Huey, not mentioning the Loyola radio station, promises the committee that the new dental college will have the finest faculty in the world. It will enable young men to study dentistry at very low cost.

"How about the low cost to the taxpayers?" speaks up young Williamson.

"The little fellow won't feel it," Huey explains. "It will cost the corporations a little more, but we have to take care of the poor people.

From those that have shall be taken away." Later a bill is approved which increases the tax on corporation franchises from $1.50 to $2 a thousand, the proceeds to be earmarked for the new colleges.

One bill is rejected during the sitting, not by the committee, but by the "visiting" Senator. The chairman hands it up to him, he looks at it, frowns. "We don't want this. Let them come to us." With this cryptic remark he hands the bill back. The committee is told no more, but it formally shelves the measure. There is a bill aimed to prevent companies with pension schemes from discharging an employee just before his pension is due, requiring them to pay a proportion of the pension in such cases. Huey refers to a company within view of the committee window. (The Standard Oil Company refinery is smoking out there. Huey has fought Standard Oil all his political life.) Young Williamson remarks that the bill may lead all companies to abandon their pension schemes.

"Whoever goes out of the pension system because of this law just admits he is a crook," says Huey. The bill is approved. Once Huey finds the draft of a measure defective and scribbles an amendment himself, leaning over the table, writing rapidly on a large sheet of yellow paper while the committee waits. But even this delay does not spoil the record; thirty-five bills are acted on in seventy minutes, thirty-four approved, one shelved. This was the pace at the last session, and no doubt will be the pace so long as Huey's machine holds together. Two minutes for a law; this is dictatorship.

America has never seen anything more brazen or more slick. It is an object-lesson in the ease with which the form of democratic government can be twisted to serve the reality of one-man rule. The legislature meets, it pretends to initiate and enact laws, to scrutinize and debate them, and yet the operation has no more merit than it would have if these men moved in hypnosis.

What happens in the later sessions is that Huey makes further inroads into the broken lines of his opponents. By a ruse he gains control over the appointment of school teachers. He takes powers to remove the elected Mayor of Alexandra, the one town which had the temerity to shower him with eggs when he spoke there in the last campaign. The parish of Baton Rouge, which he did not capture at the polls, is subdued by a law which gives the state control of the "police jury," or local-government board, through the appointment of extra members. Huey explains he will make the parish into a District of Columbia, to safeguard the vast wealth of the state there situated. Standard Oil is at last subjected to an "occupational" tax for refining oil. The principle is resented by all business men and during Long's four years as Governor they kept him from applying this tax. Now it is slipped in unheralded and cannot be blocked. It will cost Standard Oil a million a year. Nor is this the end; there is talk of a further session in January, and beyond that of a new constitutional assembly to rewrite the basic law of the state to suit Huey's purposes.

To witness such a session is an almost unbelievable experience. It bristles with elements hard to comprehend. Why do these committee members take it lying down? This legislature is composed of men who are most of them ordinary, nice human fellows. How can they stomach Huey Long? How can they put up with his bullying, his unsavory, blasphemous, overbearing language? They do not seem to be afraid of him; they appear to like him. Psychology explains the dictators of Europe as appealing to the innate yearning for father-authority in most people. But Huey Long is no father-figure. He is a grown-up bad boy.

* * *

. . . He is not a fascist, with a philosophy of the state and its function in expressing the individual. He is plain dictator. He rules, and opponents had better stay out of his way. He punishes all who thwart him with grim, relentless, efficient vengeance.

But to say this does not make him wholly intelligible. One does not understand the problem of Huey Long or measure the menace he represents to American democracy until one admits that he has done a vast amount of good for Louisiana. He has this to justify all that is corrupt and peremptory in his methods. . . . Taken all in all, I do not know any man who has accomplished so much that I approve of in one state in four years, at the same time that he has done so much that I dislike. It is a thoroughly perplexing, paradoxical record.

If he were to die today, and the fear and hatred of him died too, and an honest group of politicians came into control of Louisiana, they would find a great deal to thank Huey Long for. He has reshaped the organism of an archaic state government, centralized it, made it easy to operate efficiently. Most important of all, he has shifted the weight of taxation from the poor, who were crippled under it, to the shoulders that can bear it. He has increased the debt of the state from $11,000,000 to nearly $150,000,000, the second largest per capita debt in the Union. But each stage of debt increase has been financed with new taxation. While the state has benefited from most of the money spent and its credit has been maintained at a high level, he has relieved the poor from many taxes and arranged for an early exemption of all property of $2,000 or under. This means that most Negroes in Louisiana and more than half the whites will be tax free, save for what they pay in taxes on tobacco, liquor, and gasoline. Further, his law postponing the payment of debts, though its effectiveness in practice still is to be demonstrated, makes him appear as the debtor's savior. He has laid out a system of highways and bridges that will lift Louisiana out of the backwoods tradition and make it coherent and accessible. Since 1924 two thousand miles of concrete roads, eleven hundred of asphalt, and thirty-seven hundred of gravel have been built, according to A. P. Tugwell, chairman of the State Highway Commission. Then, surprisingly, he has devoted himself to the cause of education. He has remodeled the school system of the state. His legislation has made it possible for a full eight-month term to be maintained in the poorest parishes. The burden of school attendance has been lightened by the state's providing all textbooks free of charge, a measure which has added around 15,000 to school attendance. (This is not to deny that school classes are far too large, or to condone dragging the schools into politics.) His enthusiasm for Louisiana State University, say his enemies, is the result of a feud with Tulane University, just as the new dental school is described as a punishment for Loyola. Leaving that aside, Louisiana State now is a flourishing, wealthy institution, with a first-rate faculty, doing work which marks it Grade A among the universities of the country. It has 4,000 students, as against 1,500 when Huey became Governor. Its equipment is superb, and it is taking a leading place in education in the South. Huey added a medical college to the university; the building was begun in January, was opened in October, the faculty was assembled, and the following May it won the grade of A among medical schools. Moreover, Tulane itself is improving its work in the face of this competition.

In the first year of his term as Governor, Huey put his shoulder behind the campaign to stamp out illiteracy. Louisiana was near the bottom of America's disgrace list. The late Julius Rosenwald, who paid out $50,000 for this campaign, deserves much of the credit. More than 100,-000 adults, white and black, learned to read and write in a single year. (The work is now proceeding under the federal relief authorities.) Huey has fought the public-utility companies during his whole political career and has won important victories. Power and telephone rates have been reduced, and will be reduced further if he has his way. He is now fighting to lower electricity rates in New Orleans, the highest in the country for a city of its class. It must be recorded that his brother, testifying before the Senate committee investigating the Overman election, denied the sincerity of Huey's fight against the corporations, and this denial is vigorously supported by his enemies in Louisiana. But I am not attempting now to judge his motives, but rather to summarize his achievements as they appear to the majority in the state who support him. Even the $5,000,000 Statehouse, about which so much that is derogatory has been said, would be considered a boon without Huey and his henchmen in it. Most of it is in good taste, all of it is useful, and rearing its lofty tower beside the Mississippi it symbolizes the strength and even the dignity of a modern commonwealth. Behind Huey's record is not the enunciated social philosophy to be found, say, in Wisconsin, but he has lifted Louisiana from a backward position to one that in many respects is advanced. I have said that until this is appreciated, the menace he represents to democracy in America cannot be measured. The man has good works to offer in return for his dictatorship. One needs only to think a moment to realize that without the good works he would be no menace whatever.

* * *

Huey Long in his well-tailored brown suit, ruling over his legislature, is one manifestation, but Huey in his green pajamas, holding court in his bedroom, is the natural man. He received the commander of the German cruiser Emden in pajamas, and created an international incident, since the visitor mistook a routine wardrobe for a deliberate insult. But everyone here understands that the green pajamas are Huey's ordinary apparel for political duties at certain hours of the routine day. He has been known to don them in the middle of the afternoon, climb into bed, and receive a stream of callers till late into the night. But the rule is to confine these pajama audiences to the evening. Thus he confers with, or rather declaims at, his henchmen. He does not stay in bed, but as the excitement wells up in him, he leaps out barefooted, and giving his pajama pants a yank, parades and rants like an orator before a vast audience. Hitler (not in pajamas) also cannot converse; he must orate. But Hitler looks through a solitary listener and goes into a near-trance, forgetting everything except the flow of ideas which pours from him. Huey does not ignore his listener; he stands over him shouting, prods him with a gesticulating finger, thumps him with an articulate fist. If the normal thing is to speak quietly and persuasively with a few men in a small room, then Huey either is abnormal or is acting. But his manner is not put on; this perpetual stump speaker is the real man.

At these sessions he is not imperious, for he lets the other fellow talk, too. His subordinates speak right up to him; they call him "Kingfish" (from Amos and Andy), and argue and disagree. But quickly he prevails, and he alone decides. A session with his workers may last for hours and cover a wide field. I sat in a corner of Huey's bedroom during a "conference" with a group of local leaders from an important parish. The topics discussed ranged from a decision to build a fence around a pasture at a state institution and the most insignificant details of patronage to important strategy for the next campaign. Huey knew the parish as well as any of his workers; the man's memory for a world of detail is almost mythical. There was no order of business, but in the course of two hours some twenty decisions were made. No matter how trite the issue, Huey burned and declaimed, now in bed, now parading the room in his pajamas and bare feet, hitching up the pajama pants, and waving his long windmill arms, striking all the attitudes familiar from his photographs.

* * *

Such a conference is a distressingly noisy business. One point settled, Huey climbs back into bed. He lies down flat—his bed is without a pillow—until the next point is mooted. An idea ignites in his mind; he sits up suddenly. Then as the fire develops, he leaps from bed. His men interrupt him, even differ from him, but he overwhelms them with the stentorian passion of his shouted arguments. At the end of the session, just as his henchmen are leaving, Huey recapitulates every decision reached. "I will do this; you will do that; this man is to be fired; that contract is to be pushed through." Twenty-odd decisions, rattled off verbatim.

Thus he carries the state's business in his head to the most trivial item. He knows every district, an incredible number of citizens by name and history and how they stand, and precisely what vote turned out for him in each district in the last elections. He knows what he will do in each parish, how he will finance this or that little matter, and so on to the woven whole of the commonwealth, which is there in his mind as though fully conceived in the abstract and being transformed into reality by his unquenchable passion. Everything springs from his brain, is molded by his will alone. When Huey leaves the state, his machine develops defects, his supporters slip away, his plans are clogged. No wonder, for he is functionally not a leader, he compels. And when he is not there no one else can subjugate for him. A man is not great, it has been said, who does not know how to delegate power. Huey, the embodiment of the appetite for power, probably will never have enough to be willing to yield any of it to another.

The scene in the bedroom is noisy; it also is profane. Anything Huey says in pajamas is likely to be punctuated with swear-words. Whether profanity is ordinarily a signal of contempt for manners or merely a substitute for better-expressed emphasis, it is both for Huey. His profanity is not imaginative or colorful; it is just ordinary vulgar cussing. Certainly he has no breeding, and no respect for it. Because his oysters were not fried to suit him he threw them on the floor at the restaurant of the Heidelberg Hotel the other day. He is one of those twisted spirits who must snarl or bawl at waiters. In this he differs from Hitler, who is a meek fellow to meet, and sees that you have an easy chair, and makes you feel that he is thinking of your comfort. Huey is rude as though impoliteness somehow were a necessitous kind of self-expression. Those around him are used to it; for them the Kingfish is only having his little joke.

*   *   *

Huey seldom forgets a slight or forgives an injury. I was told that he carries with him a little book (a "son-of-a-bitch book") of those he is going to "get," with a note of their offenses. Whether or not he goes to the trouble of writing them down, he gets his man, as all Louisiana will testify. The newspapers can speak as eloquently as anyone, for they are now fighting in the courts his tax levy of 2 per cent on the gross receipts from advertising. This was a spite tax to punish the larger newspapers for having fought him, though most of them have been with him at some time or other, thanks to the factional seesaw of Southern politics. "The lyin' newspapers" are a by-word in Huey's vocabulary. "This tax," he states in one of his circulars, "should be called a tax on lying, 2 cents per lie." The papers are fighting the measure as a revival of the old British practice of licensing and taxing the press to restrain its freedom, and the brief now before the federal court is an important contribution to the history of the free press in America.

He is uneducated and devoid of culture today, but let there be no mistake, he is a precociously intelligent man. His chief, perhaps his only intellectual interest is the law. America has more polished lawyers but it knows few today with greater talent. He has been praised by Chief Justice Taft and Justice Brandeis for briefs before the Supreme Court. Almost fabulous tales are told of how he will sit up all night preparing a brief that has been too much for his colleagues, and win his case in court the next morning. He is not a trial lawyer; it is the abstractions of the law which absorb him. And he has the strength to work year in and year out with little sleep, ceaselessly at it. The mind which grasps swiftly the abstruse points of law seizes as swiftly on the essentials of knowledge. He knows the smallest details of the business of the port of New Orleans (second largest in America), of banks, of industries he has had to study. His is a mastering as well as a masterful mind, which goes far to explain the unstinting admiration of his followers. They are used to his bad manners, they forgive the ruthlessness of his political methods, they condone the corruption of his regime, they overlook his innumerable impetuous blunders, because the man has the gift of an amazing, almost baffling mental ability. He towers over them, he out-smarts them, he knows. He is the hill-billy come into power, with the crudity of the hill-billy and his native shrewdness multiplied tenfold. Hill-billies have been the under-dogs of the South; now through Huey Long they are supreme in Louisiana.

*   *   *

"Huey Long is the best stump speaker in America. He is the best political radio speaker, better even than President Roosevelt. Give him time on the air and let him have a week to campaign in each state, and he can sweep the country. He is one of the most persuasive men living." This is the opinion not of a Long supporter, but of one of the key men in the fight against the Kingfish in Louisiana. The North, he said, is misled into dismissing him as a clown, and has no conception of Huey's talents and of his almost invincible mass appeal. Mrs. Hattie Caraway of Arkansas can testify to his powers, for when she entered the primary asking to succeed her late husband in the United States Senate, she was generally expected to run last among five candidates and to poll not more than

2,000 votes. The four men against her were experienced and able. But Huey took his sound van into Arkansas for one week, and though he could not get into every county, he made a circular tour during which he spoke six times a day. Instead of 2,000 votes Mrs. Caraway won a majority over the combined opposition in the first primary, tantamount to election in a Democratic state. An analysis of the vote showed that the districts where Huey did not appear virtually ignored her, while those which he toured gave her a landslide.

When his hour strikes, Huey will attack the rest of America with the same vehemence. That probably will be during the campaign of 1936. His platform will be the capital levy, strangely enough his exclusive possession as a political theme. He will speak more violently than Father Coughlin against the money interests of Wall Street and against the evil of large fortunes. He will pose as a misunderstood man, and to most listeners he will give their first information of what he has accomplished in Louisiana. He will be direct, picturesque, and amusing, a relief after the attenuated vagueness of most of the national speaking today. He will promise a nest egg of $5,000 for every deserving family in America, this to be the minimum of poverty in his brave new world. He rashly will undertake to put all the employables to work in a few months. He will assail President Roosevelt with a passion which may at first offend listeners, but in the end he might stir up opposition of a bitterness the President has not tasted in his life. Obviously, he cannot succeed while the country still has hopes of the success of the New Deal and trusts the President. Huey's chances depend on those sands of hope and trust running out. He is no menace if the President produces reform and recovery. But if in two years, even six, misery and fear are not abated in America, the field is free to the same kind of promise-mongers who swept away Democratic leaders in Italy and Germany. Huey believes Roosevelt can be beaten as early as 1936, but he is prepared to agitate for another four years. In 1940 he will still be a young man of forty-six.

Over the radio, if he follows the technique he uses at home, Huey will begin something like this: "Hello, friends, this is Huey Long speaking. And I have some very important revelations to make. But before I begin, I want you to do me a favor. I am going to talk along without saying anything special for four or five minutes, just to keep things going. While I'm doing that I want you to go to the telephone and call up five of your friends, and tell them Huey Long is on the air, and has some very important revelations to make." Thus he builds up an audience. He then can hold it for an hour or even two, weaving a speech of argument and anecdote and special pleading which is entertaining and informative, and quietly eats away any latent prejudice of his listeners. The country will make his acquaintance over the air before it does on the stump. Louisiana State University is to have a new radio station of fifty-kilowatt power, strong enough to reach all but distant states. L. S. U. is Huey's university, and this will be his station. It is a basic factor in his national plan. (Since this was written he has given the first of two talks over a National Broadcasting Company network, introduced as described above and including a strong attack on the President.)

He does not expect the support of the press. But the "lyin' newspapers" in a contradictory sort of way are an asset. Upton Sinclair knows how it arouses instant sympathy to say you are the victim of a conspiracy of misrepresentation. And most newspaper publishers, despite their pretense of representing American opinion, do not guess how little the majority of their readers rely on them for disinterested service. Like Sinclair, Huey publishes his own newspaper, but in Louisiana he depends still more on a remarkable system of circulars. His card catalogue of local addresses is the most complete of any political machine in the world. It holds the name of every Long man in every community in the state, and tells just how many circulars this man will undertake personally to distribute to neighbors. Huey's secretary maintains a pretentious multigraph office, and it can run off the circulars and address envelopes to each worker in a single evening. Huey then mobilizes all the motor vehicles of the state highway department and the highway police. The circulars can leave New Orleans at night and be in virtually every household in the state by morning.

One may say that remarkable as that may be, it will work only in Louisiana and cannot be done throughout the United States. But in a way it can. By November the "Share Our Wealth" campaign had recruited 3,687,641 members throughout the country in eight months. (The population of Louisiana is only 2,000,000.) Every member belongs to a society, and Huey has the addresses of those who organized it. To them can go circulars enough for all members. The "Share Our Wealth" organization is first of all a glorified mailing list, already one of the largest in the land, but certain to grow much larger once the Long campaign gets under way. It is the nucleus of a nation-wide political machine. And though the movement is naively simple, its very simplicity is one secret of its success. Anyone can form a society. Its members pay no dues. They send an address to Huey and he supplies them with his literature, including a copy of his autobiography. He urges societies to meet and discuss the redistribution of wealth and the rest of his platform. He promises to furnish answers and arguments needed to silence critics.

*   *   *

I doubt whether Huey and the Reverend Gerald L. K. Smith realize that property as such cannot be redistributed. How, for instance, divide a factory or a railroad among families? Value lies in use, and if the scheme were to be realized, all property would have to be nationalized, and the income from use distributed. The income from $5,000 would not be much for each family, not more than $200 or $300, certainly not enough to make true the dream of a home free of debt, a motor car, an electric refrigerator, and a college education for all the children, which is Huey's way of picturing his millennium. And if property is to be nationalized, why not share it equally? Why give the poor only a third, and decree the scramble for the other two-thirds in the name of capitalism? If Huey were to ask himself this question, he probably would answer that since both he and America believe in capitalism, he must advocate it. But probably he has not thought the platform through. He conceived of it early one morning, summoned his secretary, and had the organization worked out before noon of the same day. It isn't meant to be specific. It is only to convey to the unhappy people that he believes in a new social order in which the minimum of poverty is drastically raised, the rich somehow to foot the bill through a capital levy. It may be as simple as a box of kindergarten blocks, but could he win mass votes, or organize nearly four million people in eight months, by distributing a primer of economics?

I doubt, too, whether Huey has studied the dictatorships of Europe, though he can hardly help thinking of himself as a coming Hitler or Mussolini of America, since the parallel between him and his European prototypes is obvious. However, it must not be drawn too closely. Huey, for instance, is not a national socialist, if that title equips him at once with a philosophy of the state as the single dominant expression of the individual. He is a vulgar American politician, who has learned to play the two-fisted, sordid game of vote-getting and patronage infinitely better than his opponents. At his worst, he is no more unprincipled than they, his sin being that he is more ruthless and successful. At his best, he is not a social thinker, certainly not as much as either Hitler or Mussolini. Hitler's "Mein Kampf" is the work of an ascetic crusader. Mussolini's autobiography palpitates with ideas. Huey's autobiography is a scratchy, smug little tale of his political victories, tossed off in two weeks. Even so, Huey is an improvement on Hitler in two respects worthy of mention. He is free of the virus of racial prejudice and he is not anti-intellectual. That is not to say that he does not have the proverbial Southerner's disdain of the colored man, but it is not the basis of his political creed. Indeed, he prides himself on having improved Negro education in Louisiana, and on the exemption of virtually all Negroes in the state from taxation. Nor will Huey Long ever burn the books of his contemporaries in a public bonfire. Like many a man deprived of an academic education, he has an almost touching faith in it, and certainly cheaper and better schooling has been one of his central objectives. However impetuously he stamped out criticism of himself in the student newspaper of L. S. U., he has seen to it that good professors have been employed by the state, and they enjoy academic freedom. The incident of the *Reveille* is to be explained not by a philosophic hostility to free speech, but by the fact that the student who wrote the critical letter was a nephew of one of his bitterest opponents. He exploded because he thought his enemies were using "his" university against him and were getting away with it. It showed well enough how little he cares about the rights of criticism, but he does not mount the platform telling people, as Hitler and Mussolini do, that individuals must be prepared to sacrifice such personal rights for the good of the community.

*　　*　　*

The assumption in the North that Huey Long is a local phenomenon, a product of conditions not to be duplicated elsewhere, rests on the fallacy that the social picture of Louisiana is unique. The same easy-going mistake is made about those foreign countries, Germany and Italy. One has only to translate conditions in any of these regions into abstractions to see how little external distinctions really matter. Given a land in which the great majority are in want or in fear of it, in which democracy has not produced wise leadership or competent organs to conduct public affairs, in which "big interests" have far more than their share of power, the easiest sacrifice that society seems ready to make, if only its prejudices can be stirred, is of its democratic freedom. In Louisiana the dictatorship already is absolute; Huey controls all three functions of government, executive, legislative, and judicial. Is it resented? Certainly, by some people, just as Hitler and Mussolini are resented by some people in Germany and Italy. But not by all the people one might expect. This was brought home to me here, in a conversation with a young instructor at Louisiana State University. "I am troubled, too," he admitted. "There are many things Huey does that I don't approve of. But on the whole he has done a great deal of good. And if I had to choose between him without democracy and getting back the old crowd, without the good he has done, I should choose Huey. After all, democracy isn't any good if it doesn't work. Do you really think freedom is so important?"

This was not a German talking to me about Hitler, or an Italian about Mussolini. The argument was the same, the perplexity the same, the conclusion the same. I have heard scores of such confessions from equally intelligent Germans and Italians. The only new fact was the geography of the conversation. I was walking across the campus of an American university. And here it was I came face to face with the full menace of Huey Long. I repeat, he is no menace if Roosevelt succeeds, if he brings security to the lives of those who constitute the great majority of our people, if he redistributes wealth and democratizes economic power, if he establishes honest and efficient government. But if he fails, the man is waiting who is ruthless, ambitious, and indeed plausible enough to Hitlerize America.

6

Hodding Carter: American Dictator

Swing's views were typical of those of a swelling stream
of correspondents, at once fascinated and repelled, who visited
Lousiana during 1934 and 1935. The equally critical observations
that follow are those of a Louisiana native, Hodding Carter, who
published the anti-Long weekly Courier *in Hammond, Louisiana,*
from 1932 to 1936. Carter was later to achieve prominence as editor
and publisher of the Greenville (Mississippi) Delta Democrat-Times,
winning a Pulitzer Prize in 1946 for his courageous editorials in
support of racial moderation. In the following recollection he re-
veals not only the extreme pressures generated by Long's drive for
power, but also the desperation of the anti-Longs, their readiness
to resort to violence, and the curiously disparate nature of the anti-
Long coalition.[1]

In the spring of 1932 I turned from reporting to start a small daily
newspaper in Hammond, Louisiana. By then, Huey Long was immovably
established as Louisiana's junior Senator in Washington and Louisiana's
Kingfish at home. From the first issue of our newspaper I editorially
criticized his tightening grip upon the state and the corruption which
accompanied it. The initial reaction of his district lieutenants was a fairly
mild annoyance. Ours was a puny, insecure newspaper. Doubtless it
would welcome help. A man whom I had known since childhood, a
friend of my family, came to me with the suggestion that I get right.
Surely I needed better equipment for my newspaper, and better equipment could be procured for the friends of the administration. There were
constitutional amendments to be printed, political advertising, security,
permanence. Just get right.

Later the approach was to change. I still have the threatening, un-
signed letters. Get out of town, you lying bastard, if you know what's
good for you. Intermittently, for four years, I received threats by letter

[1] Abridged from Hodding Carter, "Huey Long: American Dictator," *The American Mercury* (April, 1949), pp. 435–47. Reprinted by permission of *The American Mercury*, Torrance, California.

and telephone, and twice in person. I carried a pistol, kept it in my desk during the day and by my bed at night.

But violence and the threat of violence were not always one-sided. In 1934 the Congressman from our district died. The district had been consistently antagonistic to Long, although the dead Congressman had chosen to play safe with the Senator. Long did not believe that a friendly successor could be elected. So, instead of having the district Democratic Executive Committee call the mandatory Democratic primary for the election of the party nominee, he ordered this controlled group to declare the Congressman's widow the nominee, and to call a perfunctory general election with her name the only one to be printed on the ballot as Democracy's choice against any Republican, Communist, or Prohibitionist foolhardy enough to seek the office. It was a simple if illegal way to avoid a showdown in the district.

A young anti-Long judge named Nat Tycer enjoined the general election in his own judicial district, composed of four of the Congressional district's twelve parishes. Declaring, "It's a poor judge who can't enforce his own ruling," he began swearing in deputies to enforce his injunction. I became one of the deputies and wrote an angry, intemperate editorial which ended, "If ever there was need for shotgun government, that time is now."

In each of the parishes of our judicial district, deputies and unsworn volunteers took the election ballots, election boxes, and other voting paraphernalia out of the courthouses where they were stored and burned them. The Long-controlled state administration scattered thousands of leaflets throughout the district, warning of the jail sentences and fines in store for anyone interfering with elections. We kept burning ballots, adding effigies of Long to the bonfires. The administration sent in more ballots.

The night before the election was to have been held our deputies, considerably smaller in number than the hundreds who had originally been sworn in, assembled at assigned points throughout the judicial district. Some were posted at Pass Manchac, where a drawbridge links the district with the southward continuation of the New Orleans highway. They were to raise the bridge and try to fend off the militia, which, according to rumor, was being dispatched from New Orleans to insure the holding of the election. Other deputies waited in the ditch beside the highway at the border line between our district and East Baton Rouge Parish, in which the state capitol is situated. During the night, state police in trucks loaded with ballots were fired upon and forced to retire to Baton Rouge. The militia from New Orleans weren't ordered out.

All night long, scared witless, and armed with a sawed-off shotgun and a .38 revolver, I was one of a roving patrol which visited all the election booths in our parish in search of signs of political life. But not a vote was cast in our judicial district and only a comparative handful in the Congressional district itself.

Nonetheless, Long's district Democratic Executive Committee declared the widow the elected representative. In Washington, the House of Representatives eventually refused to seat her as well as our own candidate, whom we selected in a rump election a few weeks after the fiasco, in order to make a contest in Washington. And when the administration finally called a legitimate election, we defeated Huey's candidate, the Commissioner of Agriculture, a popular and perennial officeholder who had served for years before Long's advent.

Except for one victory by the Old Regular machine in New Orleans in a mayoralty campaign, this was the only major political setback suffered by Long from 1930 until his death. But the real importance of the episode is its indication of the desperation to which his tactics could drive otherwise law-abiding men. Our roles as special deputies were specious. And it was no fun to feel like an outlaw, especially when the other side had the militia, the state police, most of the judges, and a majority of the voters in the state at large.

*   *   *

For four years, from 1932 to 1936, I published my paper. It was good for neither the nervous system nor the pocketbook. Together with the repeated inducements to change sides, there were the continuing threatening letters and telephone warnings, the subscription cancellations, the refusal of some—but not a majority—of the Hammond advertisers to do business with a newspaper that fought Long. But Huey didn't get around properly to those smaller newspapers which opposed him until the summer before he was killed. Then, in a special legislative session devoted to tightening the state's straitjacket, he enacted a law for our especial undoing.

This law created a State Printing Board and empowered it to determine the eligibility of any newspaper in the state for the position of official journal. Each town and city, each school district and each parish had hitherto selected their official journals themselves for the printing of minutes, tax delinquent lists, ordinances, proceedings, and other official matters required by law to be published. For many small newspapers this legal printing meant the difference between survival and failure; and, in our case, our newspaper's selection a year before as official journal of the parish potentially added several thousand needed dollars to our revenues.

As its first act, the State Printing Board declared that our newspaper could not serve the parish as official journal. No reasons were given, just the decision. It was useless to seek redress for breach of contract in the state courts. So we sought to prove that our contract with the parish had been impaired rather than violated when the parish's governing body, the police jury, had been forced to select another journal.

Impairment of contract is a federal offense. We won our case in the United States District Court in New Orleans. The state, using a battery of lawyers from the Attorney General's office, won a reversal in the United States Circuit Court of Appeals. We appealed to the Supreme Court, which held that our contract had not been impaired but breached and that the state courts must decide the case. And it was futile to go into Huey's courts. . . .

As the Share Our Wealth chorus swelled, Huey, like a wise military tactician, took care to protect his rear. In a spectacular, degenerative series of special sessions in 1934 and 1935, his legislature reduced Louisianians almost literally to the status of Indian wards. Together with this final elimination of the actualities of democratic self-government—to the unconcern of a majority of the unconsulted electorate—came new benefits: homestead tax exemption, theoretically up to two thousand dollars; abolition of the one-dollar poll tax; a debt moratorium act; and new taxes—an income tax, a public utilities receipts tax, an attempted "two cents a lie" tax on the advertising receipts of the larger newspapers, which the United States Supreme Court pronounced unconstitutional.

Perhaps it seems inconceivable that any legislature, no matter how great the material rewards for its complaisant majority, could have so completely surrendered a people's political powers and economic and personal safety to one man. But Louisiana's legislature did. Administration-designated election supervisors were given the sole right of selecting voting commissioners, sole custody over the ballot boxes themselves, and the privilege of designating as many "special deputies" as might be necessary to guard the polls. Huey's figurehead Governor, O. K. Allen, was given the power to call out the militia whenever he—or Huey—wished. The Governor could—and did—expand the state police force into a swarm of private agents, some uniformed and some not, their number and the identity of the ununiformed alike a secret. The State Attorney General was empowered to supersede any district attorney in any trial. The State Tax Commission was given the right to change any city or county tax assessment, so that a misbehaving corporation or individual might know just who held the economic stranglehold. An ironically designated civil service board was created, with appointive control over all fire and police chiefs, and a school budget committee with the right to review the appointments of every school teacher and school employee. The Governor was even enabled to replace the entire city administration of Alexandria, a recalcitrant municipality in which Huey had once been rotten-egged. There were other repressive measures, many others. But these are sufficient to indicate what had happened to self-government in Louisiana.

. . . This hideous thing that we remember as the rough-shod reign of the Kingfish was not hideous in its beginnings. Whether or not Huey Long himself was ever sincere in his protestations for the poor and downtrodden is, basically, beside the point. For he led a social-economic revolution in Louisiana; and after his death the entire South was debated ground.

It was not his political genius and ruthlessness alone that made him possible. There were two other factors equally important.

The first factor was that, after two hundred years, the people of Louisiana were ready and waiting for a messiah who would translate their needs into accomplishments. Theirs was the ground swell of the little people, a people undisturbed by his tactics as long as they got the roads, the free bridges, the hospitals, the free school books, the public works; as long as the men whom he pilloried and broke and banished were identified with the leaders of the past, bumbling representatives of an indifferent, negative ruling class. The little people shrugged at graft because of their certainty that there always had been graft of a kind. This time, whatever the politicians skimmed off the top, they were getting theirs too. And they were getting something else. Revenge. A fantastic vengeance upon the Sodom and Gomorrah that was called New Orleans. A squaring of accounts with the big shots, the Standard Oil and the bankers, the big planters, the entrenched interests everywhere. Huey Long was in the image of these little people. He talked their language. He had lived their lives. He had taken them up to the mountaintop and shown them the world which the meek would inherit.

The second factor was the make-up of the forces actively opposed to Long. His disunited enemies had difficulty from beginning to end to maintain an alliance that had its base in military necessity alone. We were strange bedfellows: cynical spoils politicians of the Old Regular ring in New Orleans; ardent, idealistic New Dealers; inept leaders of the country parishes, turned out in short grass; nonpolitical gentility awakened from their slumbers by rude knocking; the hitherto secure representatives of Big Business; honestly disturbed, solid bourgeoisie. Our combined cries for good government made a dissonant chorus. Huey bowled us over like ten-pins, with rare misses, from the time of the failure of the impeachment proceedings to his assassination.

Looking back, I know now that part of our failure arose from an unwillingness to approve any Long-sponsored proposal for change, regardless of its merits. We offered none of our own except a plea for democratic rule, and that sounded hollow in contrast. Yet, at the end, it became the one thing of importance to Louisiana.

And Long triumphed over men far wiser politically than we. President Roosevelt and his pulse-feeler, Jim Farley, became uneasy about Long's threat soon after the Share Our Wealth movement overran the borders of Louisiana. On the Senate floor he made the most adroit, belligerent, and fluent opponent look and sound like a political fresh-man.

Even had Huey Long relied only upon his mesmeric appeal to Louisiana's masses and his ability to make promised delivery of the material things those masses wanted, it is probable that he could have dominated his state as completely and for at least as long as he did. But he was not content to rely upon these weapons alone. His compelling lust for power as such—a primary, animating force in his political life —and the intense vindictiveness which from the start characterized his public career lured him to a morally indefensible position.

When impeachment seemed a certainty in those early months as Governor, he simply bought and paid for enough legislators "like sacks of potatoes" to prevent the majority vote necessary for conviction. From then on, Long bought those whom he needed and could buy, and crushed those who had no purchase price or whose price was too high.

Nor was the control of a governor, a majority of legislators, a court majority enough. It should be repeated that no public officeholder, no teacher, no fire chief or fireman, no police chief or policeman, no day laborer on state projects held his job except in fee simple to the machine. Except among the political job holders, he used his economic power sparingly. Yet even private citizens made their living by his sufferance. Long could have taxed to extinction any business, large or small, and business knew it. Men could be—and were—arrested by unidentified men, the members of his secret police, held incommunicado, tried, and found guilty on trumped-up charges. A majority of the State Supreme Court became unabashedly his. Through his State Printing Board he cracked an economic whip over the rural and small-town press, lashing all but a few into sullen silence. A thug, making a premeditated skull-crushing attack upon a Long opponent, could draw from his pocket in court a pre-signed pardon from the figurehead Governor. Entire city administrations could be removed, not by the electorate but by legislative action.

In the end, these things indirectly destroyed Huey Long himself.

7
James Farley: Threat to Roosevelt

Although Long was only one of several popular figures
threatening Roosevelt from the left in 1935, he was judged by
Roosevelt's advisers as by far the most formidable. Brain Truster
Rexford Tugwell observed that "Father Coughlin, Reno, Town-
send, et al., were after all pygmies compared with Huey." [1] *New*
Dealers feared that Long intended to run as a spoiler in 1936,
thereby splitting the Democratic vote and defeating Roosevelt; in
the likely event that a conservative Republican would prove unable
to rally the country within four years, they reasoned, the White
House could be waiting for Huey in 1940. Roosevelt told Rex
Tugwell that Huey Long was "one of the two most dangerous men
in America" (the other? Douglas MacArthur). [2] *Roosevelt's chief*
political strategist, James Farley, reflects in the brief passage below
the New Dealers' fear of Long. [3]

I've always made an effort not to let personal bias warp my political
judgment. We kept a careful eye on what Huey and his political
allies, both in office and out of office, were attempting to do. Anxious
not to be caught napping and desiring an accurate picture of conditions,
the Democratic National Committee conducted a secret poll on a national scale during this period to find out if Huey's sales talks for his
"share the wealth" program were attracting many customers. The result of that poll, which was kept secret and shown only to a very few
people, was surprising in many ways. It indicated that, running on a
third-party ticket, Long would be able to poll between 3,000,000 to
4,000,000 votes for the Presidency. The poll demonstrated also that
Huey was doing fairly well at making himself a national figure. His
probable support was not confined to Louisiana and near-by states. On
the contrary, he had about as much following in the North as in the
South, and he had as strong an appeal in the industrial centers as he

[1] Rexford G. Tugwell, *The Democratic Roosevelt* (New York: Doubleday & Company,
Inc., 1957), p. 350.

[2] *Ibid.*, p. 35.

[3] From James A. Farley, *Behind the Ballots* (New York: Harcourt, Brace & World,
Inc., 1938), pp. 249–50. Reprinted by permission of the publisher.

did in the rural areas. Even the rock-ribbed Republican state of Maine, where the voters were steeped in conservatism, was ready to contribute to Long's total vote in about the same percentage as other states.

While we realized that polls are often inaccurate and that conditions could change perceptibly before the election actually took place, the size of the Long vote made him a formidable factor. He was head and shoulders stronger than any of the other "Messiahs" who were also gazing wistfully at the White House and wondering what chance they would have to arrive there as the result of a popular uprising. It was easy to conceive a situation whereby Long, by polling more than 3,000,000 votes, might have the balance of power in the 1936 election. For example, the poll indicated that he would command upward of 100,000 votes in New York State, a pivotal state in any national election; and a vote of that size could easily mean the difference between victory or defeat for the Democratic or Republican candidate. Take that number of votes away from either major candidate, and they would come mostly from our side, and the result might spell disaster.

8
Raymond Moley:
No Backwoods Buffoon

Huey's public posture was one of rustic simplicity. He once told the Senate: " 'I am not undertaking to answer the charge that I am ignorant. It is true. I am an ignorant man. I have had no college education. I have not even had a high school education. But the thing that takes me far in politics is that I do not have to color what comes into my mind and into my heart. I say it without varnish. I say it without veneer. I have not the learning to do otherwise, and therefore my ignorance is often not detected.' " [1] *But men who knew Long well, and especially those who feared him, were awed by his extraordinary mind. Raymond Moley, an early Roosevelt Brain Truster who later became a conservative critic of the New Deal, recalls his judgment of Long's abilities below.* [2] *Moley disapprovingly reported that in 1935 Roosevelt spoke of the need of doing something to "steal Long's thunder," thereby presaging the administration's swing to the left in the "second New Deal" initiated that year.* [3]

Largely because of the mutual distrust, not to say antipathy, that prevailed between Roosevelt and Senator Huey Long, I was delegated by the President in 1933 to maintain a contact with the Louisiana dictator.

His influence was not only supreme in Louisiana but extended into all the neighboring states. A point was reached at the summit of Long's power at which he would by his influence assure the election of his friends in both Arkansas and Mississippi. And in the Senate, while the veteran members disliked Long, there was a healthy respect for his ruthlessness in debate.

I spent many hours talking with Huey Long in the three years be-

[1] Odum, *Southern Regions*, pp. 531–32.

[2] From Raymond Moley, *The First New Deal* (New York: Harcourt, Brace & World, Inc., 1966), pp. 372–73. Reprinted by permission of the author and the publisher.

[3] Raymond Moley, *After Seven Years* (New York: Harper & Row, Publishers, 1939), p. 305.

fore his death. When we talked about politics, public policies, and life generally, he cast off the manner of a demagogue as an actor wipes off greasepaint. There could be no question about his extraordinary mental —or, if you will, intellectual—capacity. I have never known a mind that moved with more clarity, decisiveness, and force. He was no backwoods buffoon, although when the occasion seemed to offer profit by such a role he could outrant a Heflin or a Bilbo. But the state of Louisiana reveals ample evidence of his immense contributions to the happiness and welfare of its people. As his power in that state grew to be secure and absolute, the virus of success took hold. There can be no doubt of his purposes: first, the complete consolidation of his power in Louisiana; second, his use of his forum in the Senate to grasp national attention; and, finally, to direct a campaign of national "education" through the states toward a Presidential nomination for himself at some future time, perhaps in 1940.

I am unable to estimate the potential of Long's strength as he looked toward a third-party nomination in 1936. But I am certain that Roosevelt and James A. Farley entertained a healthy belief that in a close election he might throw the election to a Republican. Polls taken by Farley's National Committee gave Long 10 per cent of the preferences. This threat definitely influenced Roosevelt's policies in 1935. For after the NRA had been declared unconstitutional, Roosevelt pressed upon Congress a drastic, half-baked "share-the-wealth" tax scheme. Perhaps one of the reasons for Roosevelt's change in direction was this threat, which reached its summit just before Long went to his gaudy grave on the capitol grounds at Baton Rouge.

Many times in the course of our friendly talks I implored Huey to rise above demagoguery and use his great capacities to act like a statesman. I told him what everyone came to know after his death: that although his objectives might be sincerely held, his accomplices were unworthy of him. He always protested that he made or sought no personal gain. But there was tragedy in his deliberate squandering of his talents for tawdry ends. He misused his fine mind, battered it, as a child might treat a toy the value and purpose of which he could not understand. He used his skills for the enrichment of his shoddy friends and for petty revenge upon his enemies. He used his mind to destroy the very foundations upon which his real reforms in Louisiana could permanently rest. He destroyed many things with his mind. And among them was himself.

9
The New York Times: Obituary

Long was gunned down in Baton Rouge on September 8,
1935, and died two days later. His assassin, Dr. Carl A. Weiss, Jr.—
who fell with fifty-nine bullet holes in his body from Huey's body-
guards—was a young Louisiana physician who had never met
Long, nor had he participated in politics. But members of his
family had been prominent anti-Longs and had suffered accord-
ingly. Huey's assassination has prompted a hot and continuing
debate over whether the fatal bullet came from Dr. Weiss' pistol
(the evidence is persuasive that it did) or from that of one of his
bodyguards, whether the murder was premeditated, and over what
motivated Weiss. In his substantial recent biography, Professor T.
Harry Williams concludes that Dr. Weiss journeyed to the State
House in Baton Rouge with the intention of killing a tyrant. On
September 11, The New York Times *published the following*
obituary editorial.[1]

Of Huey Long personally it is no longer necessary to speak except
with charity. His motives, his character, have passed beyond human
judgment. People will long talk of his picturesque career and extraordinary individual qualities. He carried daring to the point of audacity.
He did not hesitate to flaunt his great personal vainglory in public.
This he would probably have defended both as a form of self-confidence,
and a means of impressing the public. He had a knack of always getting
into the picture, and often bursting out of its frame. There would be
no end if one were to try to enumerate all his traits, so distinct and so
full of color. He succeeded in establishing a legend about himself—a
legend of invincibility—which it will be hard to dissipate.

It is to Senator Long as a public man, rather than as a dashing personality, that the thoughts of Americans should chiefly turn as his tragic
death extinguisheth envy. What he did and what he promised to do are
full of political instruction and also of warning. In his own State of
Louisiana he showed how it is possible to destroy self-government while

maintaining its ostensible and legal form. He made himself an unquestioned dictator, though a State Legislature was still elected by a nominally free people, as was also a Governor, who was, however, nothing but a dummy for Huey Long. In reality, Senator Long set up a Fascist government in Louisiana. It was disguised, but only thinly. There was no outward appearance of a revolution, no march of Black Shirts upon Baton Rouge, but the effectual result was to lodge all the power of the State in the hands of one man.

If Fascism ever comes in the United States it will come in something like that way. No one will set himself up as an avowed dictator, but if he can succeed in dictating everything, the name does not matter. Laws and Constitutions guaranteeing liberty and individual rights may remain on the statute books, but the life will have gone out of them. Institutions may be designated as before, but they will have become only empty shells. We thus have an indication of the points at which American vigilance must be eternal if it desires to withstand the subtle inroads of the Fascist spirit. There is no need to be on the watch for a revolutionary leader to rise up and call upon his followers to march on Washington. No such sinister figure is likely to appear. The danger is, as Senator Long demonstrated in Louisiana, that freedom may be done away with in the name of efficiency and a strong paternal government.

Senator Long's career is also a reminder that material for the agitator and the demagogue is always ample in this country. He found it and played upon it skillfully, first of all in what may be called the lower levels of society in Louisiana. Afterward, when he began to swell with national ambition, and cast about for a fetching cry, he found it, or thought he did, in his vague formulas, never worked out, about the "distribution of wealth." For a time he seemed in this way to be about to fascinate and capture a great multitude of followers, or at least endorsers, mainly in the cities of this country. There is reason to believe that his hold upon them was relaxing before his assassination. Many observers thought that he had already passed the peak of his national influence. Be that as it may, the moral of his remarkable adventure in politics remains the same. It is that in the United States we have to re-educate each generation in the fundamentals of self-government and in the principles of sound finance. And we must have leaders able to defend the faith that is in them. When such masses of people are all too ready to run after a professed miracle-worker, it is essential that we have trained minds to confront the ignorant, to show to the credulous the error of their ways, and to keep alive and fresh the true tradition of democracy in which this country was cradled and brought to maturity.

10
Senator William Langer: In Memoriam

In 1941 the Congress unveiled and dedicated a statue of former Senator Huey Long in the Capitol's Statuary Hall. The following tribute of Senator William Langer of North Dakota testifies to the nationwide appeal of the fallen Louisiana Kingfish.[1]

Mr. President and Colleagues: I rise to pay tribute to the memory of a great statesman and friend of the common people, Huey P. Long.

The people of the Northwest, familiar with his deeds and uninfluenced by vicious newspaper propaganda, think of him today with warmest affection. It has been said that "once or twice in a generation nature spawns a great commoner"—one who combines the simple, humble, honest virtues of the common people, the inherent fairness and decency of the great mass of good folks, their quick anger at injustice and greed. He was such a man.

Perhaps the greatest reason for Huey Long's splendid leadership in the Northwest farming States was due to the times in which he lived—7-cent oats, 24-cent wheat, 11-cent rye, and 17-cent corn are farming disasters which demand an enlightened fighting champion.

In his visits to the Northwest Huey Long sensed that the people had produced enough to feed themselves for thousands of years, and yet they were on the verge of destitution, at the mercy of outside interests, and that they needed a leader who would secure for them fair prices and all the remedies covered by social insurance. Within a short time he had over 400 share-the-wealth clubs in North Dakota alone, and these share-the-wealth clubs in our State were there primarily for the protection of the family. He advocated insurance against industrial accidents, against sickness, against permanent invalidity, including blindness, against old age, and against contingencies, affecting members of the wage-earner's family—contingencies such as the dependency of the

---

[1] Senate Document No. 110, 77th Cong., 1st sess. (Washington, D.C.: Government Printing Office, 1941), pp. 63–66.

widow and orphans upon the death of the breadwinner, against sickness and burial and maternity, and also, because of the very high cost of private insurance, he seemed to the masses as the man whose program would give them permanent social security.

Because he lived several thousand miles away from us, few citizens from the northwestern agricultural sections knew Huey Long personally, but thousands heard him over the radio, read his speeches, and believed in him.

To the farming people he was the genius who would solve the grim paradox that, with our granaries bulging with foodstuffs, with our warehouses filled with shoes and clothing to overflowing, thousands of men, women, and children were going hungry and naked; and it was not only the farmers but the underprivileged one-third all over the Nation who looked to him as their long-awaited fighting leader. The men and women to whom Huey Long appealed know only too well that at any moment the worker of a family may become ill, and that the wage earner then, in addition to the loss of wages, is burdened with the expenses of doctor, medicines, and hospital care. They know only too well that being sick is one of the most expensive luxuries; that the birth of a child often drains a family income at a time when it is most needed, that the death of a child is frequently disastrous, and that the cost of the burial often results in serious debt which cannot be met for years.

Huey Long knew that the worker is weighed down by the fear of sudden death, and the prospect of leaving his wife and children utterly dependent and destitute.

It was these people, these common people, workers, farmers, and unemployed, to whom Huey Long appealed.

I doubt whether any other man was so conscious of the plight of the underprivileged or knew better the ruthlessness of those in control. And it was because Huey Long knew how to fight, knew how to fight fire with fire, knew how to combat ruthlessness with ruthlessness, force with force, and because he had the courage to battle unceasingly for what he conceived to be right that he became an inspiration for so many in their own fight for a square deal, and the object of such relentless persecution on the part of his enemies.

The fight he waged was such a desperate one that even in death he has not been immune from attack. So we find that 5 years after his body had been lowered into the grave—that grave which will forever be a shrine for those who love decency, honor, and justice—attempts are still being made to besmirch his character.

This is not fooling the farmer, the worker, the small businessman; it is not fooling the child who can read today because of the free textbooks that Huey Long obtained; it is not fooling the citizen who can vote today because Huey Long abolished poll taxes.

These people know from Huey Long's life that, as they fight for the better things, there will always be the inspiration that fighting with them in spirit will be that fearless, dauntless, unmatchable champion of the common people, Huey P. Long.

PART THREE

HUEY LONG IN HISTORY

Long's untimely martyrdom muted much of the criticism that he had received from both liberals and conservatives. His successor regime in Louisiana, headed by Governor Richard Leche, retained its predecessor's mass support and executive power, but promptly made peace both with the Roosevelt administration and with the conservative business core of the anti-Longs. Unrestrained by a watchful opposition either in Louisiana or in Washington and still endowed with extraordinary power, Long's successors proceeded to confirm Lord Acton's imperative that power corrupts, by systematically looting the state's treasury. When "The Scandals" broke in 1939, it was inevitable that the antecedents of corruption should be traced to the man who had originated the power structure. Harnett Kane in Louisiana Hayride traced the germ of the "American Rehearsal for Dictatorship" to Huey Long's doorstep.[1] Published in 1941, Kane's book reflected the widespread apprehension that the Caesarism that had engulfed Europe might take root in America.

But America was not Europe, and Louisiana was not America in microcosm. When World War II finally brought victory both over the depression at home and the fascists overseas, the class passions of the thirties waned, and historians and political scientists began to assess the meaning of those turbulent years and their dominant personalities in terms less distorted by contemporary fears. It is a truism that perspective grows with hindsight; no less true is the admonition that no historical assessment can ever be "definitive." The following four historical interpretations differ in their measure of the meaning of Huey Long, but they share the central assumption that in the remarkable career of the Kingfish are to be found profoundly important insights into the distinctive American character and its regional variations.

---

[1] Harnett T. Kane, Louisiana Hayride: The American Rehearsal for Dictatorship 1928–1940 (New York: William Morrow & Co., Inc., 1941).

11

V. O. Key, Jr.: The Seamy Side of Democracy

Before Huey Long can be assessed as a national figure,
he must first be explained as a product of Southern and Louisiana
politics. In the 1940s the late V. O. Key, Jr., led a team of political
scientists in an ambitious comparative project of studying the
patterns of political behavior in every Southern state. This un-
precedented research effort, funded by a Rockefeller Foundation
grant to the University of Alabama, was reported in Southern
Politics, *which was published in 1950 and remains the unrivaled*
"Bible" of Southern politics.[1] Key granted Huey Long's peculiar
genius but sought to explain him "in terms of the pathological
situation in which he arose"—that is, why a Huey Long in Louisi-
ana? A product of the one-party Democratic South, Huey cared
little for party and less for the supposed benefits of a two-party
system. It is ironical, then, that the most important political legacy
of his regime was to be the creation within Louisiana's dominant
Democratic party of a "disciplined bifactionalism" that shared
many of the attributes of a modern two-party system.

Few would contest the proposition that among its professional
politicians of the past two decades Louisiana has had more men who have
been in jail, or who should have been, than any other American state.
Extortion, bribery, peculation, thievery are not rare in the annals of
politics, but in the scale, variety, and thoroughness of its operations the
Long gang established, after the death of the Kingfish, a record un-
paralleled in our times. Millions of dollars found their way more or
less directly to his political heirs and followers. From the state treasury,
from state employees, from gambling concessionaires, from seekers of
every conceivable privilege, cash flowed to some members of the inner
circle.

[1] From V. O. Key, Jr., *Southern Politics in State and Nation* (New York: Alfred A. Knopf, Inc., 1950), pp. 156–68. Copyright 1949 by Alfred A. Knopf, Inc. Reprinted by permission of the publisher. Several footnotes have been omitted for reasons of space.

Huey P. Long's control of Louisiana more nearly matched the power of a South American dictator than that of any other American state boss. Many American states have had bosses whose power seemed well-nigh complete, but they were weaklings alongside the Kingfish. He dominated the legislature. He ripped out of office mayors, parish officials, and judges who raised a voice against him. Weapons of economic coercion were employed to repress opposition. When they failed the organization did not hesitate to use more direct methods. Huey, at the height of his power, brooked no opposition and those who could not be converted were ruthlessly suppressed.

Why a virtual dictatorship in Louisiana and not elsewhere in the South? Of course it may not be conceded that virtual dictatorship has been confined to Louisiana. In Tennessee Crump ruled without question only in Memphis; he had to fight for his power in the remainder of the state. And Byrd was representative in Virginia of a ruling class with a tradition of responsibility. Long, as he modestly admitted, was *sui generis*. What inner compulsion of Louisiana politics produced a Huey Long? If there had been no Huey, did conditions in Louisiana make it inevitable that some person would occupy a like position? Or should the whole episode be explained in terms of the "great man theory" of politics?

Why a Huey Long?

Early in his career, Huey Long looked like just another southern heir of Populism: an anticorporation man, a politician skilled in identifying himself with the poor farmer, a rabble-rouser in the familiar southern pattern. He gave no reason for worry, in the opinion of those philosophically disposed. Other states had had such men, most of whom had followed a well-worn course. Sooner or later they sold out to the interests they attacked or became moderate, with experience and success. They mouthed a humbuggery to capture the loyalties of the gullible and ignorant. They had no sincerity in their promises; a slush fund would quiet the barking dog.

The apostles of complacency turned out to be wrong. Huey welded to himself a following fanatically loyal. Unlike a Blease or a Ferguson, his program held more than words and sympathy. He kept faith with his people and they with him. He gave them something and the corporations paid for it. He did not permit himself, in an oft-repeated pattern, to be hamstrung by a legislature dominated by old hands experienced in legislation and frequently under corporate retainer. He elected his own legislatures and erected a structure of political power both totalitarian and terrifying. To charges that he came to terms with the interests, the reply of the Long partisan is that the terms were Huey's. He is not to be dismissed as a mere rabble-rouser or as the leader of a gang of boodlers. Nor can he be described by convenient label: fascist, communist. He brought to his career a streak of genius, yet in his program and tactics he was as indigenous to Louisiana as pine trees and petroleum.

Long dramatized himself as the champion of the people against the sinister interests and his production was by no means pure melodrama. For there are sinister interests and there are champions of the people, even though there may always be some good about the sinister and at least a trace of fraud in self-styled champions. One of his first brushes with the interests, Huey related, was at the age of 22 when he sought to advocate before a legislative committee modification of a law that severely restricted the right of recovery for injury or death incurred in the course of work. When he requested the right to speak the committee chairman asked,

"Whom do you represent?"

"Several thousand common laborers," Long replied.

"Are they paying you anything?"

"No," he replied.

"They seem to have good sense." [1]

Such episodes rankled, and early Long proclaimed the basic ideas that later flowered into his "share-the-wealth" program. In 1918, in a letter to the New Orleans *Item*, he asserted that two per cent of the people owned from 65 to 70 per cent of the nation's wealth and that the concentration of wealth was proceeding apace. He saw the greatest cause for "industrial unrest" in tremendous inequality in educational opportunity. "This is the condition, north, east, south and west; with wealth concentrating, classes becoming defined, there is not the opportunity for Christian uplift and education and cannot be until there is more economic reform. This is the problem that the good people of this country must consider." [2]

Huey set out to help the good people of this country consider the problem. In 1918, at the age of 25, he won election to the state railroad commission, as the utility regulatory body was then styled. He began a running fight, to last through most of his career, with Standard Oil. The major oil producers, through their control of pipelines, threatened to squeeze out independent producers by denial of access to market, an ancient form of piracy. Long, himself a stockholder in several independent companies, undertook to bring the majors to task. He injected the oil issue into the 1920 gubernatorial campaign and was bitterly disappointed in the successful candidate, whom he had backed. He charged that the governor called in Standard Oil lawyers to help draft laws affecting that corporation. Long also took on the telephone company and compelled rate reductions. His battles against the interests attracted

[1] *Every Man A King, The Autobiography of Huey P. Long* (New Orleans: National Book Co., Inc., 1933), p. 27.

[2] *Ibid.*, pp. 38–49.

great attention. The next logical step for him was to run for governor and he did so in 1924.

The narrowness of his margin of defeat gave hope for the future; in 1928 he ran again and won. The campaign produced florid passages of oratory, passages that Huey's partisans enshrine among the immortal sayings of the saints. In a speech delivered under the Evangeline Oak, Long said:

> And it is here under this oak Evangeline waited for her lover, Gabriel, who never came. This oak is an immortal spot, made so by Longfellow's poem, but Evangeline is not the only one who has waited here in disappointment.
>
> Where are the schools that you have waited for your children to have, that have never come? Where are the roads and highways that you sent your money to build, that are no nearer now than ever before?
>
> Where are the institutions to care for the sick and disabled? Evangeline wept bitter tears in her disappointment, but it lasted through only one lifetime. Your tears in this country, around this oak, have lasted for generations. Give me the chance to dry the eyes of those who still weep here! [3]

And from Huey's speech, campaign oratory though it may have been, one learns, perhaps, why he was able to erect a virtual dictatorship. The tears of the people of Louisiana had in reality lasted for generations. While no measuring rod is handy for the precise calibration of the tightness of oligarchies, a plausible argument can be made that the combination of ruling powers of Louisiana had maintained a tighter grip on the state since Reconstruction than had like groups in other states. That ruling combination included elements not present, at least to the same degree, in other southern states. The New Orleans machine bulked large in state politics and had established itself early. In every respect it was an old-fashioned machine, effective in its contol of the vote and, in turn, itself beholden to the business and financial interests. Add to the mercantile, financial, and shipping interests of New Orleans, the power wielded by the sugar growers, an interest peculiar to Louisiana, then add the cotton planters of the Red River and the Mississippi. The lumber industry constituted perhaps a more powerful bloc than in any other southern state and also enacted a spectacular drama in exploitation apparent even to the most unlettered. Later came oil. Like other industries it hoped to minimize taxation, but in Louisiana state ownership of oilbearing lands gave petroleum a special interest in politics. Add to all these the railroads and gas and electrical utilities, and you have elements susceptible of combination into a powerful political bloc.

[3] *Ibid.,* p. 99.

The stakes of the game and the relative greater strength of the upper-bracket interests in Louisiana probably laid the basis for a more complete and unbroken control of public affairs than in any other southern state. As good a supposition as any is that the longer the period of unrestrained exploitation, the more violent will be the reaction when it comes. Louisiana's rulers controlled without check for a long period. Even the Virginia machine suffered setbacks from time to time and had to trim its sails. In other states there arose spokesmen for the masses who gave the people at least hope. Louisiana had no Blease or Watson or Vardaman to voice the needs and prejudices of ordinary men. It had its rabble-rousers to be sure, but its annals include no outstanding popular hero acclaimed as the leader of the common cause.

Whether such men of other states did anything for their people may be, in a way, irrelevant in comprehending Louisiana politics. They at least functioned as a safety valve for discontent, and the common people felt that they had a champion. Louisiana, on the other hand, was a case of arrested political development. Its Populism was repressed with a violence unparalled in the South, and its neo-Populism was smothered by a potent ruling oligarchy. It may be that the crosscurrents introduced into Louisiana politics by the presence of a large French Catholic population contributed to the prevention of the social catharsis of expression of discontent. Differences between the Protestant north and the Catholic south furnished a convenient advantage to those who, with their eye on the main chance and unencumbered by ecclesiastical prejudice, would divide and rule. Perhaps, too, the religious, linguistic, cultural division of the people itself made it difficult for a leader to arise who understood both groups, who constituted a common denominator capable of giving full-throated voice to the common unhappinesses and aspirations of both peoples in rip-roaring political campaigns—after which everyone could go back to work.

The explanation of why Louisiana—rather than some other southern state—provided the most fertile soil for a Huey Long, requires demonstration that the ruling oligarchy of Louisiana really pressed down harder than did the governing groups of other states. As sensitive an index as any of the efficacy of financial oligarchy—in the American milieu, at least—is the status of the education of the people. Universal education—with its promise of individual betterment—is the open sesame of American utopianism. And universal education, with its impact on the tax structure, invariably comes into conflict with the oligarchical elements in American society for fiscal if not ideological reasons.

If the status of the people's education is an index to the strength of an economic elite, the Louisiana governing class excelled in exploiting of its position. In Louisiana, as late as 1940, 14.8 per cent of the rural, native white males over 25 years of age had not completed a single year's schooling. About one out of seven rural white men probably had never been to school a day. The proportion of rural white men without a year's schooling more than doubled that of the next ranking state, Virginia, almost tripled that of Texas, and was about five times that of Mississippi. Another 25 per cent of Louisiana rural white males over 25 had not had more than four years' schooling. Thus, in Louisiana in 1940 about four out of ten farm men had not gone beyond the fourth grade. Though Long won the loyal support of many of these people, it does not follow that fanatical loyalty must be based on illiteracy. The status of education is cited only as a probable indicator of the effectiveness of the ruling clique in holding down public services.

* * *

In winning the governorship in 1928 Long scored heavily in the old Populist areas. In state after state in the South an impressive continuity of attitude has existed in the areas in which agrarian radicalism was most marked in the 1890's. Even today a candidate in the Populist tradition can win a relatively heavy vote in the old Populist counties. In 1928 a fairly close relation prevailed between the distribution of Long's popular strength and that of the Populist candidate for governor in 1896. In the northern half of the state the relation was closest, with Long weakest in the Mississippi River counties and in the counties with larger towns and cities, as the Populist candidate had been.

As governor, Long recommended concrete programs of action and did not hesitate to run roughshod over opposition to obtain their adoption. In his free-schoolbook legislation he dealt with the Protestant-Catholic issue by furnishing books to school children rather than to schools, and thereby avoided the constitutional inhibition of state assistance to private institutions. The constitutional dodge did not hurt him with French-Catholic voters. By his program for construction of highways and free bridges he won popular support and, incidentally, took a swing at one group of political antagonists, the owners of toll bridges and ferries. All these programs required money, and another group of Huey's antagonists, oil and other natural resource industries, found justification for their alarm in boosted taxes.

In the maintenance of its power and in the execution of its program, the Long organization used all the techniques of reward and reprisal that political organizations have employed from time immemorial: patronage, in all its forms, deprivation of perquisites, economic pressure, political coercion in one form or another, and now and then outright thuggery. Beyond these short-range tactics, Long commanded the intense loyalties of a substantial proportion of the population. The schoolbooks, roads, bridges, and hospitals were something more than campaign oratory. The people came to believe that here was a man with a genuine concern for their welfare, not one of the gentlemanly do-nothing governors who had ruled the state for many decades.

Long's erection of a structure of power based on mass loyalty was aided by the new channels of communication not available to neo-Populist leaders who came on the scene earlier in other states. Long had the radio and means to reach the people with printed matter quickly. Normally the mails were used, but when speed was essential—as in his campaign to beat the 1929 impeachment move—a system of direct distribution was put in motion. If necessary, Long said, "a document prepared by me in the evening could be printed and placed on the porch of practically every home in the State of Louisiana during the morning of the following day." [4]

Such systems of communication were made necessary by the practically universal opposition of the press, which, incidentally, Long attempted to counter with a special tax on advertising. It is an elementary rule of southern politics that most large newspapers will oppose any candidate who seriously threatens the perquisites of the dominant economic interests. The politician who seeks mass support perforce must maintain his own channels of communication with the electorate. The press works itself into the position by which its endorsement tends, somewhat like a CIO endorsement, to be a kiss of death. The little people observe that the newspapers oppose all whom they believe would befriend them; to them it follows, not by impeccable logic, that all whom the newspapers support are enemies of the people. Huey Long gave currency to a new word, "lyingnewspapers," and his people would believe him in preference to the newspapers. And in 1948 Huey's son, Russell, running for the Senate, pictured himself as a battler for the people against the press.

The business of politics takes money and thereby hangs the tale of the Long organization. A candidate pledged to policies acceptable to the major economic interests has ample political financing. Politicians not so financed have to find other sources of funds and in so doing they often get into trouble. Long had the support of a few men of wealth. They were mainly mavericks of one sort or another who did not "belong" because of their ancestry, the sources of their money, or their accent. Such a person was Robert S. Maestri, who provided money at critical times early in Long's career, became a power in Long's organization, and, after Long's death, mayor of New Orleans. If a political leader cannot annex the support of a segment of the economic upper crust, once in office he can manufacture a new economic elite attached to the regime. Public purchases provide one means. In Louisiana state control of petroleum production permitted favoritism worth millions. Louisiana's gambling habits make gambling concessions profitable. Frankie Costello, one-time New York slot-machine czar, got the New Orleans slot-machine concession and developed, says Kane, "a million and a quarter annual business." [5]

By these and other methods the Long organization created its own vested interests, which were tied to it by golden bonds and could help pay the cost of politics. Other revenues were not neglected. Assessment of public employees was justified, with the familiar rationalization that this type of financing was far better than reliance on the corporations. The distinctions of Robin Hood morality, however, were hard to maintain and political and personal finances became mixed, with the inevitable results in neglect of politics through the pursuit of private advantage.

After Huey's assassination in 1935 his prediction that his associates would go to the penitentiary if he were not around to hold them in check began to come true. In 1936, Maestri and his New Orleans associates held the whiphand in the formation of the Long organization ticket, which won in the primary. The Long ticket included Richard W. Leche, for governor, Earl Long, who had often fought his brother, for lieutenant governor, and Allen Ellender, for the United States Senate. During Leche's administration scandals broke, and Leche resigned to be succeeded by Earl Long. In the prosecutions after Huey's death not so many men were sent to the penitentiary as should have been. Now that Huey was dead, the organization saw no point in continuing his battle against the Roosevelt Administration. In turn, the Administration saw no point in carrying out criminal prosecutions on income-tax charges of organization leaders and hangers-on. The arrangement was dubbed the "Second Louisiana Purchase." The Federal authorities, however, pushed their civil cases and collected about $2,000,000.[6] Later, under a new Attorney General, Federal prosecutors returned to the fray and, if they sent but few to prison, they at least ventilated irregularities.

Of Huey Long, most interpretations are too simple. They range from the theory that he and his crowd were ordinary boodlers to the notion that here was a native fascism. Boodling there was, to be sure. Fascism? Huey was innocent of any ideology other than the sort of indigenous indignation against the abuses of wealth current in the epoch of William Jennings Bryan. The Long phenomenon must be explained in terms of the pathological situation in which he arose, in terms of traditional anticorporationism, plus the genius of the man himself in political manipulation and organization.

The Louisiana Voter's Dilemma

Before Long, so the folklore of Louisiana goes, the voters had no choice. They could vote for one of two candidates, neither of whom

[5] Harnett T. Kane, *Louisiana Hayride* (New York: William Morrow and Co., Inc., 1941), p. 401.
[6] *Ibid.*, 184.

would do anything for the people. Since Long, the people have the alternative of a venal administration with a dynamic program, or an honest, do-nothing administration belonging to the corporations. Like most popular myths, these notions are sharpened by exaggeration yet, perhaps also as popular myths often do, they contain an element of truth.

Since Long the state has had, with some deviations, a bi-factional fight between, on the one hand, the "good government" or "better-element" crowd and, on the other, the Long faction, or at least a group claiming to be the heirs to the mantle of the martyred Huey. In 1940 Sam H. Jones, the reform candidate, ran to victory in the wake of revelations of corruption, although his victory depended partially on a split in the old Long following. In 1944, the best the "better element" could do by way of a candidate was Jimmie ("You Are My Sunshine") Davis, he of the dance band, but Jimmie was enough to defeat Lewis Morgan, the Long candidate. In 1948 the Long faction regained control in the election of Earl K. Long, Huey's brother who quarreled with him in life but has been his zealous political ally in death. Later in the year Huey's twenty-nine-year-old son, Russell, confirmed the return of the Longs by gaining election to the Senate.

The business interests tend to line up with the "good government" faction, although they are ordinarily more concerned about policies affecting business than about good government in the abstract. Taxation is usually a live issue, with the natural resource industries the most nervous about the severance tax. The broad issue, however, is not cast as one of liberal versus conservative. The conservatives label themselves as the champions of good government and the liberals rarely call themselves radicals.

When political disputes are put as battles between good and bad government—as they often have been in southern states—class differences between Populist-agrarian and business tend to be cloaked in moralities. And indeed, real moral issues may be involved—between thieves and relatively honest men—but they are often paralleled by moral issues of a higher order, viz., for whom is a government to be run. The debate between good and evil subtly divides the electorate along class lines, although a substantial proportion of the electorate may be quite unconscious that anything other than honesty and good government are at stake.

The southerner regards himself, if one gives weight to W. J. Cash's perceptive generalizations about *The Mind of the South*, as a hell-of-a-fellow. The hell-of-a-fellow complex has captured the lesser rural peoples more completely than the planter or town class. And, by this fact, the Populist-like candidate, with an earthy, occasionally profane, rip-roaring appeal, colored by disrespect if not ridicule of the nicer people, enjoys great advantage on the hustings in wooing the vote in the uplands, at the forks of the creek, and along the bayous. Contrariwise, the conservative, respectable candidate tends to direct his appeals to citizens not so imbued by the hell-of-a-fellow complex, and in doing so makes all sorts of pretensions of moral superiority. Campaigns become at times great moral dramas in which good battles evil, and evil, being so attractive to a hell-of-a-fellow, almost invariably wins. The morality duel glosses over a blurred class politics, made articulate not in terms of economic policy but in terms that the people best understand, right and wrong. And the poor-white hell-of-a-fellow, a man of native shrewdness, often sees through the gloss and votes for evil and neo-Populism, at least when he has the choice.

Louisiana, like Texas in an earlier day, has campaigns in which competent, conservative candidates identify themselves with good government, honesty, efficiency, and all the related virtues. In 1948 Sam Jones, opposing Earl K. Long for governor, proclaimed at New Orleans: "I have been part and parcel of the fight for good government since 1940." [7] Governor Jimmie H. Davis declared that Sam Jones was "a man who is capable, a God-fearing man and a man who is honest and sincere in purpose." [8] At Alexandria, Jones warned that "a terrible moral issue lies beneath all the surface issues of performance and economic health. These are surface issues compared to the threat of permanent moral blight which in sober truth hangs over the state." The question was "proud progress or depravity." [9]

"It is the age-old struggle," Sam Jones argued in a radio broadcast, "between good and evil. On one side is Maestri and the hot-oil crowd, aided and abetted by Costello and his racketeers. On the other side is the ordinary, everyday God-fearing Christian people." [10] His supporter, Mayor deLesseps Morrison of New Orleans, predicted that the people would "vote for the proposition that government should be honest, fair and above purchase." [11] Jones, on returning to New Orleans from a stumping tour, reported gains: "The people who want to continue good government will vote for one candidate—for one ticket. That is the Sam Jones ticket." [12]

The candidate thrown into the role of the protagonist of evil generally makes electoral capital thereby. Earl Long berated his opponents for calling him names: "They're calling me Earl Kangaroo Slickum Crookum Long. That don't hurt me at all, but believe me, I don't want to rob a man of his good name just to win an election. I don't want to be

[7] *Times-Picayune* (New Orleans), January 15, 1948.
[8] *Ibid.*, November 28, 1947.
[9] *Ibid.*, January 30, 1948.
[10] *Ibid.*, January 26, 1948.
[11] *Ibid.*, January 28, 1948.
[12] *Ibid.*, December 22, 1947. Louisiana observers, it should be noted, regard the reform aspect of the conservative faction as tinged with humbuggery.

governor that much." [13] To charges that about $45,000 in "dee ducts"
from employees' salaries had gone to Long, his reply was, the *Times-
Picayune* said: "Is it worse to take contributions from the little people
so we can give them the benefits, or have the big shots put up the money
so they can control the government?" [14] Or such a candidate diverts the
argument. "A lot of people cuss Huey Long and a lot of people cuss
Roosevelt. Do you know why? Well, if you touch some peoples' pocket-
books you strike their heart. Just relieve them of a few dollars to help
some poor devil, and you will hear them yell." [15]

Against roughhouse tactics on the stump, the respectable candidate
often becomes a reed blown by the hilarious laughter of the hell-of-a-
fellow, gusty and lusty man that he is. Thus, one of the most elegant
descriptions of Sam Jones in his 1940 race against Earl Long: "He's High
Hat Sam, the High Society Kid, the High-Kicking, High and Mighty
Snide Sam, the guy that pumps perfume under his arms." [16] What can
one say in reply to that sort of thing? Jones, in a 1948 campaign speech,
conceded that he had campaign weaknesses "because it has always been
hard work for me to cultivate the politician's knack for easy back-slap-
ping, for the convivial bottle, for the obscene joke and the windy, un-
fillable promise." [17] And better-element candidates often retire from the
fray, beaten, with sombre reflections on the unwisdom of getting into
a name-calling contest with a polecat and the opinion that politics is
no game for gentlemen.

The choice of the Louisiana electorate is not in reality clearly one
between black and white, between a do-nothing government and a venal
administration with a program, as some observers would have us believe.
Long left a lasting imprint on the conservative element in the state by
showing the people that government could act. By the defeat of the machine in 1940, the voters did not kill Longism. The conservatives adopted
much of Long's program, and Sam Jones, the conservative leader, in his
1940 campaign in strong Long localities did not whisper when he re-
marked, "My pappy was for Huey." A corporation lawyer of humble origins, his father had indeed been an ardent Long supporter. And Sam,
himself, in a way "was for Huey" because the better-element group has
had to champion much of the program that Long sold to the people
and, like their counterpart, the Republican party in the nation, to
promise to administer it better. The people, though, have lingering suspicions that the better-element leaders are not really honest tories and
have, in their campaign promises, unexpressed reservations.

If the conservative element has accepted some of Longism, the suc-

[13] *Ibid.*, December 7, 1947.
[14] *Ibid.*, January 4, 1948.
[15] *Ibid.*, December 22, 1947.
[16] Kane, *Louisiana Hayride*, p. 434.
[17] *Time-Picayune* (New Orleans), January 31, 1948.

cessors to Long have also made their peace with business—or at least with some segments of the business community. Of a country bank in the 1948 campaign: "Everybody connected with the bank from the chairman of the board to the janitor will vote for Earl Long." And other businesses, sensitive to the necessity of amicable relations with those who win, manage to have a friend in the Long camp. And others, perhaps as one cynical observer tells us, have never been with the "better element." "They got their snoot in the trough before 1940 and wanted to keep it there."

The 1948 victory of Earl Long meant at bottom that a majority of Louisiana voters preferred the promises of a Long, backed by a history of action, if not always pretty action, to the pronouncements of a Jones who posed for goodness and virtue but accomplished little to help humble citizens. They saw through the façade of "good government." (Later on in the year Sam Jones turned out to be a Dixiecrat.) They preferred the hazards of buccaneer government to the conservatism of "reform" rule. Like good citizens everywhere, Louisianans hoped that the democratic process would one day produce a candidate not only devoted to the welfare of the mass of the state's citizens but able to serve them through economical and efficient government. Some thought that Judge Robert Kennon, an independent candidate in both the gubernatorial and Senate races of 1948, offered such a hope. In the Senate race he barely lost to young Russell Long, and in the earlier run-off for governor many were sure that he would have fared better against Earl Long than did Jones. Perhaps the Louisiana voter will find a way out of his dilemma. At least the processes of democracy are in ferment in Louisiana.

12

T. Harry Williams: The Politics of the Longs

T. Harry Williams, professor of history of Louisiana State University, has written the most comprehensive and scholarly biography of Huey Long. In the analysis that follows, Williams favorably contrasts the "coldly realistic" politics of Long to the romanticism of the Old South and the Lost Cause that has traditionally shackled the Southern political tradition to nostalgic but essentially unrealistic visions of the past.[1] He emphasizes Long's consistent avoidance of the traditional but "unreal" issues of race and religion, and dismisses the familiar labels of fascism and dictatorship as irrelevantly European in their connotations. To Williams, Long was far more than a typical Southern demagogue; he was a modern mass leader, a thoroughly American political boss who was endowed with extraordinary political acumen. Professor Williams does not deny Key's charge that Long "erected a structure of political power both totalitarian and terrifying." But he seeks to view Huey's self-aggrandizement within the political and historical context of a tragic Southern dilemma—so as to avoid "the derision visited upon Huey Long by liberals who had no realization of the dilemmas of liberalism in the South."

Once Huey Long was asked if he saw any resemblance between himself and Hitler. His reaction was immediate, blunt, and revealing. "Don't compare me to that so-and-so," he bellowed. "Anybody that lets his public policies be mixed up with religious prejudice is a plain God-damned fool." He touched on the theme of religion in politics on another occasion. In 1934 the Ku Klux Klan, or some of its representatives, attacked him and his program. He hoped not to be drawn into a fight on grounds of the Klan's choosing. "I have always avoided any religious fight," he said, "for the sake of the good I have tried to do for every-

[1] From T. Harry Williams, "The Politics of the Longs," *Romance and Realism in Southern Politics* (Athens, Ga.: University of Georgia Press, 1961), pp. 65–84. Reprinted by permission of the University of Georgia Press.

body. I have never stepped aside to denounce a Klansman or anti-Klansman, always hoping to have all of the people understand what I was trying to do and to help me in that effort." As it turned out, in the Klan business he would have to denounce somebody, and none other than the head Klansman, Dr. Hiram Evans, who threatened to campaign against Long in Louisiana. Long issued a public statement reflecting unmistakably on the Imperial Wizard's ancestry and pledging that he would never set foot in Louisiana.

But Long did not speak out until, in effect, he was forced to by a voiced threat to his position. His reluctance did not spring from any lack of courage, for many times he would demonstrate that he possessed ample amounts of political courage and audacity. Rather, it was that he did not want to get involved in a controversy over questions which in his view were false or unreal issues. The implications of his statements quoted above are fascinating. Religion had no place in politics, not because it was intolerant or un-American to inject it, but because in politics an issue of religion was unimportant, because a discussion of religion sidetracked the issues that were important. In Long's thinking the only issues that mattered, the only issues that were real were ones concerning power and economics. Early in his career he set his sights on definite goals—the erection of a power structure without parallel in American government and the enactment of a politico-economic program positively undreamed of in Southern politics—and during his short but explosive life he moved relentlessly toward his goals, always sublimating what he considered irrelevant issues, whether of race or religion. He is the supeme example in recent Southern politics of the coldly realistic operator. His successors in the enduring faction he created in the Louisiana Democratic party would follow the general outlines of the strategy he laid down, although varying their tactics to fit new situations. They would face forces of opposition that in some ways were more intensive than those of his day, and they would record achievements that were as remarkable as his.

In the years after Reconstruction the pattern of politics in Louisiana was broadly similar to that of other Southern states. A hierarchy representing the upper-income classes emerged to grasp the sources of power. The Louisiana hierarchy exhibited the usual elements present in a Bourbon or conservative power structure plus some peculiar to the local scene. In addition to the usual planting interests, there were important business groups: lumber, sugar, railroads; and centered in New Orleans shipping, gas, and electrical concerns. Eventually overshadowing all the business factions was oil. In the 1920's the Standard Oil Company became a major economic and political force in the life of the state. Last, there was what could not be found any other place in the South, a genuine big city machine. This was the organization known as the Old Regulars or the Choctaw Club that reigned in New Orleans in alliance with the city's business and financial powers. The Old Regular machine performed much the same functions, desirable and undesirable, as city machines in the North, and it carried elections by much the same techniques. Old Regular bosses were accustomed to boasting that as late as the night before an election they could arrange to throw enough votes to carry any contest. Usually in a gubernatorial election the machine would endorse a candidate with a strong country following in return for a pledge of control over state patronage in the city.

Such then was the Louisiana hierarchy, conservative in make-up and outlook, devoted to the past and satisfied with the present, dedicated to the protection of privilege, and staidly corrupt. For fifty years after Reconstruction it ruled almost without challenge. Populism offered only a brief threat before subsiding, and no demagogue of the Tillman type appeared to advance even mild reforms. There was not even a Blease to demand some of the places reserved for members of the oligarchy.

It was upon this serene scene that Huey Long burst like a bombshell in the 1920's, and thereafter things would never be the same. Long came from Winn parish in the north-central part of the state. Winn was undeniably, in the economic sense, a poor parish, featuring small farms, cutover timber lands, and lumber mills. It would be a mistake, however, to suppose, as practically all writers of the popular school who have written about the Longs have, that the family was abjectly poor or trashy or without culture. The Longs were of a familiar Southern type—middle-class hill farmers, proud, independent, with a respect for learning and often a pathetic desire to acquire it. Practically every so-called demagogue emerged from precisely such a background. The Longs were economically a cut above the average in Winn, and every member of the large family received some kind of college education.

Winn parish did have, however, a historical heritage different from most Southern communities. In 1861 the delegate from the parish opposed secession, and the mass of the people displayed a feeling toward the Confederate adventure that was more than cool; the consensus seemed to be that this was a rich man's war and let the rich fight it. Later Winn became the center of Populist strength in the state, and after the demise of Populism a surprisingly strong Socialist party emerged, representing a rural brand of Socialism, to be sure, but still bearing a label not customarily worn in the rural South.

There is an obvious relation between Long's environment and his political thought. The program he would advocate was a later version of Populism. But was his strong sense of realism a product of the unrelieved starkness of Winn parish or of something in his inner self? We cannot know. But it is of great significance that in his entire career he never seriously mentioned the two great Southern legends, the Old South and the Lost Cause. At a time when most politicians attempted to assuage the misery of the masses by spinning tales of past glories—

the lovely South before Sumter, Jeb Stuart's dancing plume, the boys in gray plunging up the slopes at Gettysburg—Huey Long talked about economics and the present and the future.

After a spectacular career on the Public Service Commission, where he made a name attacking the big oil companies, Long ran for governor in 1924. He failed, ran again in 1928 and was elected, and then proceeded to remake completely the political pattern of the state. Before his advent on the scene governors were elected by "leaders," who were usually the sheriffs of the parishes. The successful candidate was the one who could line up the largest number of country leaders and then make a deal with the New Orleans machine. Abruptly, rudely, and with a great deal of zest, Long erased this arrangement. In his two gubernatorial campaigns he would often invade a local area and attack the boss. There was calculated design in this. He knew that in some cases he could not get the boss's support anyway, but more often he did not care. He was out to break the power of the leaders by going over their heads to the voters. For the first time a candidate for governor systematically stumped the whole state, and for the first time the masses, the people at the forks of the creeks, heard a candidate appeal to them for support and promise a program designed to benefit them. The comparative ease with which Long succeeded demonstrates that the masses were waiting for such a leader. "Overnight, one might say, the leaders found themselves without followers," said one almost incredulous opponent, "and the mob was in control."

Long then proceeded to create his own state and local organization. On the parish level he was always careful to name a committee of leaders, instead of having just one. His purpose here was, as intimates frankly and admiringly admit, to prevent one man from becoming too powerful. With several leaders, each one would watch the others, and all would compete to exercise divided authority. "He cut out the middleman in politics," said one associate. "That's a system you can't beat." It is a mark of Long's artistry as a student of power that sometimes in a parish where he had a large popular following, enough to carry a state election, he would leave an anti-Long sheriff in office—to prevent his own leaders from becoming too powerful and to keep them hungry for future victories. But if Long had stopped with forging a machine of his own, no matter how elaborate and effective, he would have merely followed the course of previous popular leaders, and would have met the same frustrating fate. He went a long step farther.

As W. J. Cash was probably the first to notice, Long was the first Southern demagogue, or to use a more satisfactory term, the first mass leader to set himself, not to bring the established machine to terms, but to overwhelm it and replace it with one of his own. In the words of V. O. Key: "He did not permit himself, in an oft-repeated pattern, to be hamstrung by a legislature dominated by old hands experienced in legislation and frequently under corporate retainer. He elected his own legislatures and erected a structure of political power both totalitarian and terrifying." When Long first went into office, he took with him only a minority of pledged supporters in the legislature. His immediate problem was to create an organization to pass his legislative program. In the lower chamber he could count on only nineteen votes whereas, as many of his measures had to be cast in the shape of constitutional amendments, he needed a two-thirds majority or sixty-seven. It was the same problem that had frustrated other liberal governors of the period, in both the South and the North. Blocked by their legislatures, they ended up by coming to terms with the opposition or by dissipating their energies in impotent crusades for sham issues.

Huey Long encountered his reverses, but defeat only intensified his determination to win through to his objectives. In fact, the techniques employed by the opposition, which sometimes included the crassest kinds of material pressures, and the violence of the reactions against him, which often took the form of fighting a bill merely because he had proposed it, had the effect of making him more fiercely implacable and of driving him to greater excesses in the use of power than otherwise would have been the case. Eventually he built up a disciplined majority in the legislature. The cost was high. In the frank words of one associate: "They all didn't come for free." Again, the process illustrates Long's sheer artistry as a manipulator of power.

The basis of his structure was patronage. First, he extended his control over existing boards and departments, and then through the constant creation of new agencies to perform new functions he continually enlarged the patronage at his disposal. That is, the job well did not dry up after the first distribution but always remained full. Finally Long was able to deprive the opposition of almost all political sustenance and to bring even the New Orleans machine to its knees. In 1935 in a radio address he said that when he ran for governor in 1928, the opposition was fighting for "our ground." Now, he announced grimly: "We are fighting for their ground. They say today they want peace. Well, they'll get peace when they get peaceful." At the end he was preparing to fit all pieces of the Democratic party into his organization. The opposition would have a place and would receive the rewards suitable to its role, but Long would determine both the place and the rewards. Not even the most gifted political operators of other times or other sections had thought in such daring terms or envisioned a machine so powerful.

Perhaps the most remarkable feature of the Long power structure— it was unique in Southern politics—was its material basis, or, put in blunter words, the techniques used by the organization to raise the money to sustain itself and to perform the welfare functions expected of machines in the pre-New Deal era. The Long organization did not ask for money or promise anything in return for contributions. It demanded and took what it needed, and was in effect self-sustaining. During Long's administration the state undertook a vast road building program. The road contractors and contractors on other public works were assessed for regular contributions in elections; so also were the distributors of highway machinery and the companies that wrote the state's insurance. For obviously good reasons all these interests met their obligations. The number of state employees was deliberately maintained at a high level, the jobs being spread around lavishly, and the holders had to contribute a percentage of their salaries to the machine campaign fund. Some of the top officials had to render monthly payments, but in Long's time lower salaried workers were assessed only before elections. In addition, there were approximately a thousand men, leaders and beneficiaries, who stood ready to supply money for emergency needs such as paying up poll taxes or covering the accounts of officials who had been tempted off the narrow path. Surviving Long leaders will frankly detail these financial manipulations. Not only that, they will insist passionately that the organization's methods of raising money were moral, and certainly more moral than the methods of the opposition. The opposition, and for that matter machines in other states, they say, went to corporate interests and asked for money under the table and hence were subject to some kind of control. But the Long machine exacted money openly and was accountable only to itself and to the voters.

During Long's lifetime the charge was flung freely at him, in Louisiana and out, that he was a dictator, a Mussolini of the bayous, a Hitler of the swamps, and the label has survived to the present. In liberal intellectual circles today it is fashionable to dismiss Long as an American Fascist. The appellation may serve the purpose of those who use it, either as a convenient smear or as a substitute for serious analysis, but as a designation it is inaccurate and offers no explanation of the phenomenon of Huey Long. The trouble with the dictator or Fascist tag is that it has a European connotation and does not fit the realities of the American political scene. Whatever Long was, he was completely American and Southern and wholly native in his outlook and methods. He was, in the most descriptive phrase, an American boss. The only respect in which he differed from the familiar pattern of the boss was in his concept of power—his genius in devising power devices and his ruthless readiness to employ power to attain his ends. Most American politicians have been reluctant to use power, or, when they have used it, to admit what they were doing. But Long openly exulted in his power and was remarkably frank in explaining his exercise of it. He fits the image of the politician of "ambition and talents" that Abraham Lincoln once warned against, although in the unconscious admiration of his account Lincoln may have been projecting himself into the role: "Towering genius disdains a beaten path. It seeks regions hitherto unexplored. It sees *no distinction* in adding story to story, upon monuments of fame, erected to the memory of others. . . . It scorns to tread in the foot-steps of *any* predecessor, however illustrious. It thirsts and burns for distinction; and, if possible, it will have it. . . ."

The most sensational demonstration of Long's power techniques came when as United States Senator but still boss of the state he returned to Louisiana to operate the legislature. Special session after special session was called at his command. He would dominate committee hearings and storm into the chamber of either house while in session to shout directions at his cohorts. Laws were jammed through at a rate never witnessed in a legislative body. On one occasion forty-four bills were passed in twenty-two minutes. In seven special sessions between August 1934 and September 1935 a total of 463 bills was enacted. Some bills started out as one thing in one house and were amended to something entirely different in the other, without the opposition or most of his followers realizing what had happened. The exhibition horrified many observers. But the travesty on the legislative process was not as bad as it seemed. Before every day's meeting Long held a closed caucus of his people and went over every proposed bill in detail, and while he was adamant on general principles there was a measure of discussion and criticism. Moreover, many of his measures had to be cast as constitutional amendments and submitted to a popular vote. Thus fourteen amendments passed in one session were ratified by the voters by a margin of seven to one.

But even when these extenuations are made, one has to wonder if Long's methods comported with the spirit of democratic government. The interesting thing is that Long, a surprisingly introspective politician, wondered too, in fact, wondered about his whole role and his place in the historical process of which he was a part. "They say they don't like my methods," he once said in an address. "Well, I don't like them either. . . . I'd much rather get up before a legislature and say 'Now this is a good law; it's for the benefit of the people, and I'd like for you to vote for it in the interest of the public welfare.' Only I know that laws ain't made that way. You've got to fight fire with fire." There is some terrible sense of urgency in the psychology of politicians who are driven by a sense of mission, a gnawing fear that time may be running out on them. Associates and members of his family attest that Long was always oppressed by time. To one man who asked why he ran bills through the legislature so fast Long replied: "You sometimes fight fire with fire. The means justify the end. I would do it some other way if there was time or if it wasn't necessary to do it this way."

Running through all his justifications of his course is the theme that he had to resort to extreme and even brutal methods; the phrase of fighting fire with fire appears again and again. It is almost impossible to separate the factors that made up his thinking on the subject of power, to say which were real and which were rationalization. The thesis most often advanced to explain him, that he simply illustrates Acton's dictum of the corrupting effects of power, is not enough. He was fascinated with power and its uses, and undoubtedly toward the end he had become so accustomed to the exercise of power, to the very convenience of it, that he could not give it up.

But there is more to the story. Epitomized in Long's life is a personal and also a sectional tragedy. When he first entered office, he exhibited many of the traits of the typical liberal reformer, including a somewhat idealistic concept of human nature and the nature of politics. But the unrelenting and sometimes unreasoning opposition he encountered and the constant attempts of his foes to destroy him, especially the try at impeachment in 1929, changed him. There was something almost wistful in his description of how he had lived out his entire career under some kind of threat of forced removal from office: "I have tried for about sixteen years to have it some other way, and it has never been any other way, so now I have stopped trying to have it any other way." After the failure of impeachment he became harder and more cynical. He resolved that thereafter he would so strengthen and solidify his position that no similar attempt could succeed in the future. But as he drove toward always greater goals of power he never lost completely the fear that the old hierarchy might recuperate and block him or possibly unseat him. Perhaps the gravest indictment that can be made of conservative Southern politics is that it forced leaders like Long to become ruthless operators of power. But, it is significant to note, as with other aspects of his position, Long wondered about his power structure. As invincible as he had made it, he apparently thought that it could be only temporary because he repeatedly warned the men who would be his successors that they could not exercise his authority without tragic results.

But no matter how adept Long was in the arts of power, he could never have sustained himself or his organization merely by manipulation. He had a program. He promised something, and he delivered it. Long was the first Southern mass leader to leave aside race baiting and appeals to the Southern tradition and the Southern past and address himself to the social and economic problems of the present. He promised big, partly because that was his nature and partly because a big promise that took in the interest of large numbers was good strategy. "Do not ever," he advised, "put one of those Mother Hubbard things out that is going to accommodate just one percent."

In a short space his record can only be summarized. When he became governor, Louisiana had 296 miles of concrete roads, 35 miles of asphalt roads, 5,728 miles of gravel roads, and three major bridges within the state highway system. By 1935 the figures read: 2,446 miles of concrete roads, 1,308 miles of asphalt roads, 9,629 miles of gravel roads, and more than forty major bridges within the highway system.

In the field of education, free textbooks were provided, causing a twenty per cent jump in school enrollment; appropriations for higher education were increased; and over 100,000 adult illiterates, of both races, were enrolled in free night schools. Facilities in state hospitals and institutions were enlarged, and the services were modernized and humanized. Just as important as the material accomplishments was the impact of Huey Long on the psychology of the state. He created a new consciousness of government on the part of the masses and thereby revitalized state politics. By advancing issues that mattered and by repealing the poll tax, he stirred voter interest to a height unmatched in any other Southern state, and he left Louisiana with an enduring bifactionalism that has many of the attributes of a two-party system.

When people in Louisiana try to describe the impact of Long and his movement, they have trouble in putting their thoughts into words. They are obviously deeply moved, but they are embarrassed that they may sound emotional or exaggerated. Thus one associate telling the writer of Long's advent in politics said: "To run for office you had either to be indorsed by the sugar barons, the banks, or the railroads. Without them putting their hands on you and anointing you, you were beyond the pale. . . . And the very fact that he was able to become governor of this state without the titular rulers—they never forgave him for that. And as a result he brought the state out of the mud, gave them free school books, and hospitals. It sounds like a political speech, but if those things had not been done this state would have lagged behind until it was pushed into it by mass hysteria." Jonathan Daniels recounts a conversation with a businessman of French descent in the Cajun country. This man told Daniels that Louisiana "was the back door to China before Huey Long came. . . . Huey Long changed Louisiana from a hell hole to a paradise. He was emancipator. He brought light." Then he quoted Huey as saying: "Many are walking. Some are buggy riding. Some are in automobiles. But I'm flying." Perhaps Long had pushed too hard, this observer conceded with the realism common to many Latins: "Maybe we moved too fast in the last eight years; certainly we moved too slowly for centuries before that."

A perceptive New Orleans lawyer with a detached interest in politics went to great lengths to impress on the writer the nature of the Long appeal to the masses. Although he had never been a member of the Long organization, he agreed to run for a state office on the Long ticket shortly after Huey's death. Before, he had thought that the Longs won elections because they made demagogic speeches or manipulated the vote. But when he toured the rural areas of the state he was both shocked and enlightened by what he saw. As he describes it: "And what interested me greatly was the poverty, misery, degradation of the people in certain sections . . . the lack of good food, the lack of ordinary comfort. . . . The first experience I had: I went into a little village called

Monticello. Earl and Christenbery were with us, and there was an old man in his house, and on the mantel there were some old relics, a picture of Long and *Every Man a King*. This old man thought that these relics were his gods. There is one of the first indications of the temper of the people. Long had given them hope, had given them free ambulances, free hospitals, hot lunches, and things of that sort and the benefits. And they figured that Long was the one man for the first time in their lives that was thinking about them. . . . When I saw those old people—that is the thing I have never seen any writer get on to. The people that I met on those trips—poor. I never saw such poverty, the women with teeth so full of tartar that they looked like coral shells. They would come to those meetings at night in the cold and the wet with babies wrapped up in blankets and use a flashlight to find their way through the woods. They called them speakings."

Another lawyer tried to put over much the same thought to A. J. Liebling, finally resorting to a sports figure of speech to clinch his point. The significance of Longism, its great end result, he said, was that opportunities in the state had been opened up to people of all classes: "Huey was like the kid who comes along in a game of Chicago pool when all the balls are massed. He breaks them and runs a few and leaves the table full of shots for the other players. As long as the Longs are in, you have a chance."

Many things have been said about Huey Long, mostly bad, and while some of the criticisms have been uninformed others have been eminently right. But even after the debits are written down in blackest ink one credit stands out with peculiar significance for the record of history. He forcibly introduced a large element of realism into Southern politics. He asked the South to turn its gaze from outside devils and the imagined past and take a long, hard look at itself and the present. We have plenty of problems, he said, but we can find the strength and the resources to solve them ourselves. Gerald Johnson, who heartily disliked him, could still say that Long was the first Southerner since Calhoun to make an original contribution to the science of government. "I cherish profound suspicion of his integrity, public and private," Johnson wrote. "I regard his methods as detestable. Nevertheless, the late Huey Pierce Long has the distinction of having injected more realism into Southern politics than any other man of his generation. Huey made millions of Southerners think of the political problems of 1935 as something quite different from those of 1865."

In Huey Long's vast plans there was no room for the race issue. Racism was a false issue that would deflect and divide people from the pursuit of the important objectives of politics; that would, in the revealing phrase of Long leaders, "mess up his show." He never seriously employed the race question in any of his campaigns, either to win an election or to distract attention from any failures in his own record.

Apparently he had no personal sense of race prejudice, and he seems to have genuinely liked Negroes. By his own standards he was a segregationist, but segregation entered into his thinking only when it had to be related to politics. That is, he did not consider it as an end in itself but as something that might threaten or aid his political ends. Thus from the beginning he included the Negroes, the poorest people in the state, in his welfare programs. He did this not out of altruism or idealism but for realistic economic reasons. As one Long leader explained it to the writer: "You can't help poor white people without helping Negroes. But that's all right." At the same time, for realistic political reasons he made no move to give the vote to the Negroes, not because he had strong feelings one way or the other on the subject, but because the attempt could have no political significance. He would have encountered fierce resistance, and he did not need the Negro vote. On one occasion he discussed the race situation in Louisiana for a Northern interviewer. The reporter asked how he would treat Negroes under his plan. "Treat them just the same as anybody else," Long replied; "give them an opportunity to make a living." Would he let them vote? "I'm not going into that. I'd leave it up to the States to decide as they want to. But in Louisiana a Negro's just the same as anybody else; he ought to have a chance to work and to make a living, and to get an education."

What Long did give the Negroes was more than they were getting in other Southern states. Being the realistic operator that he was, he knew that his course might stir white objections. He adopted a strategy of voicing publicly the familiar white attitudes on race relations and from behind this cover giving the Negroes some of the things they wanted. Unlike the businessmen of Reconstruction and the Populists, he did not label what he was doing; he seemed to be a complete segregationist. Once he explained to a Negro leader how he had managed to get better medical care for colored people: "Why, down in Louisiana . . . the whites have decided niggahs have got to have public health care. Got to give 'em clinics and good hospitals. Got to keep 'em healthy. That's fair and it's good sense. I said to them: 'You wouldn't want a colored woman watching over your children if she had pyorrhea, would you?' They see the point."

Sometimes the technique had a double edge. When the new Charity Hospital was built in New Orleans, some Negro leaders complained to Long that there were no colored nurses, when at least half the patients were Negroes. Huey said he would get their nurses in, but they would not like his method. He visited the hospital and then called a press conference. He was shocked at what he had found, he announced—white women were waiting on colored men, and it had to be stopped. Negroes might object to his method, indeed, and also white liberals, but he achieved his purpose by the only way that he could.

Huey's brother and first political heir, Earl Long, who would win the governorship three times, either owned or copied Huey's skill in dealing with both races. In the last campaign that he made before his death Earl assured colored audiences that he would take care of the question of integrated schools for them. He said, in practically these words: "Now, don't worry. I'm not going to let them make you send your kids to schools with white kids, where they'll lord it over 'em. You're going to have your own schools."

Since Huey Long's death in 1935 elections in Louisiana have been fought out between the two Democratic factions of Longs and anti-Longs, although splinter factions often appear in the first primary. Factional candidates for governor run at the head of a full ticket of suitors for lesser offices, a practice rarely employed in other Southern states, and the two principal factions are so specifically defined as to constitute the equivalent of regular parties. While the personality of a candidate may have some influence, campaigns revolve almost entirely around the issues laid down by Huey Long—taxation of the corporate interests, extension of social welfare, enlargement of the state's regulatory powers. Any candidate for governor who tries to break out of the pattern is practically doomed from the start. Thus in the election of 1960 the out-and-out segregationist aspirant, running on the sole issue of segregation, polled only seventeen per cent of the popular vote. He failed, as Earl Long, one of the shrewdest analysts in the business, predicted he would, because this issue alone was not enough in a race where every candidate supported the principle of segregation.

The later heirs of Huey Long have adopted his strategy in dealing with the race question. Under Earl Long the benefits of social welfare were more abundantly bestowed on the Negroes, who responded by voting the Long ticket. Earl Long, going a step beyond Huey, encouraged the registration of Negroes as voters, the colored vote coming eventually to compose thirteen per cent of the total. His motives, like Huey's, were mixed and are not easily separated. Obviously the fact that he received the Negro vote had something to do with his thinking, but beyond that he seemed to feel, although he could never exactly define his reasons, that qualified Negroes should vote as a right. But essentially he was trying to do in a more difficult period what Huey had done, to subordinate the race issue to problems he considered more important. Earl Long always contended he did more to preserve the basic fabric of segregation than all the segregationists—and that the way to do it was by turning the attention of both races to normal political issues. Long leaders in the parishes have assured the writer that they have succeeded in blunting Negro militancy by dealing the Negroes into the suffrage and the welfare rewards.

When Earl Long had his tragic and much publicized collapse, he was trying to get a bill through the legislature that would have made it difficult for the segregationist groups to purge Negro voters from the rolls. Presumably his action qualified him for a place in the liberal heaven, but his purpose was not mentioned in the Northern press. Here, ran the accounts, was another comic Southern politician playing the usual part of the clown, acting as a Southern demagogue was supposed to act. Whatever Earl Long should have been criticized for, he was subjected to ridicule beyond his meed. It was the same sort of ridicule heaped upon the Populists by Northern commentators who had no conception of the obstacles against which the Populists had to fight. It was the same kind of derision visited upon Huey Long by liberals who had no realization of the dilemmas of liberalism in the South. The South will doubtless continue to wrestle with all its ancient problems and will move toward some solution. It can expect many pressures from the majority section, but it should look for little understanding. As Huey Long had known, it must find the answer in its own inner strength.

13

Arthur M. Schlesinger, Jr.: The Messiah of the Rednecks

Arthur M. Schlesinger, Jr., author of The Age of Jackson, The Age of Roosevelt, *and* A Thousand Days, *is a Pulitzer Prize-winning historian whose liberal Democratic sympathies have consistently been mirrored in his histories of the Democratic administrations of Jackson, Roosevelt, and Kennedy. A warm admirer of Franklin Roosevelt and the New Deal, Schlesinger reflects in the passages that follow the New Dealers' alarm at Long's burgeoning threat on the radical left. His portrait of the "Messiah of the Rednecks" contains a harsh judgment; deftly drawn, it pictures Long as a talented but exceedingly dangerous and even vicious man who threatened not only Roosevelt and the New Deal, but ultimately the very liberal fabric of the American reform tradition from which Long's crusade ostensibly emerged.[1] Lacking the ideological preoccupations necessary to a Hitler or a Mussolini, Long resembled, in Schlesinger's view, more of a Latin American dictator—a Vargas or Perón. His Louisiana was less Southern than Caribbean—an underdeveloped banana republic in revolt against economic colonialism. "Like them, he stood in a muddled way for economic modernization and social justice; like them, he was most threatened by his own arrogance and cupidity, his weakness for soft living and his rage for personal power."*

Thus ferment held out opportunity to those who could imprint their personalities on despair and offer distressed people an assurance of the millennium. The question remained whether the unrest would shoot off in different directions under a multitude of leaders or whether one man could gather it all unto himself. For all their talents, neither Father Coughlin nor Dr. Townsend was in the tradition of major po-

[1] Abridged from Arthur M. Schlesinger, Jr., *The Politics of Upheaval* (Boston: Houghton Mifflin Company, 1960; London: William Heinemann, Ltd., 1960), pp. 42–68. Copyright © 1960 by Arthur M. Schlesinger, Jr. Reprinted by permission of the author and the publishers. Footnotes have been omitted for reasons of space.

litical achievement. If anyone could organize the discontent on a national basis and use it to propel himself into power, it would more probably be, not a priest nor a doctor, but a politician. The most likely candidate was surely the Senator from Louisiana, Huey Pierce Long, Jr.

*   *   *

In his manners, values, and idiom, Huey Long remained a backcountry hillbilly. But he was a hillbilly raised to the highest level, preternaturally swift and sharp in intelligence, ruthless in action, and grandiose in vision. He was a man of medium height, well built but inclining toward pudginess. His dress was natty and loud. His face was round, red, and blotched, with more than a hint of pouches and jowls. Its rubbery mobility, along with the curly red-brown hair and the oversize putty nose, gave him the deceptive appearance of a clown. But the darting popeyes could easily turn from soft to hard, and the cleft chin was strong and forceful. At times it was a child's face, spoiled and willful; he looked, noted John Dos Passos, "like an overgrown small boy with very bad habits indeed." At times, it was the face of the cunning yokel about to turn the tables on the city slickers around him. At times, it became exceedingly hard and cruel.

In relaxation, Long had the lethargic air of an upcountry farmer. He liked to slump drowsily on a chair or stretch out on a sofa or loll on a bed. In certain moods, he would talk quietly, grammatically, and sensibly, with humor and perception. But he was always likely to explode into violent activity, leaping to his feet, hunching his shoulders, waving his arms, roaring with laughter or rage, emphasizing points by pounding furniture or clapping people on the back. "The phone rang every minute or so while we talked," said James Thurber, "and he would get up and walk through a couple of rooms to answer it and come back and fling himself heavily on the bed again so that his shoulders and feet hit it at the same moment." The jerkiness of his movements reminded one observer of the flickering figures rushing across the screen in early silent films. This very intensity underlined his coarse and feverish power.

His weakness for conducting business in bed won him his first national notoriety. On a Sunday morning in March 1930, while Huey was recovering from the diversions of the night before in his suite at the Hotel Roosevelt in New Orleans, the commander of the German cruiser *Emden*, in dress uniform, accompanied by the German consul in morning coat, paid a courtesy call on the Governor of Louisiana. Hearing that guests were outside, Huey flung a red and blue dressing gown over green silk pajamas, shuffled on blue bedroom slippers, and ambled affably into the next room. His visitors left somewhat stiffly. Soon after, the German consul complained that Long had insulted the German Reich by his attire and demanded an apology. Long, somewhat amused, explained that he was just a boy from the country. "I know little of diplomacy and much less of the international courtesies and exchanges that are indulged in by nations." The next day, having collected all the elements of formal morning dress except a top hat, the Governor, in tail coat but with a snappy gray fedora, boarded the *Emden* and made his apologies.

The incident delighted the press across the nation, and Huey became for the first time a front-page figure outside Louisiana. It may also have given him some ideas. For the first time he was receiving friendly notices. All the world loved a character; might it not be that the disguise of comedy could make people overlook or forgive much else? He had always been a jocose figure, given to ribald language and homely anecdotes. From this time forward he began to cultivate a public reputation as a buffoon. And the new public persona happily acquired a name. In the ribbing which took place around the Executive Mansion, Huey took to calling one of his gang "Brother Crawford," after a character in the Amos 'n' Andy radio program; in return he was called "Kingfish," after the head of Amos and Andy's lodge, the Mystic Knights of the Sea. Once someone questioned his right to be present at a meeting of the Highway Commission. "I looked around at the little fishes present," Long explained later, "and said, 'I'm the Kingfish.'" The title stuck. Huey himself used to claim that the name "Long" was hard to get over the telephone, so that it saved time to say, "This is the Kingfish." Also, he added, it substituted "gaiety for some of the tragedy of politics." In the same vein, he started a mock debate over whether cornpone should be crumbled or dunked in potlikker—the liquid left at the bottom of the pot after boiling vegetable greens and pork fat. This became a national issue. Even Franklin D. Roosevelt, Governor of New York but a Georgian by adoption, joined the argument. Roosevelt was a crumbler. Long, a dunker, finally agreed to a compromise.

But all the Kingfish's clowning could not conceal his more formidable qualities, especially his power and speed of mind. His intelligence, Raymond Moley once said, was an instrument such as is given to few men. As Governor, he was an efficient administrator, sure in detail, quick in decision. On his legal mettle, before a courtroom or arguing the case for seating his Louisiana delegation at the Democratic convention of 1932, he displayed a disciplined and razor-keen analytical ability. Still, he did not value his gift. As Moley said, "He misused it, squandered it, battered it, as a child might treat a toy. . . . He used his mind so erratically as to seem, a great deal of the time, not only childish but insane." Alben Barkley once told him, "You are the smartest lunatic I ever saw in my whole life!" (Long rejoined, "Maybe that is the smartest description I've ever had applied to me!")

He was not a nice man. When his brother Julius asked him in 1930 to give their aged father a room in the Executive Mansion, Huey complained bitterly about "base ingratitude and threatened holdups" and refused. "I swear," Julius said later, "that I do not know of a man, any human being, that has less feeling for his family than Huey P. Long has." The yes men and hoodlums who clustered around him were bound to him by fear or by greed, not by affection. He knew he was much smarter than anyone else, and he could not conceal his contempt for others. He told legislators to their faces that he could buy and sell them "like sacks of potatoes." He called officeholders "dime-a-dozen punks." He rejoiced in deeds of personal humiliation. Revenge was always prominent in his mind. His flippant brutality was both evidence of his mastery and a further source of his power.

On the hustings, he played on his listeners with intimate knowledge, deriding them, insulting them, whipping up emotions of resentment and spite, contemptuously providing them with scapegoats. He knew what to say to produce the response he wanted, and, knowing, said it. "If he went in a race up North," Julius Long said, "he would publish up there that there is part nigger in us in order to get the nigger vote."

Vilification was his particular weapon. His blistering frontier invective provided the link between his own superior intelligence and the surging envy of the crowds before him. He expressed what his hearers had long felt but could not say. He was their idol—themselves as they would like to be, free and articulate and apparently without fear. It was only when he had left the platform, when hard-faced bodyguards closed in around him, shoving his admirers back and moving in a flying wedge toward the black limousine, it was only then that it became evident that Huey Long was a coward—the "yellowest physical coward," his brother Earl said, "that God had ever let live."

He carried these qualities to Washington—the comic impudence, the gay egotism, the bravado, the mean hatred, the fear. He was a man propelled by a greed for power and a delight in its careless exercise. "The only sincerity there was in him," said Julius Long, "was for himself." He talked broadly about the need for redistributing the wealth, but these were words. When a reporter tried to discover deeper meanings, Long brushed him off: "I haven't any program or any philosophy. I just take things as they come." Yet, for all this, there remained the sense in which his qualities and his ambitions were those of the plain people of his state writ large—the people from the red clay country and the piny woods, from the canebrakes and the bayous, the shrimp fishermen and the moss fishermen, the rednecks and the hillbillies and the Cajuns. Once, standing before the Evangeline Oak, he spoke to the Acadians of southern Louisiana and recalled the legend of Evangeline, weeping for her vanished lover. She was not, Long said, the only Acadian thus to have waited and wept.

> Where are the schools that you have waited for your children to have, that have never come? Where are the roads and the highways that you

spent your money to build, that are no nearer now than ever before? Where are the institutions to care for the sick and disabled? Evangeline wept bitter tears in her disappointment. But they lasted only one lifetime. Your tears . . . have lasted for generations.

His conclusion seemed to come from the heart: "Give me the chance to dry the tears of those who still weep here."

His strength, observed Sherwood Anderson, lay in "the terrible South that Stark Young and his sort ignore . . . the beaten, ignorant, Bible-ridden, white South. Faulkner occasionally really touches it. It has yet to be paid for." That terrible South was exacting the price of years of oppression. Huey Long was its man, and he gave it by proxy the delights it had been so long denied.

One day late in January 1932, while Jim Watson of Indiana, the Republican leader in the Senate, was idling on the floor, a man dealt him a smashing blow with open hands on his chest and said explosively, "Jim, I want to get acquainted with you!" Staggered by the blow, Watson said, "Well, who in the hell are you?" "I," the answer came, "am Huey Long." The Senator from Louisiana, a year late, was coming to claim his seat.

His debut was all too typical. From the start, he violated every rule of the club. He picked an immediate fight with his Louisiana colleague, who thereupon refused to escort him when he took his oath. Instead of relapsing into the decorous silence expected of a first-termer, he spoke expansively on all subjects. When Joseph T. Robinson, the Democratic leader, refused to back his share-the-wealth resolution, Long called for new party leadership and dramatically resigned all his committee assignments. (Robinson called this a "comic opera performance unworthy of the great actor from Louisiana"; other senators resented it as an escape on Long's part from the hard work of the Senate.) When Carter Glass brought in his banking bill at the end of the year, Long filibustered against it and launched a scornful personal campaign against Glass. And, when his attendance was needed in the Senate, he was always likely to be dashing off to more important business in Louisiana.

It seemed plain that Long could hardly have a lower opinion of the body which regarded itself as the greatest deliberative assembly on earth. He made certain exceptions, especially George W. Norris and Burton K. Wheeler; "they were the boldest, most courageous men I had ever met." But he treated the others like a collection of stuffed shirts. The more revered they were in the club, like Robinson, Glass, and Pat Harrison, the more Long needled and tormented them. Huey in debate, said Alben Barkley, was like a horsefly; "he would light on one part of you, sting you, and then, when you slapped at him, fly away to land elsewhere and sting again." Sitting at a desk where John C. Calhoun had once sat, wearing white flannels, pink necktie, and orange kerchief or some other bizarre combination, Long posed and strutted and stung until most of his colleagues could not endure him. He knew this, and in certain moods regretted it. Then he would bid for popularity by trying for laughs in speeches or by geniality in the cloakroom, or else talk wistfully of resigning because he had "no friends" in the Senate.

But he bided his time in the hope that the new administration would change things. Long had not originally wanted Roosevelt. "He failed with Cox," Long said, "and that should end him. Al Smith would be entirely satisfactory." But Norris brought him around, and Long played an important role in holding southern support for Roosevelt at Chicago. He wanted to play an equally important part in the campaign. When Jim Farley refused to provide him a special train to go from state to state, promising immediate payment of the bonus, Huey, in bad temper, said, "Jim, you're gonna get licked. . . . I tried to save you, but if you don't want to be saved, it's all right with me." Finally he accepted a less ambitious schedule which took him into states where Democratic strategists thought he would do a minimum of harm. Everywhere he went, he was a great success. Farley wrote later, "We never again underrated him."

At first, Long was—or seemed—enthralled by Roosevelt. "When I was talking to the Governor today," he told a newspaperman in October 1932, "I just felt like the depression was over. That's a fact. I never felt so tickled in my life." After the election, he expressed a constant fear that the new administration might be captured by the reactionaries; but his personal susceptibility to Roosevelt remained undiminished. In January he called on the President-elect at the Mayflower in Washington. "I'm going to talk turkey with Roosevelt," he shouted to reporters, "I am going to ask him, 'Did you mean it or didn't you?' Goddam it, there ain't but one thing that I'm afraid of—and that's the people." He then pounded at the door of Roosevelt's suite, an action he obligingly repeated for the photographers. Half an hour later Huey emerged jubilant. "I come out of this room happy and satisfied," he said. "We've got a great President." Some one asked whether Roosevelt intended to crack down on him. "Crack down on me?" said Long. "He don't want to crack down on me. He told me, 'Huey, you're going to do just as I tell you,' and that is just what I'm agoin' to do."

But it was not that easy. Long retained deep suspicions of some of Roosevelt's associates. A day or two before the inauguration, he came to Moley's room at the Mayflower, kicked the door open, chewed on an apple, and said pugnaciously, "I don't like you and your goddamned banker friends!" (Everyone was struck dumb; after Long departed, Moley found a senator hiding in the bathroom.) During the Hundred Days Long's suspicions steadily mounted. He disliked the conservative measures of the first month, such as the Economy Act, strongly supported the inflation drive of April, and in May denounced the administration on the ground that it was dominated by the same old clique of bankers who had controlled Hoover. "Parker Gilbert from Morgan & Company, Leffingwell, Ballantine, Eugene Meyer, every one of them are here—what is the use of hemming and hawing? We know who is running the thing." The National Recovery Act completed his alienation.

Long's ideological disillusionment was accompanied by—indeed may well have been the result of—an intense if covert political conflict with the administration. In August 1932 Roosevelt had already called Long one of the two most dangerous men in America. In January, reassessing Long's troublemaking potentiality, he suggested to Rex Tugwell, of all people, that an effort should be made to bring him round. There was an apparent period of appeasement. Presumably with Roosevelt's assent, the Senate Committee on Campaign Expenditures, which had been looking into the recent senatorial election in Louisiana, abandoned its inquiry. Nothing was done to reopen a Treasury Department investigation of Huey's income tax, begun under the Hoover administration. But Long grew insistent, particularly on questions of federal patronage. At the same time, the White House was receiving hundreds of complaints about the Long organization from Louisiana.

Sometime during the spring, Roosevelt decided to write Long off—a decision expressed in a determination to deny him patronage. The reasons for this decision are obscure. Long's power in his own state, his national appeal as a rabble rouser, his capacity to make mischief in the Senate—all this argued for a serious effort to keep him in the New Deal camp. Moreover, Roosevelt was quite prepared to get along with tyrannical bosses like Frank Hague of New Jersey or with popular demagogues like Father Coughlin. Yet the President may well have been genuinely persuaded that Long was far more dangerous to the country than the Hagues or Coughlins. If this were so, then he would not let federal patronage or presidential favor strengthen the Louisiana despotism further.

In June 1933 he asked Farley to bring Long over for a talk. Huey breezed into the White House in a light summer suit. On his head was a straw hat with a brightly colored band. He sat down in the presidential office, and the three men began a superficially genial conversation. Then Farley noticed that Long was keeping his hat on. "At first I thought it was an oversight, but soon realized it was deliberate." Farley looked apprehensively at the President. Roosevelt was plainly well aware of what was going on. Huey occasionally took off the hat to underline points, tapping Roosevelt with it on the knee or elbow. But the President declined to be annoyed. His sole interest, Roosevelt kept saying, lay in seeing that good men were named to public office. After a time, Long knew that he could not break through the ring of cool and gracious phrases. As he left the White House, he told the press, "The President and I are never going to fall out. I'll be satisfied whichever way matters go." But he muttered to Farley, "What the hell is the use of coming down to see this fellow? I can't win any decision over him." "I'm never goin' over there again," he told a reporter. His grandfather, Long added, once had a man working for him who picked twice as much cotton as anyone in the entire history of the farm. Naturally grand-pappy fired him, saying "You're so smart that if you stayed around here fust thing I know I'd be working for you." "That's the way I feel about Roosevelt," Long said. "He's so doggone smart that fust thing I know I'll be working fer him—and I ain't goin' to."

Soon he defined to his satisfaction the difference between the Hoover and Roosevelt administrations. Hoover, Huey said, was a hoot owl, Roosevelt, a scrootch owl. A hoot owl banged into the roost, knocked the hen clean off, and seized her as she fell. "But a scrootch owl slips into the roost and scrootches up to the hen and talks softly to her. And the hen just falls in love with him, and the first thing you know, *there ain't no hen.*"

In 1930 and 1931 the Bureau of Internal Revenue had begun to re-ceive letters from Louisiana charging illegal activity on the part of the Long machine. In July 1932, Elmer Irey, chief of the Treasury Depart-ment's Intelligence Unit, sent in an agent to case the situation. In a few weeks, the agent reported back. "Chief," he said, "Louisiana is crawling. Long and his gang are stealing everything in the state . . . and they're not paying taxes on the loot." Irey despatched a force of thirty-two agents to push the investigation. Long responded with heavy pressure on the Hoover administration to call the Treasury off. After the 1932 election, Ogden Mills asked Irey whether he had enough evi-dence to warrant indictment. When Irey said that his people had not had enough time, Mills said, "Very well, then. Suspend your investiga-tion immediately and write a full report of what you have done and what you propose doing and submit it to my successor. After all, the Senator is one of their babies; let them decide what to do with him."

Irey accordingly stopped the investigation and filed the report. For the first months of the New Deal, he heard nothing about Long. Then in August, a few weeks after Long kept his hat on in the presidential office, the Commissioner of Internal Revenue told Irey that the White House wanted to know why the Intelligence Unit had investigated Long; wasn't it a job for the FBI? Irey pointed out that Long was vulnerable as an income-tax evader, which made him Treasury business. Then silence again, until Henry Morgenthau, Jr., became Secretary of the Treasury. "Why have you stopped investigating Huey Long, Mr. Irey?" the new Secretary asked Irey brusquely one day. Irey explained that Mills had told him to stop and no one since had told him to resume. "What's the matter, Mr. Irey, are you afraid of Huey Long?" "I'm awaiting instructions," said Irey. "Very well, then," said Morgenthau. "Get all your agents back on the Louisiana job. Start the investigation of Huey Long and proceed as though you were investigating John Doe. And let the chips fall where they may."

The resumption of the investigation was only one of Long's headaches. A comic episode in August 1933 further complicated his life. One night Gene Buck, the song writer, took the Kingfish to spend an evening at the Sands Point Club on Long Island. Long was drunk and offensive. It is not clear what precipitated the denouement—whether his free comments to a woman at a neighboring table, or an ingenious but misguided effort to urinate between the legs of the man in front of him while waiting his turn in the men's room—but someone, goaded beyond endurance, hit Long in the face and opened a cut over his left eye. There was considerable merriment over the Kingfish's humiliation; medals were offered to the assailant, lists printed of men who regretted they had not committed the assault themselves. Long did not help his own case by asserting that it was a Wall Street plot and that three or four men with knives had ganged up on him, nor by subsequently writing an open letter to Al Capone, then in retirement at the Atlanta penitentiary, suggesting that Wall Street would doubtless arrange to give Capone his freedom if the great racketeer would confess to having planned the Long attack.

At this moment, the Kingfish even seemed in trouble at home. His hand-picked successor, Governor O. K. Allen, impressed no one. As Earl Long put it, "A leaf once blew in the window of Allen's office and fell on his desk. Allen signed it." And everyone regarded him as Huey's responsibility. "There is not a dishwasher here," said Julius Long, "that is more subservient to his master than Oscar Allen is to Huey Long." Mutters against "Long Island Huey" were rising through the state. The Mayor of New Orleans, with whom the Kingfish had patched up an alliance, turned against him. The Senate committee reopened the investigation of the 1932 election. When Long attacked Roosevelt at the South Louisiana State Fair, the crowd broke into a storm of boos. From behind twenty highway policemen, Long screamed back at the hecklers, "Come down here out of that there grandstand and I'll man-to-man it with you. And I won't have five or six men [the number was multiplying] jump on you like they did to me at Sands Point! . . . Come on down here, and I'll make you giggle! I'll give you a dose of castor oil and laudanum!"

The Mayor of New Orleans was re-elected early in 1934 over Long's envenomed opposition, and it looked as if the Kingfish were at last on the ropes. But once again his enemies underestimated Long's resourcefulness. He fought back in two ways. By pushing an ever more radical program through the state legislature—including the abolition of the poll tax, exemptions for the poor from the general property tax, a debt moratorium, and new levies on business—he reawakened support among the poor whites. At the same time, by extending his personal control over the apparatus of government at every level, he transformed the state government into a virtual dictatorship.

The legislature was wholly under Long's domination. Once it shouted through forty-four bills in twenty-two minutes. The Kingfish wandered about the floor, waved aside objections, and briskly declared that whatever he wanted had been passed. "He was like a young father on a romp in the nursery," wrote Raymond Swing after seeing him in action. "Anyone could see how much fun it was being a dictator." Few dared to protest. Even Long's personal life was sacred. As Westbrook Pegler commented after a visit to Baton Rouge, "They do not permit a house of prostitution to operate within a prescribed distance of the state university, but exempt the state Capitol from the meaning of the act."

In a series of seven special sessions in 1934 and 1935, the legislature obediently transferred nearly every vestige of authority from towns and parishes to the state, which meant to Huey. By 1935 local government was virtually at an end. No municipal officer—policeman or fireman or schoolteacher—could hold his job except by Long's favor. If elected officials defied the Long machine, the state could force their resignations by withholding public funds. Another law gave the Governor power to make new appointments once the offices were vacated. If communities continued defiant, the Governor could call out the militia and declare martial law without accountability to anyone. Indeed, Long broke the resistance in New Orleans in 1934 by sending in the National Guard for a long period of military occupation. To insure against an uprising at the polls, the state government had exclusive authority to name all election commissioners; this enabled the machine to count the votes. And the Kingfish's Supreme Court certified the constitutionality of his program. Every man was a king, but only one wore a crown.

In return, the people of Louisiana got a state government which did more for them than any other government in Louisiana's history. The power of the oligarchy, which had for so long sucked the people dry, was now broken. Schools, hospitals, roads and public services in general were better than ever before. Poor whites and even Negroes had unprecedented opportunities. Though Long had standard Southern racial views, he played very little on racist emotions. He regarded the Klan, for example, with contempt; and, when its leader offered to enter the state and campaign against him, Long told reporters, "Quote me as saying that that Imperial bastard will never set foot in Louisiana, and that when I call him a son of a bitch I am not using profanity, but am referring to the circumstances of his birth." He was rather proud of his achievements for the colored people: "Lincoln didn't free the slaves in Louisiana; I did." His greatest pride was what he had done for education, from the free textbooks and school buses in the elementary schools to the new university of Louisiana State. He led the brass band at State, meddled with the football team, and invented the Sugar Bowl. At the same time, he built up a first-class medical school, tried to get men like Wayne Morse of the University of Oregon Law School and Thomas G. Corcoran to become dean of his law school, and subsidized one of the best highbrow quarterlies in the country, the *Southern Review*. (A young man in the English Department at State named Robert Penn Warren was fascinated by the phenomenon of Long; the result was the astute and compassionate novel, *All the King's Men*.) In a way, Louisiana State summed up the Long paradox. Able people pursued their studies without hindrance, and the professional schools flourished; but the president of the University, a Columbia Ph.D. and Long stooge named James Monroe ("Jimmy Moron" or later "Jingle Money") Smith, was meanwhile using half a million dollars in university funds for private speculation in the wheat market.

Long achieved much—certainly more than the oligarchy ever had. But his achievement should not be overestimated. Like an ancient emperor or a modern dictator, he specialized in monuments. He sprinkled the state with roads and buildings. But he did little or nothing to raise wages for the workers, to stop child labor, to reduce the work day, to support trade unions, to provide pensions for the aged, to furnish relief to the unemployed, even to raise teacher's salaries. He left behind no record of social or labor legislation.

Moreover, if within Long's limits government was benevolent and fairly efficient, it was still intricately and hopelessly corrupt. In 1934, to take an example, Long and several close associates set up the Win or Lose Corporation. The state government considerately made it possible for the new corporation to acquire properties in the natural gas fields; the corporation then persuaded natural gas companies to buy the properties by threatening to increase their taxes if they didn't. Using such persuasive sales methods, Win or Lose cleared about $350,000 in 1935. And, where local talent was inadequate, Long invited outside experts into the state to assist his projects of sharing the wealth. Thus he summoned Frank Costello, the New York gangster, to take over the Louisiana slot machine concession.

Government was also increasingly cruel. Those who dared criticize the regime risked not only political and economic reprisals but threats, beatings and kidnappings. The new order, wrote Westbrook Pegler, was "reducing to the political status of the Negro all of the white people of Louisiana who oppose Der Kingfish." Newspaper critics, like Hodding Carter of the *Hammond Courier*, went armed day and night. And as the corruption and the tyranny spread, the opposition, denied legal means of expression, began itself to contemplate desperate measures. "If ever there was need for shotgun government," Carter wrote, "that time is now. . . . Let us read our histories again. They will tell us with what weapons we earned the rights of free men. Then, by God's help, let's use them."

Toward the end of 1934 the legislature enacted an occupational tax on oil refining—the same tax which had led to Long's impeachment five years before. In response, a group of Standard Oil employees, joined by indignant citizens like Hodding Carter, formed the Square Deal Association, put on blue shirts, conducted military drill, and talked of overthrowing the dictatorship. In January 1935 Long's militia dispersed the Square Dealers in an abortive engagement at the Baton Rouge airport. Later in the year, when the anti-Long leaders met secretly in a New Orleans hotel, they could only say to each other despairingly, "I wish somebody would kill the son of a bitch."

Nothing helped Long more than the bankruptcy of his opposition. It included many brave and gallant individuals; but, as an organized political force, it seemed only the old oligarchy again—hardly more honest than Long himself, and far more boring, stupid, and reactionary. "Part of our failure," Hodding Carter wrote years later, "arose from an unwillingness to approve any Long-sponsored proposal for change, regardless of its merits. We offered none of our own except a plea for democratic rule, and that sounded hollow in contrast." But Carter could rightly add, "Yet, at the end, it became the one thing of importance in Louisiana."

Long thus built his kingdom—the nearest approach to a totalitarian state the American republic had ever seen. And Louisiana was only the beginning. Now that Frank-lin De-La-No Roo-Se-Velt (as he called him, giving unctuous emphasis to each syllable of the hated name) had turned out to be a stooge of the bankers, the Kingfish was out to save all America.

The ideological basis for his national movement lay deep in Long's experience—back to the letter to the *New Orleans Item* in 1918, farther back to the poor white Populism of Winn Parish ("Didn't Abe Lincoln free the niggers and not give the planters a dime?" his father said. "Why shouldn't the white slaves be freed?"), back to the twenty-fifth chapter of Leviticus, the year of jubilee, when liberty would be proclaimed throughout all the land unto all inhabitants thereof, and all property would be redistributed, and every man would be returned unto his possession, and no man would oppress another.

As Long looked at America, he conceived the maldistribution of wealth to be the cause of all social and economic distress. "When one man decides he must have more goods to wear for himself and his family than any other ninety-nine people, then the condition results that instead of one hundred people sharing the things that are on earth for one hundred people, that one man, through his gluttonous greed, takes over ninety-nine parts for himself and leaves one part for the ninety-nine."

But one man could not eat the food intended for ninety-nine people, nor wear the clothes, nor live in the houses. And, as the rich grew richer and the poor poorer, the middle class was threatened with extinction. "Where is the middle class today?" Long asked in 1933. "Where is the corner groceryman, about whom President Roosevelt speaks? He is gone or going. Where is the corner druggist? He is gone or going. Where is the banker of moderate means? He is vanishing. . . . The middle class today cannot pay the debts they owe and come out alive. In other words, the middle class is no more." Its only hope of resurrection, Long suggested, was to follow him.

His actual program underwent a succession of versions. The share-the-wealth resolution of 1932 proposed that the government take by taxation all income over $1 million and all inheritances over $5 million. In 1933 he added a capital levy which would reduce all fortunes to somewhere around $3 million. By 1934 he was emphasizing the result more than the method: government would furnish every American family with a "homestead allowance" of at least $5,000 and an annual income of at least $2,000. There were, in addition, fringe benefits. Hours of labor would be limited. Agricultural production and consumption would be balanced through government storage and the control of planting. Everyone over sixty would receive an "adequate" pension (this was first to be $30 a month, but the competition of Dr. Townsend changed that; as Gerald L. K. Smith, the director of Long's movement, explained, "We decided to put in the word 'adequate' and let every man name his own figure. This attracted a lot of Townsendites to us"). Boys and girls of ability would receive a college education at government expense. And no one need worry about money; "taxes off the big fortunes at the top will supply plenty of money without hurting anybody."

Share-the-wealth was, in short, a hillbilly's paradise—$5,000 capital endowment without work, a radio, washing machine, and automobile in every home. It was the Snopeses' dream come true. It had almost no other quality. While Coughlin and Townsend at least went through the motions of economic analysis, Long rested his case on rhetoric and the Scriptures. "I never read a line of Marx or Henry George or any of them economists," he once said. "It's all in the law of God." In 1935 he was still using the same statistics he had used in 1918. He wildly overestimated what the government would gain from confiscation; he underestimated the number of families who would need to have their income jacked up to the $5,000 limit; he ignored the problems involved in redistributing nonmonetary wealth; and he showed little interest in such a mundane issue as economic recovery.

And yet, as economic fantasy, it produced a response. Wealth *was* un-fairly distributed. Many of the poor were consumed with envy and rancor. The New Deal seemed awfully complicated and, to some, very far away. Encouraged, the Kingfish decided in January 1934 to convert his aspiration into a crusade. He launched the Share Our Wealth Society and called on Americans everywhere to organize local chapters. "Be prepared for the slurs and snickers of some high ups," he warned. ". . . Be on your guard for some smart aleck tool of the interests to come in and ask questions. . . . To hell with the ridicule of the wise street corner politician! . . . Who cares what consequences may come following the mandates of the Lord, of the Pilgrims, of Jefferson, Webster and Lincoln? He who falls in this fight falls in the radiance of the future."

Gerald L. K. Smith, his chief assistant in the movement, was a fundamentalist preacher and political sensationalist who, a year before, had been writing William Dudley Pelley offering to set up "the first Silver Shirt storm troop in America." But he shifted quickly enough to Long, whom he worshipped (or did when Huey was alive; Smith, writing his spiritual autobiography in 1952, noted that he had experienced a "call" in 1933, but did not mention the name of the caller). "Huey Long," said Smith, "is a superman. I actually believe that he can do as much in one day as any ten men." To Raymond Swing, Smith explained Louisiana democracy as "the dictatorship of the surgical theater. The surgeon is recognized as being in charge because he knows. Everyone defers to him for that reason only. . . . They are not servile, they believe in the surgeon. They realize he is working for the welfare of the patient." "No great movement has ever succeeded," Smith once said, "unless it has deified some one man. The Share-the-Wealth movement consciously deified Huey P. Long."

Smith was, if possible, a greater spellbinder than Huey himself. On the platform, his mighty voice sounded for blocks. Sweat stained his blue shirt and streamed down his face, his arms flailed in the air while he denounced the Kingfish's foes as "dirty, thieving drunkards" or, in a swift change of pace, invoked Christ on the Cross. A favorite Smith device was to ask his audience: "All of you that ain't got *four* suits of clothes raise your two hands." As arms shot up, he would ask again, "Three suits?—two suits?" Then, a sob in his voice: "Not even two suits of clothes! Oh, my brethren, J. P. Morgan has two suits of clothes. He has a hundred times two suits of clothes." He could continue in this vein for two hours. "Share, brothers, share," he would conclude, "and don't let those white-livered skunks laugh at you." From the crowd would come a chorus of "Amens" as they surged forward to sign up for Share Our Wealth. H. L. Mencken, a connoisseur of oratory, pronounced Smith more impressive than Bryan. Throw together, Mencken said, "a flashing eye, a hairy chest, a rubescent complexion, large fists, a voice both loud and mellow, terrifying and reassuring, *sforzando* and *pizzicato,* and finally, an unearthly capacity for distending the superficial blood vessels of his temples and neck, as if they were biceps—and you have the makings of a boob-bumper worth going miles to see."

By July 1935 Smith claimed seven million adherents for Share Our Wealth. This was wild exaggeration, but there could be no question that Long was having an impact. Early in 1935 Dan Tobin of the Teamsters expressed his concern to Louis Howe about the increase in Long's popularity. "I have several letters from our members," he said, "most of them decent and honest fellows inquiring about and asking me if they should proceed to organize clubs." And Louis Howe, passing on Tobin's letter along with a letter from a Montana banker describing Long as "the man we thought you were when we voted for you," said to Roosevelt, "It is symptoms like this I think we should watch very carefully."

As for Huey, he saw his movement more and more as the alternative to the major parties. The Democrats and Republicans, he said, reminded him of the patent-medicine vendor with two bottles, one marked High Popalorum, the other Low Popahirum. When asked the difference, the vendor explained that High Popalorum was made by taking the bark off the tree from the ground up and Low Popahirum, by taking the bark off the tree from the top down. "And these days the only difference between the two party leaders in Congress that I can see is that the Republican leaders are skinning the people from the ankle up, and the Democratic leaders are taking off the hide from the ear down. Skin 'em up or skin 'em down, but skin 'em!"

More and more people sang Huey's song:

> Ev'ry man a king, ev'ry man a king,
> For you can be a millionaire
> But there's something belonging to others.
> There's enough for all people to share.
> When it's sunny June and December too,
> Or in the winter time or spring
> There'll be peace without end
> Ev'ry neighbor a friend
> With ev'ry man a king.

At the beginning of 1935, in his forty-second year, Long gave off a sense of destiny. Would there be a third party in 1936? "Sure to be. And I think we will sweep the country." Foreign visitors found him impressive, though unattractive. Rebecca West detected the steely intelligence behind the Mardi Gras mask of his conversation: "He is the most formidable kind of brer fox, the self-abnegating kind that will profess ignorance, who will check his dignity with his hat if he can serve his plans by buffoonery." She said later, "In his vitality and his repulsiveness he was very like Laval." He reminded H. G. Wells of "a Winston Churchill who has never been at Harrow."

Yet the nature of this destiny remained obscure, even to him. All he had was a sense of crisis and of opportunity. Once during the Hundred Days he had said to a group in the Senate cloakroom, "Men, it will not be long until there will be a mob assembling here to hang Senators from the rafters of the Senate. I have to determine whether I will stay and be hung with you, or go out and lead the mob." ("That statement," Senator Richard B. Russell reported later, "evoked very little laughter.") Was he a demagogue? "There are all kinds of demagogues," he said. "Some deceive the people in the interests of the lords and masters of creation, the Rockefellers and the Morgans. Some of them deceive the people in their own interests." He often said, with his impish grin, "What this country needs is a dictator." But he also said, "I don't believe in dictatorships, all these Hitlers and Mussolinis. They don't belong in our American life. And Roosevelt is a bigger dictator than any." Then again: "There is no dictatorship in Louisiana. There is a perfect democracy there, and when you have a perfect democracy it is pretty hard to tell it from a dictatorship." He told a gullible interviewer from the *New Republic,* "It's all in Plato. You know—the Greek philosopher. I hadn't read Plato before I wrote my material on the 'Share the Wealth' movement, and when I did read Plato afterwards, I found I had said almost exactly the same things. I felt as if I had written Plato's 'Republic' myself."

In 1935 some people wondered whether Long was the first serious American fascist. Long himself, when George Sokolsky asked him about it, laughed it off: "Fine. I'm Mussolini and Hitler rolled in one. Mussolini gave them castor oil; I'll give them tabasco, and then they'll like Louisiana." But he was no Hitler or Mussolini. He had no ideological preoccupations; he never said, "When the United States gets fascism it will call it anti-fascism," nor was he likely to think in such terms. Read *Mein Kampf,* and one sees a man possessed by a demonic dream which he must follow until he can purge all evil from the world. Read *Every Man A King,* and one finds a folksy and rather conventional chronicle of political success. Read Long's *My First Days in the White House,* ghost-written by a Hearst reporter in 1935, and one has a complacent picture of painless triumph, with Rockefeller, Mellon and the du Ponts backing President Long in his project of sharing the wealth (the book did have one engaging impudence: in choosing his cabinet, Long appointed as his Secretary of the Navy Franklin D. Roosevelt). Long's political fantasies had no tensions, no conflicts, except of the most banal kind, no heroism or sacrifice, no compelling myths of class or race or nation.

He had no overriding social vision. According to Raymond Daniell, who covered him for the *New York Times,* he did believe in Share Our Wealth "with all his heart"; but it was as a technique of political self-aggrandizement, not as a gospel of social reconstruction. Part traveling salesman, part confidence man, part gang leader, he had at most a crude will toward personal power. He had no doubt about becoming President: the only question was whether it was to be in 1936 or 1940. He told Forrest Davis that he planned to destroy both major parties, organize a single party of his own, and serve four terms. To Daniell he disclosed "the whole scheme by which he hoped to establish himself as the dictator of this country." His hero was Frederick the Great, and he no doubt saw himself as a kind of Frederick the Great from the piney woods. ("He was the greatest son of a bitch who ever lived. 'You can't take Vienna, Your Majesty. The world won't stand for it,' his nitwit ambassadors said. 'The hell I can't,' said old Fred, 'my soldiers will take Vienna and my professors at Heidelberg will explain the reasons why!' Hell, I've got a university down in Louisiana that cost me $15,000,000, that can tell you why I do like I do.")

At bottom, Huey Long resembled, not a Hitler or a Mussolini, but a Latin American dictator, a Vargas or a Perón. Louisiana was in many respects a colonial region, an underdeveloped area; its Creole traditions gave it an almost Latin American character. Like Vargas and Perón, Long was in revolt against economic colonialism, against the oligarchy, against the smug and antiquated past; like them, he stood in a muddled way for economic modernization and social justice; like them, he was most threatened by his own arrogance and cupidity, his weakness for soft living and his rage for personal power.

And, like them, he could never stop. "I was born into politics," he once said, "a wedded man, with a storm for my bride." A man of violence, he generated an atmosphere of violence. Early in 1935 Mason Spencer, one of Long's last foes still on his feet in the Louisiana legislature, sent the Kingfish a solemn warning.

"I am not gifted with second sight," Spencer said. "Nor did I see a spot of blood on the moon last night.

"But I can see blood on the polished floor of this Capitol.

"For if you ride this thing through, you will travel with the white horse of death."

14
Allan P. Sindler: One Man
Wore the Crown

A political scientist, Allan Sindler complains that "the flamboyant figure of Huey Long, the Louisiana Kingfish, has bedazzled commentators who otherwise would have attempted to examine, more or less systematically, the underlying structure and process of state politics." [1] *Sindler argues that students who analyze Louisiana politics by focusing on Long implicitly adopt a "Great Man" view of politics that necessarily clouds their understanding of the unique political milieu from which he emerged. By analyzing the rise and dominance of Long in the broad framework of a continuing movement of class protest having origins in nineteenth-century Louisiana and extending beyond his death in 1935, Sindler seeks to avoid one-dimensional judgments that polarize toward one-man rule in the name of the people or oligarchic rule in the name of good government. Sindler contends that the popular assessment of Long as just another Southern demagogue, albeit a highly successful one, begs the crucial question of the relationship of means to ends, for irrationality or emotionality is a constant factor in all mass appeals and emotionalism in politics carries a neutral value. "From the perspective of the political leader," Sindler observes, "the difference lies in the desire to be a leader of the people in contrast to the desire to lead the people somewhere."*

To great numbers of Louisianians, Huey Long was either the salvation or the ruination of Louisiana. It is not surprising, therefore, that most judgments of the Kingfish, whether derived from adulation or detestation, are essentially one-dimensional. A more accurate view of Huey must stress the mixture of types he actually was and the many-sided impact of his reign on succeeding state politics. The importance of a full understanding of Long scarcely can be exaggerated, for to

[1] From Allan P. Sindler, *Huey Long's Louisiana: State Politics, 1920–52* (Baltimore: The Johns Hopkins Press, 1956), pp. 98–116. Reprinted by permission of the Johns Hopkins Press. Footnotes have been omitted for reasons of space.

him must be attributed much of the form and content of recent Louisiana politics through 1952.

Temperament and Tactics

Even those who deplored his actions and objectives recognized in the Kingfish a man of unusual talents. Raymond Moley has written that his feeling, on Long's death, ". . . was a sense of tragedy—a tragedy of wasted talent. . . . He had, combined with a remarkable capacity for hard, intellectual labor, an extraordinarily powerful, resourceful, clear and retentive mind, an instrument such as is given to very few men. No one can tell what services he could have rendered his state and nation had he chosen to use that mind well." Will Percy, the vigorous Mississippi planter spokesman, put the same thought less elegantly, "[Huey Long] was . . . a moral idiot of genius."

Too much of the daringness and imaginativeness which Huey brought to his career was devoted to devising ways to punish his political foes. Long understated the streak of vengefulness in his nature when he observed in his autobiography, "Once disappointed over a political undertaking, I could never cast it from my mind." His rudeness and his predilection for engaging in personal abuse, both stemming from his egocentricity, merited the observation that ". . . Huey P. Long . . . would not have been allowed to live a week if the code duello had still been in force."

Yet the vilification and occasional crucifixion of his political adversaries were part of that intense personalization of politics by which Huey was able to erect and maintain a highly personal dictatorship. Many Louisianians idolized Long: some of the Kingfish's devoted Catholic followers, for example, unofficially canonized him. The state presented a statue of Huey as one of its two great sons entitled to recognition in Statuary Hall in Washington, purchased Long's New Orleans home for a museum, and made his birthday a legal holiday. By capitalizing on the political potency of Long's name, his successors in 1936 were able to retain the loyalty of his following while at the same time to mock his memory by enacting a state sales tax and by burying Share-Our-Wealth. In his campaigns for office following Huey's death, brother Earl always has had to explain away the accusations he had made against Huey in the 1932 Senate investigation of Overton's election.

The emotional loyalties which Huey Long aroused, in Louisiana and in the nation, reflected the fact that, at his oratorical best, Huey expressed the yearnings of the "have-nots" for a material level of living consonant with the equality of citizens proclaimed in the Constitution. In the midst of the depression, here was a homely philosopher who applied, in the vernacular of the uneducated man, the verities of the Bible and the American Constitution to the terrifying and bewildering economic problems of the day. Here was a dedicated leader for the "forgotten men." From their viewpoint, it was a man of courage and sincerity, not a petty, vindictive tyrant, who informed his colleagues in the Senate on March 5, 1935,

> Mr. President, I am not undertaking to answer the charge that I am ignorant. It is true. I am an ignorant man. I have had no college education. I have not even had a high-school education. But the thing that takes me far in politics is that I do not have to color what comes into my mind and into my heart. I say it unvarnished. I say it without veneer. I know the hearts of the people because I have not colored my own. I know when I am right in my own conscience. I do not talk one way in the cloakroom and another way out here. I do not talk one way back there in the hills of Louisiana and another way here in the Senate. I have one language. Ignorant as it is, it is the universal language of the sphere in which I operate. Its simplicity gains pardon for my lack of letters and education.
>
> Nonetheless my voice will be the same as it has been. Patronage will not change it. Fear will not change it. Persecution will not change it. It cannot be changed while people suffer. The only way it can be changed is to make the lives of these people decent and respectable. No one will ever hear political opposition out of me when that is done.

That Huey could alternate between vindictiveness and disarming rusticity testified to his capacity to adapt skillfully his tactics to his objective and his audience. Particularly noteworthy was his deliberate exploitation of a comic role through which he sought favorable press attention to enhance his class leadership and to obscure the uglier aspects of his regime. Huey observed of his sobriquet, "Kingfish," derived from "Kingfish of the Mystic Knights of the Sea" from the "Amos and Andy" radio show, that "it has served to substitute gaiety for some of the tragedy of politics." Outrageous burlesque, however, also was a most useful disguise for grim purpose. The Sands Point incident marred an otherwise consistent pattern of the Kingfish basking in the warmth of friendly national laughter, his antics successful in disarming, not repelling, most people.

Back home in Louisiana, however, in view of the events of state politics, Long's pose of comic relief was a bit difficult to sustain. The press in Louisiana, therefore, was raped rather than seduced. By ridiculing the urban press as biased spokesmen for "the interests," Long not only minimized the impact of their anti-Longism but also made them suspect as prejudiced reporters of the political news of the day. The country parish weekly press supported the Long faction, either willingly or because they were in too precarious a financial position to withstand intimidation by the state administration. Not content with undermining the influence of the daily newspapers and with controlling the weekly press, Long spread the gospel through his own organ, the *Progress*, "the most cheerfully venomous regular publication in the nation." For those special occasions when Long's viewpoint had to be communicated swiftly to all parts of the state, Huey perfected an efficient system of direct distribution of circulars which involved the use of state printing equipment, the state highway police, and factional leaders in the parishes. Long's treatment of the Louisiana press helped explain his creation of a dictatorship based upon mass loyalty to his person. As Huey liked to boast, "When I lie from the stump, I lie big, because no matter what the newspapers say, 90 per cent of the people will believe me."

Long applied a similar heavy hand, for the most part, in solving the troublesome problem of political finances. Huey's power and magnetism attracted the backing of some wealthy adventurers and businessmen, most prominent of whom was Robert S. Maestri, appointed by Huey as Commissioner of Conservation and by Huey's heirs as Mayor of New Orleans. Financial contributions also were forthcoming from the usual groups anxious to do business with the state, particularly since Huey's bent for power assured the partisan administration of many functions of government. Another important source of funds was suggested by the admission of Seymour Weiss that commissions from Louisiana highway surety bonds were held for the benefit of the Long political machine. The public boast of the Long forces that theirs was a people's movement applied quite clearly to the raising of campaign funds. Salary deductions and forced subscriptions to the *Progress* were imposed upon public employees and justified as "a legitimate and honorable way of raising funds from people who owe their jobs to the administration and who would have nothing otherwise. . . ." Besides, averred the Longites, was it preferable to rely upon big business for the money necessary to win elections?

On balance, it was the brazenness of Long's tactics more than any other feature of his dictatorship which distinguished his rule from the practices of other American political bosses. The following comment, accurate so far as it goes, misses entirely the significance of Huey's rather unique combination of retention of mass appeal while in open pursuit of a concentration of personal power. "His [Long's] political methods, as developed in Louisiana, are the methods of orthodox American politics of the machine school, plus a little gaudy drama. When he takes personal command of the Louisiana Legislature and of its committee hearings, shouts down opposition, drives through bills that nobody has read, and plays the legislature like a pack of cards, he is only doing a little more openly what many another political boss has done more quietly over his office-telephone." It would have been better for Louisiana if Long had been either the old-fashioned despot who dispensed with the Legislature, the courts, and the ballot box or the hidden boss who pulled the strings via his office telephone. Either way would have been less demoralizing to Louisianians than Long's version of absolute power, which was lawlessness, not merely legally entrenched but highly visible and candid in its operation and enjoying continued popular endorsement. These circumstances suggest the pertinence of the story of Huey P. Long to those who are concerned about the capacity of constitutional democracy to endure.

A Spotty Record of Performance

An objective evaluation of Huey's record of highway expansion, doubtless his most publicized achievement, must entertain some doubts which would be of little concern to adulatory Longites. Governor Sanders deserves some credit for fathering the good-roads movement in the state through education of the public before Huey Long entered the scene, however inadequate Sanders' financial program was in meeting his own objective. Second, unpublicized testimony in connection with the Senate subcommittee's investigation into Overton's election suggests that Huey was an inconstant proponent of free bridges. Dudley L. Guilbeau, a former member of the Louisiana Highway Commission, testified that Overton had urged Long to support a program of seven toll bridges to be constructed by the Nashville Bridge Company, Overton's client. Governor Allen admitted that Huey had asked him to approve that program, but in the face of opposition from Allen and the Highway Commission, Huey had withdrawn his support. Third, the magnitude of Huey's road expenditures should be noted: from 1928 to 1936, about one hundred million dollars were collected by the state and some ninety-six million dollars of road bonds issued. In 1936, four cents of the five-cent gasoline tax were allocated to the payment of the highway debt, of which only eight million dollars had been retired by that year. Finally, Huey's concentration, intentionally or otherwise, on highway construction as distinct from road maintenance yielded him a maximum of political benefit and his successors a maximum of highway repair bills.

To the Louisiana citizen familiar with road conditions in the state before Long, the foregoing qualifications may appear as mere quibbles. Perhaps they are. In 1928, with a two-cent state gas tax, road district property tax funds, and federal aid, Louisiana had 296 miles of concrete roads, 35 miles of asphalt roads, and 5,728 miles of gravel roads. Only three major bridges were included within the state highway system. By the close of 1935, after a total expenditure of $133,000,000, based on a five-cent gas tax of which four cents was bonded, Louisiana had 2,446 miles of concrete roads, 1,308 miles of asphalt, and 9,629 miles of gravel roads under state maintenance. Over forty major bridges were within the state highway system. Even the hostile New Orleans press admitted in 1936, "The hard-surfaced roads reach sixty-one of the sixty-four parish seats . . . and good gravel and shell roads connect with the missing three pending the completion of hard-surfacing to them. Nearly every community in the state which is not on a hard-surfaced road is on a graveled road, and the farmers' road program, being carried out with state and federal funds, is bringing all-weather roads to the comparatively small number now without them." It was on the basis of his record, then, that Long snarled in reply to a query about graft in Louisiana, "We got the roads in Louisiana, haven't we? In some states they only have the graft."

Huey turned in a contradictory performance in his other major publicized accomplishment, public education. In the field of higher education, credit for arousing public interest in an expanded state university must be assigned again to predecessors of Long, namely Governor Parker and Colonel Boyd, President of Louisiana State University. Long, on the other hand, deserves exclusive recognition for his drive on adult illiteracy and for his free textbook program. However, while state expenditures for education climbed to more than 50 per cent of total school revenues by 1936, the proportion of total state expenses allocated to education declined from 14.4 per cent under Simpson to 9.7 per cent under Long and 12.2 per cent under Allen. Teachers' salaries in Louisiana remained low, and only long-time State Superintendent of Education Harris prevented Huey from intimidating teachers through the State Budget Committee. Huey showered material benefits on "his" State University, but some students were placed on the state payroll or on political scholarships, and although apparently a high degree of academic freedom existed, its maintenance was conditional upon the whimsical good humor of the Kingfish.

Other significant gaps in Huey's record are worth noting briefly. Share-Our-Wealth notwithstanding, Long's consumer taxes on gasoline and cigarettes were high, and his 1934 income tax law provided for only a small spread in the tax rates for lower and upper income brackets. Huey's sorry labor record typed him, at best, a rural liberal. Long enacted no pro-labor law of note, not even relative to a strengthened workmen's compensation system which he had urged when a young lawyer in 1917. Shrimp cannery supporters of the Kingfish killed a bill setting maximum hours for female workers. Long is on record as having said to a labor delegation, "The prevailing wage is as low as we can get men to take it," and in 1930 he revived the practice of farming out state prisoners at Angola to private contractors. Long's coolness toward the idea of old-age pensions has been discussed earlier; he also weakened the mothers' pension law and refused to appropriate funds for its operations during the depression. In his control of patronage Long spared not even the welfare institutions, which were so sacred to him as a candidate in 1924 and 1928. And, while Huey enforced the antigambling laws in the selective manner of most Louisiana governors, he had the dubious distinction of having invited Frank Costello to set up slot machine operations in the state. As a final point, it might be noted that Long's benefits were costly: in 1935, state revenues from some forty-five taxes, many of them burdensome nuisance levies, were $38,000,000, an increase of 75 per cent over 1927 revenues, and Louisiana had the second highest per capita state debt in the nation.

The validity of the many charges of personal corruption leveled against Long, while highly relevant to a judgment of his record, for obvious reasons is impossible to determine on the basis of public information. Among the more authoritative accusations is that of Elmer Irey, who labeled Long, on the basis of his information as head of the Internal Revenue, as the "greatest 'confidence' man in the century," and stated that the federal government was on the eve of a tax prosecution case against Huey when he was assassinated. Irey made no mention of the source of Huey's money, but two of Huey's brothers publicly charged him with selling out to the business interests he attacked from the stump. Brother Earl alleged that Huey personally had accepted a $10,000 bribe from a utilities executive in late 1927. Brother Julius testified at the Overton hearings, "As a candidate for Governor the first time [1924], Huey Long received his principal financial support from the Southwestern Gas and Electric Company and their allied interests. . . ." All in all, sadly concluded Julius, "the trust could not have a better agent than Huey Long. . . . They could not get a man that would stand hitched better." While such sell-outs by Southern lower-class leaders have not been uncommon, Huey's blanket denial rang true to his egocentric temperament. "Only stupid politicians take bribes. I'm my own boss. If I take a bribe, I accept a boss. There's no man living can tell me I must do this or that because some time in the past I put myself under peculiar obligations to him." Perhaps more to the point, the Kingfish's pursuit of money, as well as most of his other tactics, should be understood and evaluated in the larger terms of his ambitious quest for power.

What may be said of this uneven record of Long as class reformer? To some observers, Huey's policies stamped him as a precursor of the New Deal. Longite state Senator Ernest Clements asserted, "I believe Louisiana under the leadership of the late Huey P. Long pioneered America in social legislation. I believe the national pattern was taken from the social legislation enacted in the State of Louisiana." A case might be made that Long's espousal of Share-Our-Wealth caused Roosevelt to swerve to the left, but surely there was nothing in Huey's Louisiana program, except perhaps its remarkable political results, of which the New Deal was not already aware. Whether measured, then, against the New Deal or against his capacity to have the Legislature enact his policies, Long's achievements were less than spectacular.

In particular, Long's performance revealed an undue concentration on tangible and showy benefits at the expense of civic education and perhaps in ignorance of the deeper economic and social problems of his state and nation. One of Huey's stump speeches is instructive as to what "Longism" meant to its leader,

They tell you that you got to tear up Longism in Loozyanna. . . .
All right, my friends; go get you a bomb or some dynamite and blow
up that building yonder. Go out and tear up the concrete roads. Get
yourself some spades and shovels and scrape the gravel off them roads
we've graveled and let a rain come on them. That'll put 'em back like
they was before I come. Tear down the buildings I've built at the
University. Take the money away from the school boards that I've give
them to run your schools. And when your child starts out to school
tomorrow morning, call him back and snatch the free school books out of
his hand that Huey Long gave him. . . . Then you'll be rid of Longism
in this State and not till then."

A thorough program was carried through by Long in only one particular: the erection of a dictatorship. The rejoinder by the Long partisan
that Huey's life was snuffed out before the class fruits of the dictatorship
could be harvested will not stand examination. The simple and damning
answer is that no dictatorship would have been required to effectuate
an even more coherent and penetrating class program than that which
Long did perform. The guidestar of the Kingfish was politics, not service.

A Three-Dimensional Judgment of Huey Long

What may be termed the classic defense of the Kingfish was rendered by Senator Overton in his Memorial Address for Huey Long
delivered on the floor of the United States Senate on January 22,
1936. In that speech, Overton candidly recognized that "it has been
repeatedly contended by many of his critics that Senator Long rose
to political power by ruthless and unscrupulous methods." Overton
chose not to attempt denial of the truth of the charge but to blunt
its force by asserting that Long's methods had to be understood in the
context of "both the modern political history of Louisiana and the
political career of the man. . . ." The crux of the ensuing argument
was that the "ruthless warfare against Governor Long" conducted
by the discredited "political aristocracy" he had displaced, culminat-
ing in the 1929 impeachment effort, compelled Long, "in order to
save himself [and] his friends and associates from political annihila-
tion . . . to build and maintain an organization as ruthless perhaps,
as was the opposition." In short, Overton's defense was made largely
on relative grounds, with the "better elements" and the Choctaws
used as constant foils.

There was much of persuasive substance in Overton's hymn to the
memory of Huey. If, as has been argued here, the class reforms of
Long were limited both in scope and content, then the popular inflation of his reputation for liberalism commented strikingly on the
inadequacies of prior state administrations. That a majority of the
citizenry acquiesced in tyranny because of the benefits it yielded them
condemned the conservative predecessors of Huey far more than it

did the Kingfish. As Long liked to say, Louisiana had been suffering from a Tweedledum-Tweedledee administration: "one of 'em skinned you from the ankles up, the other from the neck down." Compared with past governors, Huey gave more to the people, and few of his followers looked, or apparently even cared, to see if he also took more for himself.

Perhaps that indifference of Louisiana citizens reflected their long acquaintance with malodorous political tactics. There were solid precedents for a Huey Long in the looting of Reconstructionists, the immorality of the Louisiana Lottery Company, and the maneuvers of the Choctaws. Shifting and cynical alliances among governors, the Ring, blocs of legislators, and courthouse groupings were traditional in state politics. And the urban press, roasted by Huey as partisan, indeed often was thoroughly partisan. Yet, whatever the similarities of some of Long's tactics to those of preceding governors, the fact remains that only Long erected a ruthless dictatorship. If his autocracy was not justified by reference to past politics or to his current commitment to realize a class program, then it could be justified only, as Overton had urged, by the strength and tactics of the anti-Longs. The Kingdom of the Kingfish, however, failed to pass that test.

The impeachment session of 1929 and the deadlocked session of 1930 were the high-water mark of anti-Long strength. From late 1930 on, Huey's torch flared ever brighter, while that of his opposition feebly flickered. A strange alliance of conservatives, malcontents, and those primarily disturbed by the increasing power of the Kingfish vainly sought to oppose effectively the kingdom that Huey built. "[Their] combined cries for good government made a dissonant chorus," and their continued unity was a function not of aggression but of survival. A minority to begin with, anti-Longs further limited their appeal by opposing indiscriminately any and all Longite measures, by harshly applying that extreme stand to determine friend from foe, and by refusing to offer reasonable alternatives to the class policies of Longism. In such post-1930 circumstances, political enemies of the Kingfish posed no real threat to his leadership and compelled no resort to dictatorship. It was Huey who chose not to be a democratic leader, to substitute compulsion for persuasion and to adopt domination in place of the give and take of constitutional politics. In a democracy, a minority faction without constructive program, popular appeal, or much access to the policy-making centers of government deserves compassion, not extirpation.

The fact of Huey's ruthless bossdom, admitted even by Overton, became virtually the single datum in the confirmed anti-Long's judgment of the Kingfish. Long, according to this view, was nothing but a neurotic seeker of power, a political racketeer who would have slashed his way to autocracy in any state. The inferences followed that the substance of Huey's policies did not necessarily reveal anything about the true nature of his class sympathies and that a meaningful analysis of Long should confine itself to the dissection of the techniques by which he achieved and wielded power.

To date there is not available, and perhaps there never will be available, the kinds of materials and data which would permit an assessment of the validity of the foregoing anti-Long judgment. In the opinion of this writer—and it remains only an opinion—it is highly likely that Long was possessed of deep proletarian sympathies. Those sympathies, however, became so enmeshed with a lust for power and with a determination to avenge every real or fancied personal grievance as to make futile any attempt to gauge the sincerity of his policies. It seems likely also that, far from being born with a scepter on his mind, Long did not plan much in advance, if at all, either the fact or the details of his dictatorship. Indeed, the Kingfish probably was not possessed of overweening ambition until late 1932, after Allen's and Roosevelt's elections, and coincident with the full impact of the national depression. Less speculatively, the anti-Long judgment under discussion was defective in that it adopted an "evil great man" approach to politics which conveniently divorced Huey from his Louisiana setting and thereby exonerated the anti-Longs from having contributed in any measure to the character of his regime.

The popular view of Huey Long dismisses him as little else but a highly successful member of the family of post-bellum Southern poor-white leaders loosely termed demagogues. What, then, is a demagogue? The term usually refers to a rider of discontent, one who propounds quack remedies insincerely for personal or political gain. To uncover a demagogue, the observer is supposed to pay particular attention to irrational appeals, attempts to sway emotions, attention-getting stunts and so forth. Such criteria, it may be suggested, are inadequate and misleading and have made of the term a subjective epithet to be used with abandon against the politicians one dislikes.

Irrationality, or emotionality, is a constant factor in all mass appeals. The simplification and dramatization of complex issues are essential to a democratic politics which strives to secure a continuing consent to governmental decisions through popular participation in or understanding of public actions. The restriction of demagogy to "insincere" advocates likewise provides no firm measurement. Few will deny that most politicians, indeed, most human beings, possess and act upon personal ambition in addition to principles. And what of the zealous bigot who holds to undemocratic beliefs with the tenacity of a fanatic? An unbiased application of these popularized standards of demagogy, then, would lead to the conclusion that demagogy is an inherent part of all political appeals and a tactic of most politicians.

There is a more useful standard by which to distinguish between types of political leadership. "The politician says: 'I will give you what you want.' The statesman says: 'What you think you want is this. What it is possible for you to get is that. What you really want, therefore, is the following.' . . . The politician, in brief, accepts unregenerate desire at its face value and either fulfills it or perpetrates a fraud; the statesman re-educates desire by confronting it with the reality, and so makes possible an enduring adjustment of interests within the community." From the perspective of the political leader, the difference lies in the desire to be a leader of the people in contrast to the desire to lead the people somewhere. Every politician must have some broader cause to serve if his action is to have inner strength.

Within this broader category of demagogy as distinguished from statesmanship, emotionalism in politics has a neutral value. Since irrationality is a universal theme of politics it is morally neutral, and must be judged in terms of its consequences, by the kinds of emotional responses elicited. Assume the initial irrationality of a complaint. It is a longing, a feeling, an unconscious grievance or felt tension, an aggressive frustration. To some extent the reformer, the revolutionary or the leader sublimates and socializes the complaint, to some degree he intellectualizes the complaint to a higher plane of awareness, and calls for a revision of some part of the social, economic, or political framework as the necessary solution. The demagogue personifies the complaint, intensifies the original irrational elements or merely relieves tension by expressing feeling. By so doing, he seduces his followers into an emotional attachment to his person which effectively blocks any group awareness of either the real sources of their discontents or the real areas of solution.

There was much in Huey Long's career which qualified him for inclusion within the category of "demagogue" as here redefined. But there were other aspects of Long's record and impact which suggest that, if the judgment of demagogue is retained, Long should be credited with having been one of the most useful and effective demagogues produced by the new South.

Unlike Mississippi's Bilbo and South Carolina's Ben Tillman, Georgia's Tom Watson and Eugene Talmadge, Huey Long eschewed "nigger-baiting," the most common tactic of Southern demagogues. While Long was no active friend of the Negro in terms of helpful legislation, he did not echo Tillman's call for repeal of the Fourteenth Amendment nor Bilbo's plan for the mass emigration of Negroes to Liberia. His Share-Our-Wealth movement erected no racial barriers, not even in Louisiana, and his stump speeches customarily made no reference to the race issue. Indeed, Long himself was on occasion the victim of racial alarums inspired by the opposition, as in the case of poll tax repeal in 1934. In similar fashion, Long did not follow the lead of Tom-Tom Heflin of Alabama in his baiting of the Pope, though the bi-religious setting of Louisiana gave the Kingfish little choice on the matter.

In company with other poor-white leaders, though, Huey did bait corporations and urbanites, the "better elements" and the professional politicians, marking him as a legitimate heir of the suppressed dirt-farmer movements of the nineteenth century. Indeed, as one astute student of Southern history has argued: ". . . perhaps these despised 'upstarts' [rural demagogues], as spokesmen of the agrarian interests, more nearly represented a continuation of the political and economic ideas of the ante-bellum South than did the 'developers of resources,' who were engaged in forming a New South." Crushed as Populists and un-touched by the urban progressivism of Wilson, lower-class rural whites in Louisiana found themselves voiceless until the entry of Huey Long into state politics.

The mere presence in office of the vitriolic Kingfish gave an outlet to the accumulated resentments of the dirt-farmer community. Long's castigation, for example, of "Turkey-Head" Walmsley, "Feather-Duster" Ransdell, "Donny-boy" Ewing, and "Prince" Franklin Roosevelt fulfilled beyond the wildest of expectations the symbolic role required of him by his class leadership. His supporters could applaud vicariously as the Kingfish guffawed and "cut the Big Boys down to size," for "it was as if they themselves had crashed the headlines."

It was the fact that Huey went beyond serving only or primarily as a catharsis for his following that distinguished him from many another Southern demagogue. Pappy O'Daniel and Eugene Talmadge also claimed to be neo-Populist rebels, only to effectuate opposite policies. Talmadge jettisoned the New Deal because it went too far; Long osten-sibly because it did not go far enough. Long may have been, as his bitter foe Sanders characterized him, "a pigmy disciple of radicalism," but his free-spending and heavy-taxing ways strongly contrasted with political leadership elsewhere in the South. The brazen dictatorship which Huey constructed and ran should not hide his substantial accomplishment of redeeming some of his promises of lower-class benefits.

By keeping at least partial faith with his supporters when in office, Long provoked a rural lower-class protest which exceeded that of Popu-lism in intensity and durability. The fury and substance of Longism stimulated the interest and participation of masses of whites, and made them aware of the relevance of state politics to the settlement of their demands. Huey captured in his state the hitherto nonvoting elements which the New Deal had attracted on a national scale. Such a change in the composition of the electorate by itself heralded a different con-tent of politics than in the pre-Long days.

More crucially, Longism itself set both the form and content of sub-sequent politics. The distracting appeals of localism and personality common to multifactionalism were reduced to minimal proportions as the bulk of voters affiliated themselves, in a close approximation to a two-party system, with the two major factions, Long and anti-Long.

Candidates for state offices and many of the candidates for Congress and for parish and local offices publicly proclaimed their loyalty to one or the other faction. Factional lines within the state Legislature became firmly drawn; when combined with the customary majority support for the incumbent administration, this gave to Louisiana governors a control over legislation unequalled in most other Southern states. Huey's heavy-handed injection of realism into the content of state politics was carried forward by brother Earl so that the Long forces gained a continuity of headship normally denied to personal factions.

Longism thus was no flashing meteor of Populism, brilliant but transient. It aroused the politically quiescent have-nots and showed them unforgettably the total victory that was theirs for the balloting. It unified the fragments of politics—expectations, candidates, institutions —by means of one deeply felt adherence, pro- or anti-Longism. It came closer to the salient issues of the day than had a raft of "good government" predecessors of Huey. The policy impact of Longism was strikingly attested to in the state office campaign of 1940, when the anti-Longs, despite the involvement of the Longites in the corruption of the "Scandals," saw fit to pledge liberal measures which, in toto, made Huey's performance eight years earlier appear conservative. The persistence of the factional loyalists and the issues created by the Kingfish thus accounted in large part for the content and form of post-Huey politics in Louisiana.

It is no small entry on the credit side of Huey's ledger to conclude that the pervasiveness, durability, and substantive meaning of recent Louisiana bifactionalism owe much to his charismatic demagogy. In terms of total judgment, however, the immorality of his regime, neither deniable nor justifiable, tips the scales in the opposite direction. By his wholesale bribery of some communities and his ruthless raping of others, Long promoted cynicism in all as to the legitimacy of constitutionalism and its values. The anti-Longs were provoked to violence, the Longites to a countenancing of corruption and dictatorship. As defiantly phrased by Longite disciple Ellender, "I repeat, we had neither a dictator nor dictatorship in Louisiana. If dictatorship in Louisiana, such as was charged to Huey Long, will give to the people of our nation what it gave to the people of my native state, then I am for such a dictatorship." Widespread popular acceptance of the principle that the ends justify all means thus was Huey Long's morally enervating legacy.

Ironically, then, in the final analysis the overriding factor in the judgment of Long becomes the hollow anti-Long battle-cry of "decency versus degradation." Yet surely the moral cost of pre-Huey state government also had been too high. Big business, the planters, and the Choctaws also had looked upon the forms and processes of government as manipulatable means to a desired selfish end. Neither pro- or anti-Longs, in truth, had a high regard for the value of constitutional machinery.

The Kingfish's abuse of democratic forms was but the more dramatic and conspicuous, since aggressive changes in the status quo required a greater co-ordination of state institutions than did conservative inaction. A plague on both their houses then. Neither upper-class rule before Huey nor one-man rule by Huey in the name of the lower classes can be adjudged satisfactory substitutes for vigorous democracy.

Afterword: The Enigma
of Huey Long

It is not our purpose here to attempt a brief summation or conclusion that suggests an emergent historical consensus. Were such a task not impossible, it would clearly be undesirable, for each generation is impelled to rewrite its own history according to its ideological predispositions and its peculiar circumstances. Further, students of history within any given generation will perforce interpret differently a common body of evidence because differing assumptions about the nature of man and society must logically lead to divergent interpretations.

Even so, we are not thereby condemned to total and permanent disarray, for a limited area of consensus has already emerged to form a minimal but important assessment that is not seriously in dispute. Clearly, no close student of Long takes seriously his dissembling professions of naive hillbilly ignorance. Critics and partisans alike remain awed by the powers of his mind and question only the uses to which it was put. Few dispute that Huey's political intuition was both keenly sensitive and genuinely creative; whether or not he was a statesman, he was an astute politican of the first magnitude. Similarly, the public record testifies undisputably to Long's talented recourse to demagogic appeals on the stump and to his erection of an unprecedentedly authoritarian regime—indeed, of a dictatorial, if not a totalitarian one, in Louisiana. There is a further area of agreement, however reluctant and qualified and even partially justified on the part of his defenders, that Long was possessed of an inclination toward vindictiveness and even ruthlessness that betrayed a taste for the sweetness of revenge.

But even Long's detractors concede that unlike the typical Southern demagogue with which he is so often invidiously compared, Huey Long was unique in largely shunning the common tactic of race-baiting and religious bigotry that was central to the appeal of the Bilboes and Heflins. Further, hindsight has led critics of the Kingfish largely to abandon the malevolent analogies to Hitler or to Stalin that had captured the imaginations of so many of Long's contemporary detractors. Finally, fair-minded historical critics are inclined to grant that part of the blame for whatever alleged evil flowed from Long's ascent must rest upon the shoulders of Louisiana's dominant conservatives, who for generations had ground the faces of the poor and had reaped the whirlwind.

Far less agreement obtains, however, concerning crucial questions of motivation and historical significance. What can we learn from Long's open contempt for the two-party system about the dynamics of the one-party system in the South? Were the accomplishments of which he boasted in Louisiana merely, as his critics have claimed, public monuments—erected in the manner of an Nkrumah or Sukarno? Was Long sincere in his professed selflessness and in his insistence that the Share Our Wealth program represented a realistic and workable solution to the depression? How significant and enduring was his contribution to American political life?

Our impatience with the interminable debate over Huey Long's appropriate label should not be interpreted as a conclusion that the debate itself is meaningless. To the contrary, is it not a compelling puzzle that Long's contemporaries could not decide whether to label him with a left term, like radical democrat, or a right term, like fascist? Indeed, the term "demagogue" itself is politically ambiguous, for the traditional Southern demagogues were both racists *and* reformers. And Huey Long was the least racist and the most effective reformer of them all. Why are the politics of left and right paradoxically so closely associated in the rural South?

Long's economic radicalism was clearly of a leftist democratic variety, and his career raises another compelling question: why has radical left-wing politics been such a hard road in America, and especially in the impoverished South? Consider the toll these heavy odds extracted from Huey Long. In order to overcome the almost unanimous opposition of the conservative mass media, Long had to establish his own newspapers and circular system. In order to overcome the crushing apathy of the lower classes, Long had to act a clown. In order to combat the massive financial advantages of the entrenched conservatives, Long had to establish a system of involuntary "deducts" from the paychecks of public employees. To be sure, Huey crushed the opposition ruthlessly, but the traditional Southern demagogues had made little imprint with their reforms, and the reformers themselves had traditionally sold out.

All this is not to suggest that Huey Long should be exonerated for his highhanded exploits, but rather to raise a broader question, the implications of which are quite contemporary and extend far beyond the biography of one extraordinary man. The conservatives attacked Long for having pandered to the ignorant masses, for having debauched republican due process with populist democracy. Their lament is as old as Juvenal's despairing cry that two things only do the people desire: bread and circuses. But when a moral cause fueled by long years of inequity and neglect confronts a rigid political structure, what are one's responsibilities? And when due process takes a beating, how should we apportion the burden of guilt?

These hard questions did not die with Huey Long. They were raised once again by the desegregation movement of the 1950s, and again by the student antidraft and antiwar movements of the 1960s. And the conservatives themselves raised them in the antisubversion movement led by another crusading senator, Joseph McCarthy of Wisconsin. So the sword cuts both ways. Americans of all political persuasions have historically demanded liberty and equality, but liberty and equality are often contradictory goals. By opting for equality, Huey Long inevitably enmeshed himself in this most ancient of American—and human— dilemmas. That he did not emerge from the fight unblemished or even, in the long run, triumphant, is not to say that he should not have tried.

Bibliographical Note

The career of Huey Long provides a dynamic focus for the study of local, state, regional, and national history during the first third of the twentieth century. Students of Louisiana, Southern, and national political and social life from the Progressive era through the Depression and the New Deal, as well as connoisseurs of biography, can profit from tracing and analyzing Long's ascent. The primary evidence for such inquiry is extensive, although it does not apparently include the traditional collection of personal manuscript evidence that is necessary for authoritative research. The Long family still controls whatever personal evidence Huey Long may have accumulated, but the archives of Louisiana State University has amassed fifty-seven volumes of Huey Long scrapbooks containing newspaper clippings and similar evidence covering the years 1923–1939.

Other useful public sources include the *Congressional Record* (Long spoke constantly and at considerable length in the Senate from 1931 through 1935, once filibustering for 15½ hours against a bill to extend the NRA); Louisiana and national newspapers (the *New York Times* index is especially useful); Long's own newspapers, the *Louisiana Progress* (1930–1932) and the *American Progress* (1933–1935); and his numerous campaign circulars. He published his autobiography, *Every Man A King* (New Orleans: National Book Co.), in 1933; and *My First Days in the White House* (Harrisburg, Pa.: Telegraph Press) was published posthumously in the fall of 1935. Long dictated the outlines of the latter book, which described how he would lead the nation out of the depression by directing an implausible coalition containing such financial and corporate giants as Rockefeller, Mellon, Ford, and the Du Ponts (with Hoover as Secretary of Commerce and Roosevelt as Secretary of the Navy!). The text was revised by his secretary, Earle Christenberry, and political reporter Ray Daniel of the *New York Times*. It was clearly designed as a presidential campaign tract and is useful primarily as an index of Long's ambitions and of his contempt for the two-party system.

Fortunately, the Long family cooperated with Louisiana historian T. Harry Williams in his preparation of what is by far the most substantial and authoritative Long biography, *Huey Long* (New York: Knopf, 1969). Williams had earlier outlined his essentially sympathetic interpretation of Long in "The Gentleman from Louisiana: Demogogue or Democrat," *The Journal of Southern History* (February, 1960). Williams' biography retains this sympathetic posture, but he has not removed the warts. He compensated for the paucity of personal manuscript evidence by conducting 295 interviews.

Several contemporary biographies of Long appeared in the 1930s; although none approaches Williams' either in scope and authority or in sympathy with their subject, they do display in varying degrees the contemporary fascination with and general hostility toward the Kingfish. The polemical John Kingston Fineran made no attempt at objectivity in *The Career of a Tinpot Napoleon* (New Orleans: John K. Fineran, 1932). More balanced but curiously neutral is Webster Smith (pseudonym for a member of the Long faction), *The Kingfish: A Biography of Huey P. Long* (New York: Putnam, 1933). Forrest Davis, *Huey Long: A Candid Biography* (New York: Dodge Publishing Co., 1935), and Carleton Beals, *The Story of Huey P. Long* (Philadelphia: Lippincott, 1935) are unfriendly but attempt to be fair-minded. Less useful is Thomas O. Harris, *The Kingfish—Huey P. Long, Dictator* (New Orleans: Pelican, 1938).

These early journalistic biographers generally rated Long a demagogue, as did Hilda Phelps Hammond, whose *Let Freedom Ring* (New York, Farrar & Rinehart, 1936), reflects both the hostility of a prominent Louisiana anti-Long and the pious condescension of the "good government" conservatives. Comparative biographical sketches which assess Bilbo, Upton Sinclair, Milo Reno, *et al.* can be found in The Unofficial Observer (pseudonym), *American Messiahs* (New York: Simon and Schuster, 1935); Raymond Gram Swing, *Forerunners of American Fascism* (New York: Julian Messner, 1935); Raymond Moley, *Twenty-Seven Masters of Politics* (New York: Funk and Wagnalls, 1949); Reinhard H. Luthin, *American Demagogues* (Boston: Beacon Press, 1954); Donald R. McCoy, *Angry Voices: Left of Center Politics in the New Deal Era* (Lawrence, Kans.: University of Kansas Press, 1958); and Daniel M. Robinson, "From Tillman to Long: Some Striking Leaders of the Rural South," *The Journal of Southern History* (August, 1937).

The artist's insights into the psychological and tragic dimensions of the Long phenomenon may be derived from Robert Penn Warren, *All the King's Men* (New York: Harcourt, 1946). Although Warren has denied that his protagonist, Willie Stark, is modeled after Huey Long, a most convincing case to the contrary is made by Ladell Payne, "Willie Stark and Huey Long: Atmosphere, Myth, or Suggestions?," *American Quarterly* (Fall, 1968). Another excellent article is Burton L. Hoteling, "Huey Pierce Long as Journalist and Propagandist," *Journalism Quarterly* (March, 1943), which traces Long's considerable efforts in journalism.

Long's battles in Louisiana and his surge to national prominence inspired scores of magazine and journal articles describing his colorful antics and attempting to interpret him. Among the best are, in addition to those by Raymond Swing and Hodding Carter that are reprinted in this volume, Walter Davenport, "Yes, Your Excellency," *Colliers* (December 12, 1930); Hermann B. Deutsch, "Huey Long of Louisiana," *New Republic* (November 11, 1931); Hamilton Basso, "Huey Long and His Background," *Harper's Monthly* (May, 1935); and Gerald W. Johnson, "Live Demagogue, or Dead Gentleman," *Virginia Quarterly Review* (January, 1936).

Interest in the circumstances of Long's assassination has been rekindled by three recent books: Richard Briley, *The Death of the Kingfish* (Dallas: Triangle, 1960); David B. Zimman, *The Day Huey Long Was Shot* (New York: Ivan Obolensky, 1963); and Hermann B. Deutsch, *The Huey Long Murder Case* (New York: Doubleday, 1963).

Huey Long launched a Long dynasty in Louisiana politics. Subsequent to his assassination his younger brother, Earl, was elected once lieutenant-governor, thrice served as governor, and had been elected to the U.S. House of Representatives when he died in 1960. Huey's son, Russell, has served in the U.S. Senate since 1948, and several other Longs have held lesser posts in Louisiana. The first book to trace the dynasty beyond Huey was Harnett T. Kane, whose *Louisiana Hayride: The American Rehearsal for Dictatorship 1928–1940* (New York: William Morrow, 1941) linked the scandals that broke in 1939 to Long's successors and indicted Huey for having forged the power they abused. The best single study of Longism remains Allan P. Sindler, *Huey Long's Louisiana: State Politics, 1920–1952* (Baltimore: The Johns Hopkins Press, 1956). Sindler sought to penetrate beyond the debate over demagoguery and analyzed Long less in terms of personality than as reflective of historic social and economic forces. A. J. Liebling's *The Earl of Louisiana* (New York: Simon and Schuster, 1961) is a splendidly written defense of Earl Long. Two recent journalistic accounts are Thomas Martin, *Dynasty: The Longs of Louisiana* (New York: Putnam, 1960); and Stan Opotowsky, *The Longs of Louisiana* (New York: Dutton, 1960). More descriptive than analytical, both are critical of Huey Long and his legacy; neither adds substantially to our knowledge of Huey.

For an understanding of Louisiana politics, useful background studies are Roger W. Shugg, *Origins of Class Struggle in Louisiana 1840–1875* (Baton Rouge: Louisiana State University Press, 1939); Garnie W. McGinty, *Louisiana Redeemed: The Overthrow of Carpetbag Rule, 1876–1880* (New Orleans: Pelican, 1941); George M. Reynolds, *Machine Politics in New Orleans 1897–1926* (New York: Columbia University Press, 1936); Perry H. Howard, *Political Tendencies in Louisiana, 1812–1952* (Baton Rouge: Louisiana State University Press, 1957); and Grady McWhiney, "Louisiana Socialists in the Early Twentieth Century," *Journal of Southern History* (August, 1954).

Several unpublished theses and dissertations focus on various aspects of Long's career: Emile B. Oder, "An Analysis of the Campaign Techniques and Appeals of Huey Long," Master's thesis, Tulane University (New Orleans, 1942); Leo Glens Douthit, "The Governorship of Huey P. Long," Master's thesis, Tulane University (New Orleans, 1947); Elsie B. Stallworth, "A Survey of the Louisiana Progress of the 1930's," Master's thesis, Louisiana State University (Baton Rouge, 1948); Martha M. Schroeder, "The Senate Career of Huey Long," Master's thesis, University of Texas (Austin, 1965); and Edward F. Renwick, "The Longs' Legislative Lieutenants," Doctoral dissertation, University of Arizona (Tucson, 1967).

The most comprehensive and recent bibliographical guide is that of T. Harry Williams' *Huey Long*. But see also the the following historiographical analyses: John A. Moreau, "Huey Long and His Chroniclers," *Louisiana History* (Spring, 1965); and Henry C. Dethloff, "Huey P. Long: Interpretations," *Louisiana Studies* (Summer, 1964).

Index